German
A Self-Teaching Guide

SECOND EDITION

Revised and updated

Heimy Taylor

Werner Haas

BICENTENNIAL
1807
WILEY
2007
BICENTENNIAL

John Wiley & Sons, Inc.

Contents

How to Use This Book

German: A Self-Teaching Guide is a simplified and practical beginner's course for anyone who would like to learn German. This book lends itself easily to self-learners, students in adult education courses, and those in short-term beginning German courses.

This book can serve as a survival course for those who wish to learn only the essentials of German grammar and want to acquire some basic vocabulary for everyday life and traveling in German-speaking countries. Be assured that whatever you learn in this book, you can apply it in speaking or in writing to communicate with German-speaking people. However, it lays no claims to completeness. On the contrary, rules have been shortened, structures simplified, and the vocabulary geared toward high-frequency use. The objective of this book is to teach important communicative skills in German at the beginner's level.

Each chapter contains the following features:

Culture Notes: A cultural overview written in English

Dialoge: Dialogues in German with English translations

Kommunikation: Communication activities to practice, with answers in the back of the book

Grammatik: Explanations of German grammar

Übungen: Exercises with an answer key in the back of the book

Sprechen leicht gemacht: "Speaking made easy" activities

Wiederholung: A review with answers in the back of the book

Wortschatz: A list of words found in each chapter.

Before you begin the first chapter, take a look at the introduction, German Sounds and Spelling, to orient yourself to spelling rules and pronunciation.

Here are a few hints for using this book:

Read the Dialoge aloud and study them carefully. Always check the English translation.

Practice the Aktivitäten (Activities) in the Kommunikation section.

Study the Grammatik section and try to do the Übungen (Exercises).

Check the answers in the back and see how well you did. Do not expect to bat 1000—hardly anyone does.

Analyze your mistakes and reread the appropriate grammar explanations.

Practice the Sprechen leicht gemacht (Speaking Made Easy).

Always review by completing the Wiederholung (Repetition).

Read aloud all sentences and exercises. Don't worry about your less than perfect pronunciation. It still beats "silent mumbling."

The chapter Wortschatz (Vocabulary) will list the new words appearing for that particular chapter. If you can't find a certain word there, look it up in the German-English and English-German vocabulary lists located in the back of the book.

German: A Self-Teaching Guide will not turn you into a polished speaker of German overnight and will not enable you to deal immediately with every German text. However, it will provide you with the basic tools to understand, speak, read, and write simple German. It opens the gate to a very gratifying experience: understanding and appreciating the language and culture of the German-speaking people. "Viel Spaß mit Deutsch" (Have fun with German)!

—H. T.

—W. H.

Introduction: German Sounds and Spelling

BASIC RULES*

As you read and write German, you will notice that all nouns are capitalized—not only proper nouns like **England, Hamburg,** and **Karin Braun,** but also common nouns like **Ball, Butter,** or **Mann.** Other words used as nouns must be capitalized as well. Unlike English, though, German does *not* capitalize proper adjectives such as **englisch, amerikanisch,** and **deutsch.**

Although pronouns in German are generally lowercased (**ich, du, er**), the pronoun of formal address *Sie* (you) and the corresponding *Ihr* (formal your) must always be capitalized. When writing letters, all pronouns of direct address are capitalized: **Du, Dein.**

German uses the special letter ß to denote *ss*, as in **Fuß** (foot). This is pronounced like the *s* in *bus*: [fu:s].

German has a graphic sign known as the *umlaut* (literally, "sound transformer"), which consists of two dots (¨) placed over the vowels *a* = *ä*; *o* = *ö*; *u* = *ü*. They are pronounced differently than the regular *a, o,* and *u*. Watch out for these umlauts in speaking as well as in writing.

In German as well as in English certain syllables receive more stress than others. This stress is not indicated through a special mark, as in Spanish. Generally speaking, most German words are stressed on the *first*

---

*These simplified pronunciation guidelines are based on *SIEBS—Deutsche Aussprache* (Berlin: Walter de Gruyter & Co., 1969) and *The Oxford Duden German Dictionary* (Oxford, England: Clarendon Press, 1990).

1

syllable ('**wandern, 'trinken, 'Hamburg**). In compound words the *first* word is usually stressed more than the second ('**Autofahrer**). Words of foreign origin are usually stressed on the last syllable of the stem (**Stu'dent, Universi'tät**). Separable prefixes like *ab-, an-, aus-,* etc., are always stressed ('**abfahren, 'ankommen, 'ausgeben**). Inseparable prefixes such as *be-, ent-, er-,* or *ge-* are never stressed (**be'handeln, ent'fernen, er'kennen**).

Now let's look at the German vowel and consonant system in detail. Remember, the best way to learn to pronounce German is to imitate native speakers as accurately as possible. As you listen to the pronunciation tape, repeat all the sounds and words as carefully as you can.

Vowels

Vowels in German are either long or short (tense or lax). German spelling will help you in deciding whether a vowel should be pronounced long or short. Note the following general pronunciation rules:

A vowel is pronounced long* if:

- it is doubled

  Boot (boat): [boːt]; say *o* as in English *so*

- it is followed by *h*

  nehmen (to take): [neːmən]; say *e* as in English *nay*, but don't glide the *e*

- a syllable ends with a vowel

  haben (to have): [haːbən]; say *a* as in English*father*

- *i* is followed by *e*,

  lieben (to love): [liːbən]; say *ie*[†] as in English *see*

Caution: Although we have a tendency to glide our long vowels in English, you should avoid this glide in German.

A vowel is pronounced short if:

- it is followed by a double consonant

  Mitte (middle): [mɪtə]; say *i* as in English *mittens*

- before consonant clusters

  Fenster (window): [fɛnstər]; say *e* as in English *met*

- if followed by *ck*, or *tz*

  Ecke (corner): [ɛkə]; say e as in English *met*
  jetzt (now): [jɛtst]; say *j* as in English *you* and *e* as in English *met*

---

*A colon next to the vowel indicates that it should be long.

[†]Note: *ie* is not a diphthong but the German long *i* sound [iː]. It is always pronounced like English *ee*.

German has three diphthongs, which are easy to pronounce since they resemble our own. A diphthong is a combination of two vowels pronounced as one unit. German diphthongs are shorter than English diphthongs.

ei, ai	pronounced [ae], as in **Mai** (May): [mae]; **mein** (mine): [maen]; say *ai, ei* as the *i* in *mine*
au	pronounced [ɑo], as in **Haus** (house): [hɑos]; say *au* as the *ou* in *house*
eu, äu	pronounced [ɔø], as in **Leute** (people): [lɔøtə]; **Häuser** (houses): [hɔøzər]; say *eu, äu* as the *oi* in *oil*

Here is the German vowel system somewhat simplified.

		Spelling		Phonetic Symbol	
short	i	ü	u	ɪ	Y	U
	e	ö	o	ɛ	œ	ɔ
	a	ä		a	ɛ	
long	i	ü	u	iː	yː	uː
	e	ö	o	eː	øː	oː
	a	ä		aː	ɛː	
diphthong	au	ei		ɑo	ae	
	äu	eu		ɔø		
unstressed	e			ə		

Practice saying the following words.

German Spelling	Phonetic Symbol	Description	Examples
a (short)	[a]	Almost like the English *u* in *up, hut*	**hat** (has): [hat]
a (long)	[aː]	like English *a* in *spa*; open mouth wide and don't glide	**Tag** (day): [taːk] **Nase** (nose): [naːzə]

German Spelling	Phonetic Symbol	Description	Examples
e (short)	[ɛ]	like English e in *met*	**Bett** (bed): [bɛt] **kennen** (to know) [kɛnən]
e (long)	[eː]	like English *ay* in say, but spread lips and don't glide	**beten** (to pray): [beːtən] **nehmen** (to take): [neːmən]
e	[ə]	unstressed e as in *begin, locket*	**beginnen** (to begin): [bəgɪnən] **leben** (to live) [leːbən]
i (short)	[ɪ]	like English i in fit, mitten	**mit** (with): [mɪt] **bitte** (please): [bɪtə]
i (long)	[iː]	like English ee in *see, me, bee*; spread lips and don't glide	**Miete** (rent): [miːtə] **ihm** (him): [iːm] **tief** (deep): [tiːf]
o (short)	[ɔ]	o as in *not, lot*; don't open mouth too wide for this short o	**Tonne** (ton): [tɔnə] **offen** (open): [ɔfən] **ob** (whether): [ɔp]
o (long)	[oː]	like o in *so, foe*; say with open, round lips and don't glide	**Lohn** (wages): [loːn] **Boot** (boat) [boːt] **Not** (need) [noːt]
u (short)	[ʊ]	like u in *put, bush*	**muss** (must): [mʊs] **Hund** (dog): [hʊnt]
u (long)	[uː]	like u sound in *moon, shoe, rule*, but don't glide	**Mut** (courage): [muːt] **Huhn** (chicken): [huːn]
ä (short)	[ɛ]	like short German e or English e in *met, let, wet*	**Bäcker** (baker): [bɛkər] **Blätter** (leaves): [blɛtər]
ä (long)	[ɛː]	similar to long German e; however, don't spread lips, but open mouth wide	**Käse** (cheese): [kɛːzə] **Fähre** (ferry): [fɛːrə]
ö (short)	[œ]	tongue up front as for e, but lips rounded as for o; practice by going from short e to ö	**Helle, Hölle** (light, hell): [hɛlə], [hœlə] **Stecken, Stöcke** (sticks): [ʃtɛkən], [ʃtœkə]
ö (long)	[øː]	like long German e, but with rounded lips	**Sehne, Söhne** (tendon, sons): [zeːnə], [zøːnə]

German Spelling	Phonetic Symbol	Description	Examples
ö (long) *(con't)*			**Lehne, Löhne** (armrest, wages): [leːnə], [løːnə]
ü (short)	[ʏ]	tongue up front as for *i*, but lips rounded as for *u;* practice by going from short *i* to short *ü*	**Kissen, küssen** (pillow, to kiss): [kɪsən] [kʏsən] **Kiste, Küste** (box, coast): [kɪstə], [kʏstə]
ü (long)	[yː]	like long German *i* but with rounded lips	**Biene, Bühne** (bee, stage): [biːnə]. [byːnə] **viele, fühle** (many, feel): [fiːlə], [fyːlə]
au	[ɑo]	like English *ou-* in *house*	**Haus** (house): [hɑos] **laufen** (to run): [laofən]
eu äu	[ɔø]	like *oi* in *oil*	**Leute** (people): [lɔøtə] **Mäuse** (mice): [mɔøzə]
ei ai ey ay	[ae]	like *i* in *mine,* or *y* in *my*	**mein** (mine): [maen] **Mai** (May): [mae] **Meyer** or **Mayer** (German surnames): [maeər]

Practice:

Say the following pairs of German words several times until you are comfortable with your pronunciation. Since this is pronunciation practice only, don't worry about the meaning of the words.

kam	[kaːm]	Kamm	[kam]	Beet	[beːt]	Bett	[bɛt]
Bahn	[baːn]	Bann	[ban]	den	[deːn]	denn	[dɛn]
Kahn	[kaːn]	kann	[kan]	stehen	[ʃteːən]	stellen	[ʃtɛlən]
Ofen	[oːfən]	offen	[ɔfən]	Mus	[muːs]	muss	[mʊs]
Ton	[toːn]	Tonne	[tɔnə]	Ruhm	[ruːm]	Rum	[rʊm]
wohne	[voːnə]	Wonne	[vɔnə]	schuf	[ʃuːf]	Schuft	[ʃʊft]
Miete	[miːtə]	Mitte	[mɪtə]	Öfen	[øːfən]	öffnen	[œfnən]
biete	[biːtə]	bitte	[bɪtə]	Höhle	[høːlə]	Hölle	[hœlə]
ihnen	[iːnən]	innen	[ɪnən]	Hüte	[hyːtə]	Hütte	[hʏtə]

meine	[maenə]	Miene	[miːnə]	fühle	[fyːlə]	Fülle	[fʏlə]
Leid	[laet]	Lied	[liːt]	Maus	[maos]	Mäuse	[mɔøzə]
reimen	[raemən]	Riemen	[riːmən]	lauten	[laotən]	läuten	[lɔøtən]
Wein	[vaen]	Wien	[viːn]	Laus	[laos]	Läuse	[lɔøzə]

Consonants

Most German consonants are similar to their English equivalents. Double consonants are pronounced like the corresponding single consonants, but they generally indicate that the preceding vowel is short.

The consonants *b*, *d*, and *g* are pronounced almost the same as in English. However, their position in a word makes a difference in their pronunciation. (See the following chart.)

The consonants *p*, *t*, *k*, *f*, *m*, *n*, and *h* are pronounced much like their English counterparts.

Examples: **Platte** (record): [platə]
Tage (days): [taːgə]
Keller (cellar): [kɛlər]
Feder (feather): [feːdər]

German Spelling	Phonetic Symbol	Description	Examples
b	[b]	at the beginning of a syllable or between vowels, pronnounced like the English *b*, *d*, *g*	**Butter** (butter): [butər] **aber** (but): [aːbər] **Biene** (bee): [biːnə] **geben** (to give): [geːbən]
d	[d]		**du** (you): [duː] **dann** (then): [dan] **reden** (to talk): [reːdən] **denken** (to think): [dɛNkən]
g	[g]		**Geld** (money): [gɛlt] **gut** (good): [guːt] **Magen** (stomach): [maːgən]
b	[p]	at the end of a syllable or before *s* and *t* pronounced like English *p*, *t*, *k*	**ob** (whether): [ɔp] **gibt** (you give): [giːpt]
d	[t]		**und** (and): [ʊnt] **fliegst** (you fly) [fliːkst]
g	[k]		

Pay special attention to the following consonants:

German Spelling	Phonetic Symbol	Description	Examples
l	[l]	similar to English *l* but further to the front (tip of tongue should touch the gum ridge)	**leben** (to live): [leːbən] **als** (as): [als] **Bild** (picture): [bɪlt]
v	[f]	generally pronounced like English *f*	**Vater** (father): [faːtər]
v	[v]	between vowels, pronounced like English *v*	**Novelle** (novella): [novelə]
j	[j]	like English *y* in *you, yes,* or *year*	**ja** (yes): [jaː] **Jahr** (year): [jaːr]
w	[v]	exactly like the English *v* in *vine*	**Wasser** (water): [vasər] **Winter** (winter): [vɪntər]
s	[z]	at the beginning of a syllable and between vowels, like *z* as in *zoom*	**sagen** (to say): [zaːgən] **Rose** (rose): [roːzə] **lesen** (to read): [leːzən]
s, ss, ß	[s]	single *s* at the end of a syllable, or double *s* and *ß;* always pronounced like *s* as in *sun*	**als** (as): [als] **lassen** (to let): [lasən] **Fluss** (river): [flus] **Muße** (leisure time): [muːzə]
z	[ts]	always like English *ts* in *sits, lets;* note that English has this sound in final position, but never at the beginning of a syllable as in German	**Zoo** (zoo): [tsoː] **Zeit** (time): [tsaet] **zu** (to): [tsuː] **zwei** (two): [tsvae]

Pay particular attention to the *ch* combination in German. The pronunciation is unfamiliar to speakers of English. When *ch* follows *a, o, u,* or *au,* it is velar—i.e., pronounced in the back of the mouth (velum), where you also pronounce the *k*. However, the *ch* is much softer. If you can say "Loch Lomond" (the name of the Scottish lake) with more breath or friction, you can say the German velar (back) *ch*. Listen carefully to the examples on the tape. Note that the phonetic symbol for velar *ch* is [x]. We will follow this pattern:

Nacht (night):	[naxt]	**lachen** (to laugh):	[laxɜn]
Buch (book):	[buːx]	**Loch** (hole):	[lɔx]
Rauch (smoke):	[raox]	**Bauch** (stomach):	[baox]
hoch (high):	[hoːx]	**nach** (after):	[naːx]

After the vowels *e, i, ö, ä, ü, ei, eu* and consonants *n, r, l,* the *ch* sound is pronounced between the front of the tongue and the hard palate. It sounds very much like the English *h* in *hue, huge,* or *human* when pronounced with a lot of friction. Again, listen carefully to the tape. The phonetic symbol for palatal *ch* is [ç]. We will follow this pattern:

ich (I):	[ɪç]	**schlecht** (bad):	[ʃlɛçt]
Licht (light):	[lɪçt]	**leicht** (light):	[laeçt]
echt (real):	[ɛçt]	**München** (Munich):	[mʏnçɜn]
weich (soft):	[vaeç]	**Küche** (kitchen):	[kʏçɜ]

A FEW FINAL NOTES

The German *r* never sounds anything like our American *r.* Using an American *r* in German sounds about as bad as using a German *r* in English. Most Germans say a uvular *r* in which the back of the tongue is raised toward the uvula (the little droplet of skin that you can see in the back of your mouth). Probably the best way to learn the German *r* is by tipping your head back and trying a dry gargle. This might sound ridiculous, but it works. Don't let your tongue flip upward. Listen to the tape and try to imitate the speakers as closely as possible. Don't let the German *r* discourage you.

Rose (rose):	[roːzə]	**Rand** (edge):	[rant]
rund (round):	[rʊnt]	**Rhein** (Rhine):	[raen]
Ring (ring):	[rɪN]	**Rücken** (back):	[rʏkən]
Rest (rest):	[rɛst]	**reden** (to speak):	[reːdən]
Ruder (oar):	[ruːdər]	**raten** (to advise):	[raːtən]

Note that when German *r* is not followed by a vowel, it tends to become vocalized, that is, it is pronounced almost as a vowel-like glide. Practice these examples.

Uhr	(clock):	[uːr]	**mir**	(me):	[miːr]
Tür	(door):	[tyːr]	**fährt**	(drives):	[fɛːrt]
Tier	(animal):	[tiːr]	**spart**	(saves):	[ʃpaːrt]

Finally, the spellings *sp* and *st* at the beginning of a German word are pronounced like English *shp* and *sht,* respectively. Again, listen and practice:

spielen	(to play):	[ʃpiːlən]	**Stuhl**	(chair):	[ʃtuːl]
spannend	(exciting):	[ʃpanənt]	**stehen**	(to stand):	[ʃteːən]
sprechen	(to speak):	[ʃprɛçən]			

Also, the German spelling *sch* is pronounced like English *sh.*

Schiff	(ship):	[ʃɪf]	**Asche**	(ash):	[aʃə]
Schule	(school):	[ʃuːlə]	**waschen**	(to wash):	[vaʃən]

Greetings, Introductions, and Useful Expressions

—————————————— **CULTURE NOTES** ——————————————

The most common greeting in all German-speaking countries is **Guten Tag.** It will suffice for most "hello/hi/good day" situations during daytime. **Grüß Gott** is also a popular equivalent to **Guten Tag,** but only in southern Germany and Austria. **Grüizi** is used in Switzerland, but primarily among native Swiss.

Guten Morgen and **Guten Abend** are fitting greetings if used at the right time of the day. **Gute Nacht,** however, is strictly used as a good-bye before turning in for the night.

And then there is the universal **Auf Wiedersehen** when one leaves. It is always appropriate.

There are a number of other informal greetings used by Germans, Austrians, and Swiss: **Grüß dich** (German and Austria), **Servus** (Austria), and **Tschau** (Switzerland). Unless you are a close friend of a German-speaking person, though, you won't have much use for these greetings.

Shaking hands is a much-practiced ritual among Germans, Austrians, and Swiss. They do it a lot more often than their Anglo-Saxon counterparts. They shake hands everywhere, not just at formal events such as receptions. As a matter of courtesy, a gentleman is always supposed to wait for the outstretched hand when shaking hands with a lady.

When you introduce yourself, **Ich heiße . . .** or **Ich bin Thomas Weiß/Erika Richter** will suffice. Leave out **Herr, Frau,** and any titles before your name. However, if you introduce other people, the phrase

Darf ich Ihnen Frau/Herr/Professor/Dr. . . . vorstellen is the proper way of introduction. If you can't remember that, just pointing at the person and saying Herr/Frau/Dr./Professor . . . will do.

DIALOGE
(Dialogues)

Read the dialogues aloud in German and check the English translation.

HERR B.:	Guten Morgen. Ich heiße Rolf Berger.	Good morning. My name is Rolf Berger.
HERR C.:	Guten Morgen, ich heiße Richard Cook. Wie geht es Ihnen?	Good morning, I'm Richard Cook. How are you?
HERR B.:	Danke, gut, und Ihnen?	Fine, thank you. And you?
HERR C.:	Danke, auch gut.	Fine.

FRAU K.:	Entschuldigen Sie bitte, wo ist die Luisenstraße?	Excuse me, where is Luisen Street?
FRAU L.:	Die nächste Straße links.	The next street on your left.
FRAU K.:	Danke schön.	Thank you.
FRAU L.:	Bitte schön.	You're welcome.

FRAU M.:	Woher kommen Sie, Herr Klein?	Where are you from, Mr. Klein?
HERR K.:	Aus Frankfurt, und Sie?	From Frankfurt, and you?
FRAU M.:	Aus Los Angeles.	From Los Angeles.
HERR K.:	Wie lange sind Sie schon in Deutschland?	How long have you been in Germany?
FRAU M.:	Drei Wochen.	Three weeks.
HERR K.:	Und wohin fahren Sie jetzt?	And where are you going now?
FRAU M.:	Nach Bonn.	To Bonn.

HERR J.:	Entschuldigen Sie, bitte.	Excuse me, please.
	Wie komme ich zum Bahnhof?	How do I get to the train station?

Herr F.:	Fahren Sie mit dem Bus.	Go by bus.
Herr J.:	Wann fährt der Bus?	When is a bus going?
Herr F.:	Alle zehn Minuten.	Every ten minutes.
Herr J.:	Vielen Dank.	Many thanks.
Herr F.:	Bitte schön.	You're welcome.

KOMMUNIKATION (Communication)

Wichtige Ausdrücke (Important Expressions)

Ja.	Yes.
Nein.	No.
Bitte.	Please.
Danke *oder* **danke schön.**	Thank you.
Vielen Dank.	Many thanks.
Nein, danke.	No, thank you.
Entschuldigen Sie *oder* **Verzeihung.**	Excuse me *or* Pardon me.

Begrüßung und Abschied (Hellos and Good-byes)

Guten Morgen.	Hello (in the morning).
Guten Tag.	Hello (at any time during the day).
Guten Abend.	Hello, Good-bye (during the evening).
Gute Nacht.	Farewell (late in the evening and at bedtime), good night.
Auf Wiedersehen.	Good-bye.
Tschüss.	Farewell (used informally).
Bis später.	See you later.
Bis bald.	See you soon.

Wichtige Fragewörter (Important Question Words)

Wann?	When?	**Wie lang(e)?**	How long?
Warum?	Why?	**Wieviel?**	How much?
Was?	What?	**Wie viele?**	How many?
Wer?	Who?	**Wo?**	Where?
Wie?	How?	**Woher?**	Where from?
Wie oft?	How often?	**Wohin?**	Where to?

Häufige Fragen (Frequently Asked Questions)

Wie heißen Sie?	What's your name?
Wie geht es Ihnen?	How are you?
Wie geht's?	How are you?
Wo wohnen Sie?	Where do you live?
Woher kommen Sie?	Where are you from?
Wie lange bleiben Sie?	How long are you staying?
Was machen Sie heute abend?	What are you doing tonight?
Wer ist der Herr/die Dame/die Frau?	Who is that gentleman/lady/woman?
Wo ist die Post/eine Bank?	Where is the post office/a bank?
Wo ist ein Telefon/ein Taxi?	Where is a telephone/a taxi?
Wie komme ich zum Flughafen?	How do I get to the airport?
Wieviel kostet das?	How much does this cost?

Häufige Antworten (Frequently Given Answers)

Ich heiße Jens Kurz.	My name is Jens Kurz.
Ich komme aus München.	I am from Munich.
Ich wohne in Frankfurt.	I live in Frankfurt.
Wir bleiben vier Monate.	We are staying four months.
Ich fahre nach Hamburg.	I am going to Hamburg.
Wir gehen ins Kino.	We are going to the movies.
Das kostet fünf Euro.	That costs five euros.

Aktivität A (Activity A)

Write questions with each one of the following question words.

BEISPIEL/Example: Wie = Wie heißen Sie?

1. Wo _Wo wohnen sie?_
2. Wie _Wie komme ich zum..._
3. Wer _ist der dirigent?_
4. Was _machen sie heute?_
5. Wieviel _kostet das?_
6. Wohin _färst du heute?_
7. Woher _kommen sie_
8. Wann _färt die bim?_

Aktivität B (Activity B)

Matching: Find the appropriate answer to the questions below. Note that more than one answer may fit. Check unfamiliar words in the Wortschatz (Vocabulary) on page 28.

BEISPIEL/Example: Wie heißen Sie? = *d.* Karl Schmidt

FRAGEN: (QUESTIONS)

1. Wo wohnen Sie? C
2. Wie heißen Sie? D
3. Was machen Sie heute abend? J
4. Woher kommen Sie? I
5. Wie geht's? F/B

6. Wieviel kostet das? A
7. Wann fahren Sie nach Hause? M
8. Wie lange bleiben Sie? H
9. Wohin fahren Sie? E
10. Wo ist die Post? M

ANTWORTEN (ANSWERS)

a. Fünfzig Euro.
b. Danke gut.
c. In Chicago.
d. Karl Schmidt.
e. Ich spiele *(play)* Tennis

f. Nicht gut.
g. Am Montag.
h. Zwei Monate.
i. Aus Bonn.
j. Ich gehe ins Konzert.

k. In zwei Monaten.
l. Nach Frankfurt.
m. Die nächste Straße rechts.

Aktivität C (Activity C)

Auf deutsch, bitte. (Write in German.)

BEISPIEL/Example: What are you doing tonight?
Was machen Sie heute abend?

1. How are you? wie geht's?
   Wie geht es Ihnen ?

2. How much does this cost?
   Wieviel kostet das ?

3. What's your name?
   Wie heißen sie ?

4. What are you doing today?
   Was machen sie heute

5. Where do you live?
   Wo wohnen sie ?

6. What are you doing tonight?
   Was machen sie heute abend ?

7. Where are you going?
   Wohin fahren sie ?

8. My name is . . .
   Ich heiße ?

9. I am from (come from) . . .

Ich komme aus ?

10. I live in . . .

Ich wohne in Texas?

11. Many thanks.

Vielen dank ?

12. I am going to Berlin.

Ich fahre nach ?
Berlin

GRAMMATIK (Grammar)

1. Subject Pronoun

A _pronoun_ is a word that replaces a _noun_. The nominative case is the case of the subject. The subject is the person or thing performing the action. Look at these examples.

Wo ist Herr Braun?	Er ist in Österreich.
Wo ist Frau Graf?	Sie ist in Berlin.
Wie ist das Wetter?	Es ist warm.
Wie heißen die Kinder?	Sie heißen Martin und Karin.
Wo wohnen Sie?	Ich wohne in Chicago.

SUBJECT PRONOUN

	Singular		Plural
ich	I	wir	we
du	you (familiar)	ihr	you (familiar)
er, sie, es	he, she, it	Sie	you (formal)
Sie	you (formal)	sie	they

German vs. English Subject Pronouns

1. German **ich** is not capitalized unless it begins a sentence.

2. German **Sie** is always capitalized when it means _you_.

3. German has three subject pronouns corresponding to _you_:

$$you \begin{cases} \textbf{du} & \text{familiar singular} \\ \textbf{ihr} & \text{familiar plural, as in } you\ all \\ \textbf{Sie} & \text{formal, singular and plural, always capitalized.} \end{cases}$$

When to use _du_ or _Sie_

The formal **Sie** is used when speaking to strangers and persons you would normally address as Herr (Mr., Sir), Frau (Mrs.), or Fräulein*

---

*Nowadays, Fräulein is only used for unmarried female teenagers.

(Miss). The familiar **du** and **ihr** are used when speaking to relatives, close friends, children, animals, and generally among younger people and students. As a rule of thumb, use **du** and **ihr** with people whom you would call by their first name. If in doubt, you will always be correct to use **Sie** until you become certain that you may use **du.**

Übung A (Exercise A)

Supply the German pronoun suggested by the English cue.

BEISPIEL: _____Wir_____ lernen Deutsch. **We**

1. _____Er_____ wohnt in New York. **He**
2. _____Wir_____ tanzen oft. **We**
3. _____Sie_____ fahren nach Deutschland. **They**
4. _____Sie_____ lernt Deutsch. **She**
5. _____Du_____ spielst heute Tennis. **You,** _fam. sing._
6. _____Sie_____ sind aus Hamburg. **You,** _formal_
7. _____Es_____ ist kalt. **It**
8. _____Ich_____ fahre nach Frankfurt. **I**
9. _____Sie_____ studiert Biologie. **She**
10. _____Sie_____ arbeiten in New York. **They**

Note: **Man** is a subject pronoun, corresponding to English _one, people, you_ (but **never** to English _man_). Hier trinkt **man** viel Bier. = One drinks a lot of beer here.

---

2. The Present Tense Form of Verbs

The basic form of a German verb is the infinitive. Most German infinitives end in -**en**; a few end in -**n.** Dictionaries list verbs under the infinitive form:

kaufen = to buy **wandern** = to hike

For traveling and residing:

komm_en_	to come	**bleib**_en_	to remain
geh_en_	to go	**wohn**_en_	to live
fahr_en_	to drive, to ride	**reis**_en_	to travel

For shopping:

kaufen	to buy
kosten	to cost
zahlen	to pay

For having fun:

tanzen	to dance
schwimmen	to swim
spielen	to play

Other verbs we want to use right away:

antworten	to answer
finden	to find
fragen	to ask
trinken	to drink
heißen	to be called

wandern	to hike
arbeiten	to work
machen	to make, to do
lernen	to learn

You formal = "they" form NOT he/she/it like in spanish

	Singular	Plural
kaufen (to buy)	ich kaufe	wir kaufen
	du kaufst	ihr kauft
	er, sie, es kauft	sie, Sie kaufen

When the verb stem ends in **-d** or **-t**, a linking **-e** is inserted between the stem and the ending to facilitate pronunciation of the **du, er,** and **ihr** forms.

arbeiten	du arbeitest	er arbeitet	ihr arbeitet
finden	du findest	er findet	ihr findet
antworten	du antwortest	er antwortet	ihr antwortet

Übung B (Exercise B)

Complete the sentences with the correct verb form.

    BEISPIEL/Example: Ich _____ frage _____ viel   **fragen**

1. Wie __heißen__ Sie?   **heißen**
2. Wo __wohnt__ er?   **wohnen**
3. Woher __kommt__ sie (she)?   **kommen**
4. Ich __kaufe__ eine Lampe.   **kaufen**
5. Was __studiert__ Peter?   **studieren**
6. Wo __arbeitet__ Frau Braun?   **arbeiten**

7. Du _fragst_ viel.   **fragen**

8. Wir _wandern_ oft.   **wandern**

The most common way of saying in German that you like doing something is to use **gern** with a verb.

Ich trinke gern Orangensaft.	I like to drink orange juice.
Elke schwimmt gern.	Elke likes to swim.

If you don't like doing something, use **nicht** (not) between the verb and **gern**.

Ich trinke nicht gern Wasser.	I don't like to drink water.
Elke wandert nicht gern.	Elke doesn't like to hike.

Übung C (Exercise C)

Say that the following people like doing certain activities.

    BEISPIEL/Example: Annie likes to sing. = Annie singt gern.

1. Christian likes to dance.   _tanzt gern._
2. We like to learn German.   _wir lernen gern Deutsch_
3. I like to drink coffee (**Kaffee**).   _Ich trinke gern Kaffee_
4. They like to work here.   _Sie arbeiten gern hier._
5. Karin likes to swim.   _Schwimmt gern._
6. I like to play tennis.   _Ich spiele gern tennis._
7. You (*formal*) like to travel.   _Sie reisen gern._
8. They like to sing.   _Sie singen gern._
9. He likes to hike.   _Er wandert gern._
10. We like living in Florida.   _Wir wohnen in fironda gern._

(handwritten margin notes:)
positive
immediately after
verb gern
negative
verb nicht gern
in between

Note: If you were a native speaker of German learning English, you would have to learn three forms to express present time in English. Fortunately, German has only one.

Regular present:	We save money.	
Progressive present:	We are saving money.	(Wir sparen Geld.)
Emphatic present:	We do save money.	

---

3. The Definite Articles: *der, die, das*

Every German noun has a grammatical gender that is indicated by the definite article. English has only one definite article: *the*. German has three: **der, die, das**.

[handwritten margin notes: tät = die / ion = die / E.T. for "das"/ neuter nouns.]

der words *(m.)*		**die** words *(f.)*	
der Bus	the bus	die Frage	the question
der Mann	the man	die Antwort	the answer
der Tag	the day	die Frau	the woman

das words *(n.)*

das Jahr	the year
das Konzert	the concert
das Kind	the child

The gender of all plurals is **die**.

You should always learn a noun with its article. If you don't recognize the English meaning of these nouns, look them up in the chapter vocabulary (Wortschatz) on page 28:

Gender and sex sometimes coincide . . .

der words	**die** words
der Herr	die Dame
der Mann	die Frau
der Student	die Studentin
der Vater	die Mutter

and sometimes not . . .

der words	**die** words	**das** words
der Löffel *[handwritten: Spoon]*	die Gabel *[handwritten: Fork]*	das Messer *[handwritten: Knife]*
der Kalender	die Lampe	das Radio
der Computer	die Butter	das Haus
der Apfel	die Milch	das Geld

Here are some common nouns that you will want to use immediately:

People	**Home and Furnishings**	**Family**
der Amerikaner	das Haus	die Familie
die Amerikanerin	die Wohnung	die Eltern
der Deutsche	der Garten	das Kind
die Deutsche	der Stuhl	die Kinder, *pl.*
der Student	der Tisch	die Tochter
die Studentin	das Bett	der Sohn
das Kind	das Sofa	der Bruder
das Mädchen	die Couch	die Schwester

People	**Home and Furnishings**	**Family**
der Junge *Boy*	das Telefon *telephone*	die Geschwister
Colleague der Kollege	das Radio *radio*	*Siblings*
die Kollegin	der Fernseher *TV*	*brüder*
physician der Arzt	die Lampe *lamp*	*Schwester*
der Polizist	der Ofen *oven*	*oma/opa*
Police		*vater/mutter*
Officier	**Travel and Transportation**	

das Auto	das Taxi	das Flugzeug *plane*	das Gepäck
der Bus	der Zug *train*	der Flughafen *airport*	der Bahnhof *train station*
die Stadt *City*	die Straße *Street*	die Straßenbahn *Steetcar*	die Fahrkarte *ticket*

Übung D (Exercise D)

Write the German equivalent of the English definitions.

> **BEISPIEL/Example:** A person who heals the sick = der Arzt/die Ärztin

1. My father and mother are **meine** (die) Eltern _____.
2. You need this if you want to buy something __das Geld__.
3. Items of transportation that are spelled the same in German and English __das Auto__ or __der Bus__.
4. Person who directs traffic __der Polizist__
5. My parents' other son is **mein** __Bruder__.
6. My parents' other daughter is **meine** __Schwester__.
7. If you have one, you can talk long distance __das Telefon__ ← *ET phone home!*
8. A white beverage __die Milch__.
9. When you eat food, you usually use __das Messer__ *knife* and __die Gabel__.
10. Mr. Little comes from the United States. He is **ein** __Amerikaner__

> **Don't forget the article (unless a pronoun is given)**

4. The Gender of Third-Person Pronouns

Pronouns must have the same gender as the nouns they replace. In the list below, the corresponding pronoun becomes the subject of each sentence.

der = er   die = sie   das = es   die (*pl.*) = sie

der   die   das
er   sie   es

> "In German a young lady (*das Mädchen*) has no sex, while a turnip (*die Rübe*) has. Think what overwrought reverence that shows for the turnip, and what callous disrepect for the girl."
> —Mark Twain

Herr Schmidt lernt Deutsch. Mr. Smith is learning German.	**Er** lernt Deutsch. He is learning German.
Frau Klein wohnt in Amerika. Mrs. Klein lives in America.	**Sie** wohnt in Amerika. She lives in America.
Der Tisch ist groß. The table is large.	**Er** ist groß. It is large.
Die Lampe ist teuer. The lamp is expensive.	**Sie** ist teuer. It is expensive
Das Radio kostet zu viel. The radio costs too much.	**Es** kostet zu viel. It costs too much.

Übung E (Exercise E)

Answer "ja" (yes), replacing the noun with the appropriate pronoun.

> **BEISPIEL/Example:** Ist **das Wetter** warm? Ja, **es** ist warm.
> Is **the weather** warm? Yes, **it** is warm.

1. Ist das Konzert heute? Ja, _es_ ist heute.
2. Heißt die Dame Frau König? Ja, _sie_ heißt Frau König.
3. Studiert Karl Medizin? Ja, _er_ studiert Medizin.
4. Ist das Auto neu? Ja, _es_ ist neu.
5. Kostet der Computer zu viel? Ja, _er_ kostet zu viel.
6. Ist das Sofa alt? Ja, _es_ ist alt.
7. Sind deutsche Autos gut? Ja, _sie_ sind gut.
8. Sind John und Tim Amerikaner? Ja, _sie_ sind Amerikaner.
9. Fährt der Bus alle 15 Minuten? Ja, _er_ fährt alle 15 Minuten.
10. Ist die Goethestraße weit von hier? Ja, _sie_ ist weit von hier.

5. Using Adjectives and Adverbs

To describe someone or something, you need to know some adjectives and adverbs. Learn these, and you will be able to say a lot more.

oder = or

nur = only

Adjectives

billig, teuer	cheap, expensive
gut, schlecht	good, bad
krank, gesund	sick, healthy
intelligent, dumm	intelligent, dumb
kurz, lang	short, long
alt, jung	old, young
kalt, heiß	cold, hot
groß, klein	big, small
leicht, schwer	light, heavy
	or
	easy, hard

Adverbs

immer, nie	always, never
oft, selten	often, seldom
viel, wenig	much, little
hier, dort	here, there
wieder	again
alt, neu	old, new
warm, kühl	warm, cool
fleißig, faul	hardworking, lazy

Übung F (Exercise F)

Was passt hier? (What fits?) Choose from the words listed below.

lang / groß / wenig / schwer / teuer / warm
fleißig / selten / alt / schlecht / gesund / heiß

1. Wieviel kostet der Computer? Ist er billig oder <u>teuer</u> ?

2. Wie ist das Wetter heute? Gut oder <u>schlecht</u>?

3. Und wie ist die Temperatur? Kühl oder <u>heiß</u> ?

4. Der Arzt sagt: „Sie sind nicht krank, Sie sind <u>gesund</u>."

5. Herr Gates hat viel Geld. Aber ich habe <u>wenig</u> Geld.

6. Ist dieser Mercedes neu? Nein, er ist <u>alt</u> .

7. Ist die Übung A kurz oder <u>lang</u> ?

8. Ist die Übung B leicht oder <u>schwer</u>?

9. Gehst du oft ins Kino? Nein, ich gehe nur [only] <u>selten</u> .

10. Herr Professor, sind die Studenten faul? Nein, sie sind <u>fleißig</u> .

11. Trinken Sie Kaffee kalt oder <u>heiß</u> ?

12. Ist Martin klein? Nein, er ist <u>groß</u> .

6. Present Tense of Sein and Haben

Sein (to be) and **haben** (to have) are key verbs because they are used so often. Their forms must be memorized and practiced.

Singular		Plural	
sein			
ich **bin**	I am	wir **sind**	we are
du **bist**	you are	ihr **seid**	you are
er/sie/es **ist**	he/she/it is	sie, Sie **sind**	they, you are
haben			
ich **habe**	I have	wir **haben**	we have
du **hast**	you have	ihr **habt**	you have
er/sie/es **hat**	he/she/it has	sie, Sie **haben**	they, you have

Übung G (Exercise G)

Supply the correct form of **sein.**

BEISPIEL/Example: Wir _____ sind _____ fleißig.

1. Herr Braun _ist_ Amerikaner.

2. In Deutschland _ist_ Bier billig.

3. _Bist_ du heute krank?

4. Monika _ist_ intelligent.

5. Die Computers _sind_ neu.

luggage   6. Das Gepäck _ist_ schwer.

7. Die Kinder _sind_ fleißig.

8. Wir _sind_ aus der Schweiz.

9. _Sind_ Sie Amerikaner, Herr Brown?

10. Karin _ist_ wieder gesund.

Übung H (Exercise H)

Say that the cued subjects have something.

BEISPIEL/Example: _____ Haben _____ Sie ein Radio?

1. Wir _haben_ viel Zeit.

2. Robert _hat_ ein teures Auto.

3. Ich _habe_ ein altes Haus.

4. Karin _hat_ einen neuen Freund.

5. Das Kind _

6. _Hast_ du ei

7. _Hat_ er Ge

8. _Haben_ Herr Kinder?

Übung I (Exercise I)

Now express all sentences of Übung G and Übung H in English.

> **BEISPIEL/Example:** Die Kinder sind fleißig. = The children are hardworking (or industrious).

7. Verbs with Vowel Changes

A number of common German verbs change their stem vowel in the **er/sie/es** and **du** forms in the present tense. There are no rules; you must memorize them. This vowel change is indicated in the vocabulary in this manner: **sprechen (i), lesen (ie), fahren (ä)**.

sprechen	er/sie/es	spricht	to speak
	du	sprichst	
sehen	er/sie/es	sieht	to see
	du	siehst	
lesen	er/sie/es	liest	to read
	du	liest	
essen	er/sie/es	isst	to eat
	du	isst	
fahren	er/sie/es	fährt	to drive
	du	fährst	
schlafen	er/sie/es	schläft	to sleep
	du	schläfst	

Übung J (Exercise J)

Und andere Leute? (And other people?)
Restate the sentence to say that other people do the same activity.

> **BEISPIEL/Example:** Ich esse Hamburger. Sylvia **isst** Steak.

1. Martin und Jane sprechen Deutsch. Und Herr Eger? Er _spricht_ auch Deutsch.

2. Ich sehe dort ein Taxi? _siehst_ du es auch?

3. Ich lese gern Zeitungen. Was _liest_ du gern? Und was _liest_ Heidi gern?

4. Amerikaner essen viel Steak. In Deutschland _isst_ man viel Sauerkraut. Und was _isst_ du gern?

5. Wir fahren am Wochenende nach München. Wohin _fährst_ du? Und Erich? Er _fährt_ nach Berlin.

6. Im Hotel schlafe ich immer schlecht. Wo _schläfst_ du schlecht? Und wo _schläft_ man immer gut? _always baldly_

SPRECHEN LEICHT GEMACHT
(Speaking Made Easy)

Aktivität A (Activity A)

Say something about yourself by choosing the appropriate words from the suggested lists.

storel
business

Ich bin **Student:** Studentin, Amerikaner, Sportlerin, Lehrerin, Geschäftsmann, Hausfrau, Sekretärin, Biologin, Professor, Professorin, Musiker, Musikerin

Ich bin **charmant:** fit, jung, alt, nett, intelligent, fleißig, krank, klein, groß

Ich spiele gern **Tennis:** Fußball, Gitarre, Basketball, Golf, Klavier (piano)

Ich habe **Zeit:** Geld, Humor, Energie, Kinder, ein Auto, ein Haus, ein Boot, ein Motorrad, ein Telefon, eine Wohnung, Gepäck

Ich trinke gern **Milch:** Wasser, Kaffee, Tee, Wein, Bier, Apfelsaft, Orangensaft, Cola

Ich **spiele** gern: tanze, arbeite, trinke, wandere, reise, lerne, lese, schreibe, schwimme, studiere

Aktivität B (Activity B)

Now say something about a friend.

BEISPIEL/Example: Er/sie hat Geld, trinkt gern Cola, und spielt viel Golf.

er/sie ist . . .   er/sie hat . . .
er/sie spielt gern . . .   er/sie trinkt gern . . .

Wiederholung (Repetition)

Complete this review on a separate sheet of paper. Answers are in the back of the book.

A. How would you greet a person at . . .

BEISPIEL/Example: 2 P.M. = Guten Tag.

1. at 12 noon.   2. at 8 A.M.   3. at 7 P.M.
4. at 10 A.M.   5. at 3 P.M.   6. at 11 P.M.

B. Ask questions that would elicit the answers below.

BEISPIEL/Example: Wo . . .? Sie ist jetzt in Österreich.
Wo ist sie jetzt?

1. Wann . . . ?   Herr Schmidt arbeitet heute.
2. Was . . . ?   Martin kauft Briefmarken.
3. Wie . . . ?   Das Wetter ist warm?
4. Wieviel . . . ?   Es kostet €10,50.
5. Wo . . . ?   Frau Bieber wohnt in Bonn.

C. Write these sentences in German.

BEISPIEL/Example: When are you coming? = Wann kommen Sie?

1. I like to travel.
2. What is your name?
3. How much does the radio cost?
4. We like to play golf.
5. They have a lot of (much) time.
6. She lives in Munich.
7. Excuse me, please.
8. Where are you going now?
   wohin

D. Respond to these questions.

BEISPIEL/Example: Wie heißt der Professor?
Er heißt Professor Jensen.

1. Sind Sie Amerikaner?
2. Wohin fahren Sie?
3. Wo wohnen Sie?
4. Was machen Sie gern?
5. Wie lange bleiben Sie hier?

Wortschatz (Vocabulary)

This chapter vocabulary includes all words appearing in Kapitel 1 (Chapter 1). Subsequent chapter vocabularies will include only new words.

Nouns

Note: letters after comma indicate plural forms.

der Abschied, -e	farewell, say goodbye	die Fahrkarte, -n	ticket (for travel)
der Amerikaner, –	American, *m.*	die Familie, -n	family
die Amerikanerin, -en	American, *f.*	der Fernseher, -	TV set
die Antwort, -en	answer	der Flughafen, ⸚	airport
der Apfel, ⸚	apple	das Flugzeug, -e	airplane
der Apfelsaft, ⸚e	apple juice, cider	die Frage, -n	question
		die Frau, -en	woman
der Arzt, ⸚e	physician, *m.*	das Fräulein	Miss
die Ärztin, -nen	physician, *f.*	der Freund, -e	friend, *m.*
der Bahnhof, ⸚e	train station	die Freundin, -nen	friend, *f.*
der Ball, ⸚e	ball	der Fußball, ⸚e	football
die Banane, -n	banana	das Fußballspiel, -e	soccer (game)
die Begrüßung, -en	greeting	die Gabel, -n	fork
das Beispiel, -e	example	das Geld, -er	money
das Bett, -en	bed	das Gepäck	luggage
das Bier, -e	beer	die Geschäftsfrau, -en	business-woman
die Biologin, -nen	biologist, *f.*		
das Boot, -e	boat	der Geschäftsmann	businessman
die Briefmarke, -n	postage stamp	die Geschäftsleute, *pl.*	business-people
der Bruder, ⸚	brother	die Geschwister	brothers and sisters, siblings
die Dame, -n	lady		
(das) Deutsch	German (language)		
		das Haus, ⸚er	house
(das) Deutschland	Germany	die Hausfrau, -en	housewife
die Eltern	parents	der Herr, -en	gentleman
der Euro	euro (currency of European Community)	das Jahr, -e	year
		der Junge, -n	boy

der Kaffee, -s	coffee	der Polizist, -en	police officer
der Kalender, –	calendar	die Schweiz	Switzerland
das Kind, -er	child	die Schwester, -n	sister
das Kino, -s	movie	die Sekretärin, -nen	secretary, *f.*
das Klavier, -e	piano	der Sohn, ¨e	son
der Koffer, –	suitcase	der Sportler, –	sportsman
der Kollege, -n	colleague, *m.*	die Sportlerin, -nen	sportswoman
die Kollegin, -nen	colleague, *f.*	die Stadt, ¨e	city
der Lehrer, –	teacher, *m.*	die Straße, -n	street
die Lehrerin, -nen	teacher, f.	die Straßenbahn, -en	streetcar
der Löffel, –	spoon	die Studentin, -nen	student, *f.*
das Mädchen, –	girl	der Stuhl, ¨e	chair
die Managerin, -nen	manager, *f.*	der Tag, -e	day
der Mann, ¨er	man	der Tee, -s	tea
die Medizin	medicine	das Telefon, -e	telephone
das Messer, –	knife	der Tisch, -e	table
die Milch	milk	die Tochter, ¨	daughter
der Monat, -e	month	der Vater, ¨	father
der Montag, -e	Monday	das Wasser, –	water
das Motorrad, ¨er	motorcycle	der Wein, -e	wine
der Musiker, –	musician	die Woche, -n	week
die Mutter, ¨	mother	die Wohnung, -en	apartment
der Ofen, ¨	oven, range	die Zeit, -en	time
der Orangensaft, ¨e	orange juice	der Zug, ¨e	train
(das) Österreich	Austria		

Verbs

antworten	to answer	lernen	to learn
arbeiten	to work	lesen (ie)	to read
bleiben	to remain	machen	to make,
essen (i)	to eat		to do
fahren (ä)	to drive,	reisen	to travel
	to ride	schreiben	to write
finden	to find	schwimmen	to swim
fragen	to ask	sehen (ie)	to see
geben (i)	to give	spielen	to play
gehen	to go	sprechen (i)	to speak
haben	to have,	studieren	to study
	to possess	tanzen	to dance
heißen	to be called	trinken	to drink
kaufen	to buy	vorstellen	to introduce
kommen	to come	wandern	to hike
kosten	to cost	wohnen	to live

Other Words

alle	all	links	left
alt	old	man	one, you, people
aus	out of, from		
billig	cheap, inexpensive	müde	tired
		nach	to
bitte	please	nächst-	next
braun	brown	nah(e)	near
charmant	charming	nett	nice
dort	there	neu	new
drei	three	nicht	not
dumm	dumb	nie	never
faul	lazy	oft	often
fleißig	hardworking, industrious	rechts	right
		schlecht	bad
fünf	five	schwer	difficult, heavy
fünfzehn	fifteen		
fünfzig	fifty	selten	seldom
gern haben	to like	teuer	expensive
gesund	healthy	viel(e)	much, many
groß	big, large	von	from
häufig	frequent	wann	when
heiß	hot	warum	why
heute	today	was	what
heute abend	tonight	weit	far
heute morgen	this morning	wenig(e)	little, few
hier	here	wieder	again
immer	always	wie lang(e)	how long
jetzt	now	wie oft	how often
jung	young	wieviel, wie viele	how much, how many
kalt	cold		
klein	little, small	wo	where
krank	sick, ill	woher	where from
kühl	cool	wohin	where to
kurz	short	zehn	ten
lang	long	zwei	two
leicht	light, easy		

Idiomatic Expressions

Auf Wiedersehen.	Good-bye.	Danke (schön).	Thank you. Thanks.
Bis bald.	Till then.		
Bis später.	Until later.	Darf ich Ihnen . . . vorstellen	May I introduce . . .
Bitte schön.	You are welcome.		

Entschuldigen Sie, bitte.	Excuse me, please.	**Stellen Sie Fragen.**	Ask questions.
Grüß Gott!	Good day. (Austrian)	**Tschüss!**	Bye. Bye now.
		Verzeihung.	Excuse me.
Guten Abend!	Good evening.	**Vielen Dank.**	Many thanks.
Guten Morgen!	Good morning.	**Wie geht es Ihnen?**	How are you?
Gute Nacht!	Good night.	**Wie geht's?**	How are you?
Guten Tag!	Good day. Hello.		

Cognates

Cognates need no translations but for nouns the articles are listed.

das Auto, -s   der Garten, -   das Radio, -s

die Bank, -en   die Gitarre, -n   die Post

die Biologie   das Golf   das Sofa, -s

der Bus, -se   der Humor   der Student, -en

die Butter   das Konzert, -e   das Taxi, -s

das Cola, -s   die Lampe, -n   das Tennis

der Computer, – *same*   der Manager, – *same*

die Energie, -n   die Minute, -n   fit

   g   intelligent

    warm

Numbers: Measurements, Currencies, Sizes, and Temperature

---------- **CULTURE NOTES** ----------

When it comes to the chores of simple arithmetic, Europeans and Americans do it pretty much the same way: most use a calculator.

But the metric system—officially adopted by the U.S. Congress in December 1975 as the system of measurements for the future—is still a bit strange to many Americans, especially when traveling in Europe.

This conversion table may be helpful.

MEASURE, WEIGHTS, AND TEMPERATURE: AMERICAN MEASURE AND THE METRIC SYSTEM

Lengths

1 mm	= 0.039 in		1 in	= 2.54 cm
1 cm	= 0.394 ft		1 ft	= 30.48 cm
1 m	= 1.094 yds		1 yd	= 91.44 cm
1 km	= 0.621 mile		1 mile	= 1.609 km

Areas or Surfaces

1 sq in	= 6.45 sq cm			
1 sq ft	= 929.03 sq cm			
1 sq m	= 1.196 sq yd		1 sq yd =	0.836 sq m
1 ha	= 2.471 acres		1 acre =	4047 sq m
1 sq km	= 0.386 sq mi		1 sq mi =	2.59 sq km
	= 247.11 acres		=	259 ha

Weight

1 ton	= 2205 lb	1 oz =	28.35 g
1 kilo	= 2.205 lb	1 lb =	453.59 g
1 pound	= 500 g		
1 Deka	= 10 g		
(Austrian)			

Capacities

1 liter	= 2.114 liquid pt	1 liquid pt	= 0.473 l
	= 1.057 liquid qt	1 liquid qt	= 0.946 l
	= 0.264 liquid gal	1 liquid gal	= 3.785 l

mm = millimeter, cm = centimeter, m = meter, km = kilometer, sq cm = square centimeter, sq m = square meter, sq km = square kilometer, ha = hectare; g = gram, kg = kilogram, l = liter

Conversion Formula for Temperature

Degrees Fahrenheit (°F)

$$F = \frac{18\ (°C)}{10} + 32$$

Degrees Celsius (°C)

$$C = \frac{10\ (°F - 32)}{18}$$

The following points of reference and examples may make the metric system a bit clearer.

1 liter	= about one qt
20°C	= 68°F (fever begins at 37.5°C)
100 km	= 62 mi
3.000 m	= ca. 10,000 ft
1.000 m²	= ca. 0.25 acres
1,67 m groß*	= 5 ft, 6 in tall

German, Austrian, and Swiss currency works this way:

Germany: *Euro* (€) and *Cent*: 1 Euro = 100 Cent

---

*Note the comma in 1,67. German utilizes commas instead of decimal points, and you'll definitely notice this in currency: **Das Brot kostet €1,50.** Large numbers use decimals where we would use commas: **2.000 Kilometer.**

Austria: *Euro* and *Cent*: 1 Euro = 100 Cent

Switzerland: *Schweizer Franken* and *Rappen*: 1 Franken = 100 Rappen

European clothes sizes are quite different from ours. The table below will give you an overview:

SHOES

American									
Women's	5	6	7	8	9	10	11		
Men's		4	5	6	7	8	9	10	11
Continental	34	36	37	38	39	41	42	44	45

CHEST/BUST

American		30	32	34	36	38	40	42	44	46
Continental	40	42	44	46	48	50	52	54	56	

SOCK SIZES

American	Small	Medium	Large
Continental	36/38	40/42	44/46

DRESS SIZES

American		6	8	10	12	14	16	18
Continental	34	36	38	40	42	44	46	

SHIRT SIZES

American		14	14½	15	15½	16	16½	17	17½
Continental	36	37	38	39	41	42	43	44	

DIALOGE

Read the dialogues aloud in German and check the English translation.

B: **Die Äpfel, wieviel kosten sie?**   These apples—how much are they?

C: **Zwei Euro fünfzig das Kilo.**   Two euros fifty a kilo.

B: **Drei Kilo, bitte.**   Three kilos, please.

C: **Dreimal zwei fünfzig—das macht sieben Euro fünfzig.**   Three times two fifty—that is seven euros fifty.

A:	Wie weit ist es von Salzburg nach München?	How far is it from Salzburg to Munich?
B:	Ungefähr 170 Kilometer.	Approximately 170 kilometers.
A:	Und wie lange fährt man?	And how long does it take?
B:	Ungefähr zwei bis zweieinhalb Stunden.	Approximately two to two-and-a-half hours.

A:	Wie warm ist es heute?	How warm is it today?
B:	Ich glaube etwa fünfundzwanzig Grad.	I think about twenty-five degrees.
A:	Nein, so warm ist es nicht.	No, it can't be that warm.
B:	Oh doch, ich trage heute keinen Pullover.	Oh, yes. I am not wearing a sweater today.

A:	Wie lange bleibst du in Europa?	How long are you staying in Europe?
B:	Zwei bis drei Wochen.	Two to three weeks.
A:	Nicht länger?	Not longer?
B:	Nein, ich habe leider kein Geld mehr.	No, unfortunately I don't have any more money.

KOMMUNIKATION

Cardinal Numbers

Cardinal numbers (one, two, three, and so on) are used in *counting*. Ordinal numbers (first, second, third, and so on) show the *rank* of an item in a series.

0 null	9 neun	18 achtzehn
1 eins	10 zehn	19 neunzehn
2 zwei	11 elf	20 zwanzig
3 drei	12 zwölf	21 einundzwanzig
4 vier	13 dreizehn	22 zweiundzwanzig
5 fünf	14 vierzehn	23 dreiundzwanzig
6 sechs	15 fünfzehn	30 dreißig
7 sieben	16 sechzehn	40 vierzig
8 acht	17 siebzehn	50 fünfzig

60 sechzig	101 hunderteins	300 dreihundert
70 siebzig	102 hundertzwei	600 sechshundert
80 achtzig	103 hundertdrei	700 siebenhundert
90 neunzig	145 hundertfünfundvierzig	1.000 tausend
100 hundert	200 zweihundert	

Note an essential difference when using numbers in English and German:

Deutsch (German)	**Englisch (English)**
26 = sechsundzwanzig	26 = twenty-six
48 = achtundvierzig	48 = forty-eight
53 = dreiundfünfzig	53 = fifty-three

German compound numbers are always written as one word. And there is another difference:

eine Million	one million
eine Milliarde	one billion
eine Billion	one trillion

Aktivität A

1. Zählen Sie *(count)* von null bis 20.

2. Zählen Sie von 40 bis 60.

3. Sagen Sie alle ungeraden *(uneven)* Zahlen von 81 bis 101.

Aktivität B

Antworten Sie auf deutsch.

1. Was ist Ihre *(your)* Telefonnummer?

2. Was ist Ihre Zimmernummer?

3. Was ist Ihre Hausnummer?

4. Was ist Ihre Schuhgröße *(shoe size)*?

5. Wie viele Kilometer ist es von New York nach Los Angeles?

6. Was ist Ihre Sozialversicherungsnummer *(Social Security number)*?

Expressing Multiplication

einmal	= once	**viermal**	= four times
zweimal	= twice	**zehnmal**	= ten times
dreimal	= three times	**hundertmal**	= hundred times

Wie rechnen (calculate) *die Deutschen?*

$8 + 7 = 15$ acht plus sieben ist fünfzehn

$26 - 9 = 17$ sechsundzwanzig minus neun ist siebzehn

$4 \times 6 = 24$ viermal sechs ist vierundzwanzig

$63 \div 7 = 9$ dreiundsechzig durch sieben ist neun

Aktivität C

Nun rechnen Sie—auf deutsch, bitte. Sagen Sie es laut.

1. $33 + 14 = 47$
2. $87 - 13 = 74$
3. $7 \times 3 = 21$
4. $40 \div 8 = 5$
5. $17 + 6 = 23$

6. $5 \times 7 = 35$
7. $42 - 8 = 34$
8. $50 \div 10 = 5$
9. $12 + 9 = 21$
10. $25 - 6 = 19$

---

a. **eins** has an *-s* when it stands alone as a cardinal number, but has no *-s* in compounds.

b. **dreißig** is spelled with an *-ß,* not *-z.*

c. **sechs** is pronounced [zeks], but in **sechzehn** and **sechzig,** the *ch* sound is the same as in **ich.**

d. the *-en* is dropped in **siebzehn** and **siebzig.**

Aktivität D

Antworten Sie auf deutsch, bitte.

1. Wie groß sind Sie?

2. Wie viele Euro/Schweizer Franken bekommt man heute für einen Dollar?

3. Wie viele Brüder und Schwestern haben Sie?

4. Wie alt sind Sie?

5. Wieviel Liter Wasser trinken Sie täglich?

6. Wie hoch ist Mount McKinley? (20,300 ft)

7. Wie warm oder kalt ist es heute?

GRAMMATIK

1. A Few Rules about Basic Word Order

A. Subject-Verb (S-V)

When a sentence in German consists only of a main clause, the *subject-verb* word order is usually used.

BEISPIELE:

Subject	Verb	
Sie	fahren	nach Berlin.
Die Kinder	kommen	jetzt.
Es	ist	heute warm.

B. Verb-Subject (V-S)

In questions without question words, the verb-subject (V-S) word order is used, and the voice is raised at the end of the question.

BEISPIELE:

Verb	Subject	
Fahren	Sie	nach Berlin?
Kommen	die Kinder	jetzt?
Ist	es	heute warm?

Übung A

Change these statements into questions.

> **BEISPIEL:** Familie Roberts kommt nach Salzburg.
> Kommt Familie Roberts nach Salzburg?

1. Wir haben jetzt eine Wohnung.

   Haben wir jetzt eine Wohnung?

2. Robert hat ein Haus.

   Hat Robert ein Haus?

3. Es ist weit von Berlin nach Wien.

Ist es weit von Berlin nach Wien?

4. Wir bleiben zwei Wochen in Europa.

Bleiben wir zwei Wochen in Europa?

5. Inge hat drei Brüder.

Hat Inga drei Brüder?

6. Herr Braun hat viel Geld.

Hat Herr Braun viel Geld?

C. Question Word-Verb-Subject (Qu-V-S)

Questions in which question words (interrogatives) are used show the _question word-verb-subject_ (Qu-V-S) word order.

BEISPIELE:

Question Word	Verb	Subject
Wann	kommt	der Bus?
Wohin	fährt	der Zug?
Wieviel	kostet	der Computer?

Übung B

Use the correct question word.

   BEISPIEL: <u>Was</u> kaufst du?   **What**

1. _Wo_ ist hier das Telefon?   **Where**

2. _Wann_ kommt die Straßenbahn?   **When**

3. _Wohin_ fahren Sie?   **Where (to)**

4. _Wer_ ist die Studentin?   **Who**

5. _Wie_ geht es Ihnen?   **How**

6. _Warum_ glauben Sie das nicht?   **Why**

7. _Wie viel_ kostet das Auto?   **How much**

8. _Woher_ kommt ihr?   **Where (from)**

9. ___Was___ machen Sie heute abend?   **What**

10. ___Wie lange___ bleibt Maria in Zürich?   **How long**

Übung C

Sie fragen . . .

> **BEISPIEL:** Do you have five euros?
>> Haben Sie fünf Euro?

1. How much does it cost?

   wie viel kostet das?.

2. Do they have children?

   Haben sie Kinder?

3. Does she stay three or four days?

   Bleiben sie drei oder vier tagen?

4. Does it cost 38 euros or 83 euros?

   Kostet das achtunddreißig oder dreiundachtzig.

5. How far is it from here?

   wie länge.

6. Do you (fam. sg.) have money?

   Hast du geld?

Übung D

Sagen Sie . . .

> **BEISPIEL:** It takes (one drives) four hours.
>> Man fährt vier Stunden.

1. It costs 15 euros.

   _____.

2. I have two brothers and three sisters.

   _____.

3. He buys the radio.

   _____.

4. It is 12 degrees today.

   _____.

5. You (fam. pl.) get the money tomorrow.

   _____.

6. I don't have enough time.

   _____.

2. Formation of Noun Plurals

It is best to learn the plurals of nouns along with the singular. One cannot accurately predict what the plural form of a noun might be. However, there are some guidelines:

	Singular	Plural
no change	der Koffer	die Koffer
	das Messer	die Messer
add umlaut	der Bruder	die Brüder
	der Apfel	die Äpfel
add -e	das Beispiel	die Beispiele
	der Tisch	die Tische
add -er	das Kind	die Kinder
	das Geld	die Gelder
add umlaut and *-er*	das Buch	die Bücher
	das Haus	die Häuser
add -n	die Frage	die Fragen
	die Gabel	die Gabeln
add -en	die Frau	die Frauen
	die Zahl	die Zahlen
add -s (usually foreign words)	das Radio	die Radios
	das Auto	die Autos

3. The Accusative Case

The *accusative case* is the case of the *direct object*; the direct object is the recipient of the action.

Ask: *Whom?*   or   *What?*

Nominative		Accusative	
wer	who	**wen**	whom

> Only the masculine direct object changes.

Wen suchen Sie?	For whom are you looking?
Ich suche *den* Kellner.	I am looking for the waiter.
Ich suche *die* Kellnerin.	I am looking for the waitress.
Ich suche *das* Geld.	I am looking for the money.
Was sucht sie? *Das* Auto.	What is she looking for? The car.
Was bringt er? *Den* Wein.	What is he bringing? The wine.
Was kauft sie? *Die* Uhr.	What is she buying? The watch.

4. The Indefinite Article

As you know, the definite articles are **der, die,** and **das.** The **indefinite** article for *der* and *das* is **ein;** for *die* it is **eine. Ein** and **eine** correspond to English *a* or *an.* As with the definite article, only the *masculine* changes in the accusative.

Ich kaufe *einen* Pullover.	I am buying a pullover.
Ich kaufe *eine* Zeitung.	I am buying a newspaper.
Ich kaufe *ein* Sofa.	I am buying a sofa.

Kein = *not, not a, not any,* or *no* and is the negative of **ein**. It follows the same pattern as **ein**.

Wir haben einen Computer.	Ihr habt **keinen** Computer.
Sabine hat ein Auto.	Elke hat **kein** Auto.
Sie hat eine Wohnung.	Ich habe **keine** Wohnung.

	Masculine	Feminine	Neuter	Plural
Nominative	der	die	das	die
	ein	eine	ein	—
	kein	keine	kein	keine
Accusative	den	die	das	die
	einen	eine	ein	—
	keinen	keine	kein	keine

Übung E

Restate the sentence by replacing the definite article with the *indefinite* article.

> **BEISPIEL:** Ich kaufe das Haus.   I am buying the house.
> Ich kaufe **ein** Haus.   I am buying a house.

1. Ich nehme den Zug.

_____.

2. Wir finden das Restaurant.

_____.

3. Gregor sucht das Buch.

_____.

4. Brauchen Sie die Wohnung?

_____.

5. Kennt sie die Journalistin?

_____.

6. Maria kauft die Jacke.

_____.

Übung F

Answer in the negative.

> **BEISPIEL:** Haben Sie heute Zeit?   Do you have time today?
> Nein, ich habe heute keine Zeit.   No, I don't have time today.

1. Haben Sie ein Auto? Nein, ich habe _____.

2. Haben Sie Geld? Nein, ich habe _____.

3. Kaufen Sie einen Pulli? Nein, ich kaufe _____.

4. Trinken Sie ein Bier? Nein, ich trinke _____.

5. Sehen Sie den Bus? Nein, ich sehe _____.

6. Haben Sie Kinder? Nein, ich habe _____.

7. Essen Sie Fisch? Nein, ich esse _____.

Accusative in Action

Look at these examples:

A. Wen heiratet Daniel?
   Er heiratet . . .

eine Freundin.
eine Deutsche.
eine Lehrerin.

B. Es regnet. Was brauche ich?
   Ich brauche . . .

einen Regenschirm.
ein Taxi.
eine Tasse Tee.

C. Sie haben Durst.
   Sie trinken . . .

ein Coca Cola.
eine Flasche Bier.
ein Glas Milch.
einen Liter Wasser.
ein Glas Orangensaft.

D. Was trinkt Maria nicht?
   Sie trinkt . . .

keinen Wein.
kein Bier.
keinen Alkohol.
keine Milch.

E. Was versteht Paul nicht?
   Er versteht . . .

den Computer nicht.
das metrische System nicht.
die Frage nicht.
den Text nicht.
das Problem nicht.

F. Wen heiratet Anja?
   Sie heiratet . . .

einen Freund.
einen Mann aus Amerika.
einen Schweizer.
einen Lehrer.

G. Sie sind krank.   einen Arzt.
    Was brauchen Sie?   eine Ärztin.
    Sie brauchen . . .   ein Aspirin.
                        einen Tee.

H. Was kaufen wir heute?   ein Auto.
    Wir kaufen . . .   einen Computer.
                        eine Fahrkarte.
                        ein Sofa.
                        einen Tisch.

5. The Accusative of Personal Pronouns

Pronouns, like articles, change their form to show case.

Ich kenne Karl Müller.	I know Karl Müller.
Ich kenne *ihn.*	I know him.
Ich frage Frau Schmidt.	I am asking Mrs. Schmidt.
Ich frage *sie.*	I am asking her.
Ich sehe das Haus.	I see the house.
Ich sehe *es.*	I see it.

	Singular					**Plural**			
Nominative	ich	du	er	sie	es	wir	ihr	sie	Sie
Accusative	mich	dich	ihn	sie	es	uns	euch	sie	Sie

Übung G

Complete each sentence using the accusative form of the personal pronoun in the cue.

    BEISPIEL: (er) Ich frage <u>ihn.</u>   (he) I ask **him.**
                (wir) Sie kennen <u>uns.</u> (we) You know **us.**

1. Kennen Sie _____?   ich

2. Wir fragen _____?   sie (her)

3. Besuchen Sie _____?   wir

4. Sehen Sie _____?   er

5. Versteht sie _____?   du

6. Ich frage _____?   Sie

7. Fragen Sie _____?   sie (them)

8. Sie kennen _____?   ihr

As you know, personal pronouns often take the place of nouns. The gender of a personal pronoun is the same as that of the noun. Its case, however, is determined by its function in the sentence (subject, object).

BEISPIELE: Wie heißt der Lehrer?   Er heißt Karl Horn.   Kennen Sie   **ihn?**
Wer sind die Leute?   Sie sind Deutsche.   Kennen Sie   **sie?**
Wie heißt die Frau?   Sie heißt Maria Kühn. Kennen Sie   **sie?**
Wie heißt das Hotel?   Es heißt „Imperial."   Kennen Sie   **es?**

Übung H

Complete each sentence with a personal pronoun standing for the cue in italics.

BEISPIEL: Er . . . ist gut und ich trinke . . . ihn . . . .   der Wein

1. _____ ist neu und ich fahre _____ gern.   das Auto

2. _____ fährt alle 10 Minuten und ich nehme   die Straßenbahn
   _____ täglich.

3. _____ hält hier und ich sehe _____ schon.   der Bus

4. _____ ist ausverkauft. Wir hören _____ nicht.   das Konzert

5. _____ ist billig und ich trinke _____ gern.   das Bier

6. _____ heißt Müller und ich kenne _____.   der Arzt

7. _____ heißt Mayer und ich sehe _____ oft.   die Ärztin

8. _____ ist Schweizer und ich frage _____.   der Mann

6. Prepositions Requiring the Accusative Case*

A preposition is a word that shows the relationship of a noun or pronoun to other elements in the sentence. A number of prepositions always require the use of the accusative case. These are the most frequently used:

durch   through   Wir fahren durch die (eine) Stadt.

---

*These prepositions will not be listed again in the chapter vocabulary, only in the end vocabulary.

für	for	Ich bin für ihn.
gegen	against	Wir sind gegen den Krieg (*war*).
ohne	without	Er kommt ohne den (einen) Freund.
um	around	Sie laufen um das (ein) Haus.

In everyday speech, **durch, für,** and **um** are contracted with the definite article *das.*

durch das = durchs	Er geht **durchs** Zimmer.
für das = fürs	Ich brauche es **fürs** Auto.
um das = ums	Wir laufen **ums** Haus.

Übung I

Complete the sentence using the accusative case of the cue at right.

    BEISPIEL: (der Bahnhof)   Wir gehen durch . . .
                                 Wir gehen durch **den** Bahnhof.

1. Ich reise nie ohne _____.   ein Regenschirm

2. Wir gehen oft durch _____.   der Park

3. Ich fahre durch _____.   die Stadt

4. Karl fährt um _____.   das Geschäft

5. Wir sitzen um _____.   der Tisch

6. Inge kauft ein Sofa für _____.   das Haus

7. Es geht heute nicht ohne _____.   das metrische System

8. Sie spricht für _____.   die Kinder

7. Negation with *nicht*

Nicht means *not*. Its position in a German sentence is quite flexible. There are some rules on the word order with **nicht** but also many exceptions. At the risk of oversimplification, look at these examples and consider them as guidelines to where **nicht** should be placed. **Nicht** goes at the end when it negates the verb or the entire sentence.

Wir wissen es *nicht*.	We don't know it.
Ich kenne ihn *nicht*.	I don't know him.
Verstehen Sie das *nicht*?	Don't you understand that?

Nicht follows expressions of time.

Er kommt heute **nicht**.	He is not coming today.
Ich arbeite abends **nicht**.	I don't work at night.
Wir besuchen euch morgen **nicht**.	We are not visiting you tomorrow.

But **nicht** often precedes adverbs, adjectives, and expressions of place.

Das ist **nicht** wahr.	That's not true.
Fahren Sie **nicht** so schnell.	Don't drive so fast.
Es ist **nicht** zu spät.	It isn't too late.
Wir sind noch **nicht** in Köln.	We are not yet in Cologne.

Übung J

Now apply the given guidelines. Answer these questions by negating them with **nicht**.

BEISPIEL: Kennen Sie mich?   Nein, ich kenne Sie **nicht**.
Fährt Jens nach Wien?   Nein, er fährt **nicht** nach Wien.
Arbeiten Sie morgen?   Nein, ich arbeite morgen **nicht**.

1. Wohnen Sie im Hotel? Nein, ich wohne . . .

2. Sehen Sie es? Nein, ich sehe _____.

3. Schreibt Thomas oft? Nein, er schreibt _____.

4. Kommen Sie morgen? Nein, ich komme _____.

5. Fahren Sie schnell? Nein, ich fahre _____.

6. Sehe ich Sie heute abend? Nein, ich sehe Sie _____.

Übung K

Auf deutsch, bitte.

BEISPIEL: Don't you see her?   Sehen Sie sie **nicht**?
Siehst du sie **nicht**?

A: Is Gregor driving tonight?
B: No, I don't think so. He doesn't have a car.   *Er hat kein auto*

A: Mr. Scholz, when are you flying to Germany?

S: Tomorrow.

A: Do you have a passport?

S: Oh yes, I travel a lot.

_____

A: What is the name of the man?

B: We don't know him.

A: Does he speak German?

B: Yes, he is from Austria.

Übung L

Sie sagen . . .

> **BEISPIEL:** Martin isn't coming tomorrow.
> Martin kommt morgen **nicht**.

1. She doesn't walk fast.

   _____.

2. You aren't speaking too loudly.

   _____.

3. He doesn't work in the evening.

   _____.

4. We don't pay the bill
   (**Rechnung**).

   _____.

5. They don't eat much.

   _____.

8. The Function and Use of Adverbs

Adverbs modify or communicate further information about a verb. There are

adverbs of time:	heute, morgen, jetzt, abends, usw.
adverbs of manner:	gern, gut, leider, oft, laut, usw.
adverbs of place:	hier, dort, da, links, rechts, usw.

When a sentence contains more than one adverb, the sequence of adverbs in German is:

Time = T   Manner = M   Place = P

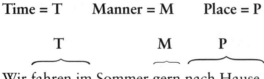

Wir fahren im Sommer gern nach Hause.
We like to go home in the summer.

Ich bleibe am Wochenende oft zu Hause.
I often stay home on the weekend.

Er fährt morgen mit dem Bus in die Stadt.
Tomorrow he is going downtown by bus.

Vocabulary Notes: Here are some adjectives and adverbs that you will need right away. For translations, see the Wortschatz at the end of the chapter or Wortchatz: Deutsch/Englisch at the end of the book.

Temperatures and the Weather	How Often	When	Where
warm	nie	jetzt	dort
heiß	oft	morgen	hier
windig	selten	heute	da
nebelig	täglich	heute abend	drüben
kühl	stündlich	sofort	links
kalt	immer	später	rechts
bewölkt	manchmal	pünktlich	

Übung M

Arrange the adverbs in an appropriate order and complete each sentence.

> **BEISPIEL:** Does he always come into the office on time?
> Kommt er immer pünktlich ins Büro?

1. Are you alone tonight?

2. Are we on time today?

_____.   _____.

3. Is he ill again?

_____.

4. Does the train go every day?

_____.

Übung N

Sie sagen . . .

    BEISPIEL: I gladly stay home today.
                 Ich bleibe heute gern zu Hause.

1. Mr. Schulz comes to the hotel on time.

_____.

2. Bettina is not home today.

_____.

3. They are staying here until tomorrow.

_____.

4. Dieter is flying home at once.

_____.

5. The bus always stops here.

_____.

SPRECHEN LEICHT GEMACHT

Die Wochentage (Days of the Week)

The word for _day_ is **der Tag, -e**

Montag, Dienstag, Mittwoch, Donnerstag,
Freitag, Samstag (Sonnabend), Sonntag } alle maskulin

Was ist heute?	What's today?
Heute ist . . .	Today is . . .
Was ist morgen?	What is tomorrow?
Was war gestern?	What was yesterday?

Aktivität A

Sie fragen, und ein Partner/eine Partnerin (real or imagined) antwortet.

1. Was ist heute?   _____.

2. Was kommt nach Dienstag?   _____.

3. Was ist morgen?   _____.

4. Was kommt vor Samstag?   _____.

5. Was war gestern?   _____.

Aktivität B

Match the questions on the left with the answers on the right. If you have a partner, try this as a partner activity.

1. Was machen Sie am Samstag?   a. Ich fahre nach Bonn.

2. Arbeiten Sie am Sonntag?   b. Nein, ich esse zu Hause.

3. Essen Sie am Freitag im Restaurant? c. Nein, ich arbeite am Sonntag nicht.

4. Wohin fahren Sie am Montag?   d. Ja, man spielt Beethovens Violinkonzert.

5. Gehen Sie am Mittwoch ins Konzert? e. Ich sehe einen Film.

Wiederholung

A. Respond to each question using the cue in your answer.

BEISPIEL: Was verstehen Sie nicht?   die Antwort
Ich verstehe die Antwort nicht.

1. Was trinken Sie?   Milch
2. Wer ist krank?   mein Freund
3. Wen sehen Sie dort?   eine Freundin
4. Wieviel Geld brauchen Sie? 100 Euro
5. Wann kommt Sabine?   am Dienstag
6. Wohin fahren Sie heute?   nach Hamburg
7. Woher kommen Sie?   aus Texas
8. Wie lange bleiben Sie hier? drei Tage

B. Supply **kein, nicht,** or **nichts.** Watch endings for **kein.**

BEISPIEL: Morgen fahre ich **nicht** nach Hause.

1. Haben Sie _____ Geld?

2. Bitte, fragen Sie _____.

3. Wir haben _____ Arzt.

4. Sie hat _____ Zeit.

5. Ich kenne ihn _____.

6. Michael versteht das _____.

7. Heute kaufe ich _____.

C. Auf deutsch, bitte.

1. 68 degrees Fahrenheit is 20 degrees Celsius.

2. Three times four is twelve.

3. One kilo has 1,000 grams?

4. What is your room number?

5. My telephone number is . . .

6. What day is today?

Wortschatz

Nouns

der Alkohol	alcohol	die Kellnerin, -nen	waitress
die Billion, -en	trillion	das Kilo, -s	kilogram
das Buch, ¨er	book	die Leute	people
der Deutsche, -n	German, *m.*	die Milliarde, -n	billion
die Deutsche, -n	German, *f.*	der Mittwoch, -e	Wednesday
der Dienstag, -e	Tuesday	der Österreicher, –	Austrian, *m.*
der Donnerstag, -e	Thursday	die Österreicherin, -nen	Austrian, *f.*
der Durst	thirst		
der Euro	euro	der Pass, ¨sse	passport
das Europa	Europe	das Pfund, -e	pound
die Flasche, -n	bottle	der Regenschirm, -e	umbrella
der Franken, –	Swiss franc	der Samstag, -e	Saturday
der Freitag, -e	Friday	die Schuhgröße, -n	shoe size
das Geschäft, -e	store	der Sonnabend, -e	Saturday
der Grad, -e	degree	der Sonntag, -e	Sunday
die Hausnummer, -n	house number	die Stunde, -n	hour
die Jacke, -n	jacket	das metrische System	metric system
der Journalist, -en	journalist, *m.*	die Telefonnummer, -n	telephone number
die Journalistin, -nen	journalist, *f.*	die Uhr, -en	watch, clock
die Karte, -n	ticket, card	die Zahl, -en	number
der Kellner, –	waiter		

| die Zeitung, -en | newspaper | die Zimmernummer, | room |
| das Zimmer, – | room | -n | number |

Verbs

bekommen	to receive, to get	hören	to hear, to listen
besuchen	to visit	kennen	to know
brauchen	to need	nehmen (nimmt)	to take
fliegen	to fly	rechnen	to calculate
halten (ä)	to stop	sitzen	to sit
heiraten	to marry, to get married	suchen	to look for
		verstehen	to understand
		zählen	to count

Other Words

allein	alone	morgen	tomorrow
ausverkauft	sold out	nebelig	foggy
da, dort, drüben	there, over there	nichts	nothing
		null	zero
dreimal	three times	pünktlich	punctual
etwa	about, approximately	schnell	quick, fast
		schon	already
		sofort	immediately
genug	enough	spät	late
hoch	high	später	later
kein	no, not a	stündlich	hourly, every hour
laut	loud		
leider	unfortunately	täglich	daily
		ungefähr	approximately
manchmal	sometimes	ungerade	uneven
mehr	more	welch-	which
mein	mine		

Idiomatic Expressions

| es gibt | there is/are |

Cognates

der Kilometer, –	der Pullover, –
die Million, -en	das Restaurant, -s
der Park, -s	das System, -e

KAPITEL **3** Food, Restaurants, and Eating

CULTURE NOTES

In the German-speaking countries, many restaurants post their menus and prices outside the establishment. A quick glance can be informative and may save you disappointment and "pocketbook aches."

Some restaurants serve hot meals only during certain hours, usually from 11:30 A.M. to 2 P.M. and from 5 P.M. to 8 P.M. Snacks are available, however, during all business hours. Many people in Germany, Austria, and Switzerland prefer to eat their main hot meal during noon hours and a smaller meal in the evening. But changing work hours and greater commuting distances, especially in urban areas, are making it more difficult to uphold this tradition of the big noontime meal (**Mittagessen**).

Except for expensive and fancy restaurants, do not wait to be seated. Find yourself a free table and sit down. If all tables are taken, you may join others at a larger table if there is still room. Simply ask:

Entschuldigen Sie bitte,
ist hier noch frei?
　　　　or　　　　　　　　Excuse me, please. Is this seat still available?
Entschuldigen Sie bitte,
ist hier noch Platz?

The prices listed on the menu include about 10 to 15 percent for the tip and the value-added tax (**Mehrwertsteuer**). Therefore, just round up the sum quoted and give it to the waiter or waitress as you pay. Do not

54

leave a tip on the table. It is customary to pay the person who served you, not the cashier. To pay, just say, „Herr Ober, bitte zahlen" (waiter) or „Frau Ober, bitte zahlen" (waitress). Remember that many waiters in Germany are guest workers (Gastarbeiter) from other countries and that their German may not be much better than yours.

Today large supermarkets have replaced most specialty or mom-and-pop stores. However, you can still find bakeries and butcher shops in many cities and most small communities. Large department stores quite often have a food section (**die Lebensmittelabteilung**) offering a wide selection of food items. Europeans still go shopping several times a week and buy in small quantities. In general, groceries are quite expensive compared to the United States. You will also notice that most small and large cities have open-air markets.

Familiarize yourself with signs like these:

Heute Ruhetag.	This is our day off.
Wegen Betriebsferien von . . .	Closed for company vacation
bis . . . geschlossen.	from . . . to . . .
Geöffnet von . . . bis . . .	Open from . . . to . . .
Geschlossen von . . . bis . . .	Closed from . . . to . . .
Parkplatz hinter dem Restaurant.	Parking behind the restaurant.
Schöner, schattiger Gastgarten.	Nice, shady yard.
Wegen Renovierung geschlossen.	Closed for renovation.

Ich habe Hunger/Ich bin hungrig. Wo ist . . .
I Am Hungry. Where Is . . .

For a regular, square meal, look for . . .

ein Hotel	hotel
ein Restaurant	restaurant
ein Gasthaus	inn
eine Gaststätte	restaurant
eine Raststätte*	restaurant

For a quick snack there is . . .

ein Schnellimbiss	snack bar, fast-food stand
eine Milchbar	dairy bar

---

*You will find **Raststätten** mostly on the **Autobahn** (freeway).

| eine Jausenstation | Austrian snack bar |
| eine Weinstube | place for snacks and beverages |

Sie fragen: Wo ist hier . . .

ein gutes/billiges/preiswertes Restaurant?
eine gute/billige/preiswerte Gaststätte?
ein gutes/billiges/preiswertes Hotel?

DIALOGE

Read the dialogues aloud in German and check the English translation.
Note where each dialogue takes place.

Im Restaurant „Schuberthof" in Graz, Österreich

GAST:	Servieren Sie jetzt Mittagessen?	Do you serve lunch now?
OBER:	Ja, schon seit 11 Uhr.	Yes, since 11 o'clock.
GAST:	Einen Tisch für vier, bitte.	A table for four, please.
OBER:	Hier in der Ecke, bitte.	Here in the corner, please.

GAST:	Herr Ober, die Speisekarte bitte.	Waiter, the menu please.
OBER:	Bitte schön.	Here it is.
GAST:	Was können Sie empfehlen?	What can you recommend?
OBER:	Das Menü* ist heute sehr gut.	The special of the day is very good.
OBER::	Möchten Sie bestellen?	Would you like to order?
GAST:	Ja bitte—eine Tomatensuppe, Gulasch mit Reis, und grüne Bohnen.	Yes please—tomato soup, goulash with rice, and green beans.
OBER:	Möchten Sie auch einen Salat?	Would you like a salad, too?
GAST:	Nein, danke.	No, thank you.

---

*Watch out: **Menü** is not the menu but the special dish of the day. It usually includes a complete meal including dessert.

GAST:	Bitte zahlen.	Check, please.
OBER:	Ja, sofort.	Yes, right away.
	War alles in Ordnung?	Was everything alright?
GAST:	Ja, ausgezeichnet.	Yes, excellent.
OBER:	Kommen Sie bald wieder.	Come back soon.
GAST:	Auf Wiedersehen.	Good-bye.
OBER:	Auf Wiedersehen.	Good-bye.

KELLNER:	Möchten Sie noch eine Nachspeise?	Would you like dessert?
GAST:	Ja, was gibt's?	Yes, what do you have?
KELLNER:	Nun, möchten Sie etwas Leichtes oder einen Kuchen?	Well, do you want something light or cake?
GAST:	Etwas mit wenig Kalorien.	Something with few calories.
KELLNER:	Dann nehmen Sie doch ein Kompott.	Why don't you take some stewed fruit?

KOMMUNIKATION

In the Restaurant: Initial Questions and Responses

Sie fragen oder sagen:

Servieren Sie jetzt Mittagessen/ Abendessen?	Do you serve lunch/dinner now?
Gibt es noch etwas Warmes zu essen?	Do you still serve hot meals?
Einen Tisch für zwei/drei/vier, bitte.	A table for two/three/four, please.
Die Speisekarte, bitte.	The menu, please.

The waiter may ask you:

Was möchten Sie essen/trinken?	What would you like to eat/drink?
Was möchten Sie bestellen?	What would you like to order?

Aktivität A: Im Gasthaus „Zum Adler"

Pretend you want to eat in the restaurant „Zum Adler." How would you respond to the questions and comments by the waiter? Choose from the list below:

BEISPIEL: KELLNER: Guten Abend.

              SIE: Guten Abend. Haben Sie einen Tisch frei?

a. Haben Sie noch das Menü?

b. Ja, ausgezeichnet.

c. Nein, ich möchte Steak und einen Salat.

d. Ja, ein kleines Bier bitte.

e. Danke schön.

f. Ich möchte zahlen.

g. Auf Wiedersehen.

    KELLNER: Hier ist die Speisekarte.

1. SIE: ____ . . .

    KELLNER: Möchten Sie bestellen?

2. SIE: ____ . . .?

    KELLNER: Nein, leider nicht.

              Ich empfehle Wiener Schnitzel mit Pommes Frites und grüne Bohnen.

3. SIE: ____ . . .

    KELLNER: Möchten Sie etwas zum Trinken?

4. SIE: ____ . . .

              Der Kellner bringt das Essen.

    KELLNER: Guten Appetit.

5. SIE: ____ . . .

    KELLNER: Möchten Sie noch etwas?

6. SIE: ____ . . .

    KELLNER: Einen Moment bitte.

              Der Kellner bringt die Rechnung.

    KELLNER: War alles in Ordnung?

7. SIE: ____ . . .

        ____ . . .

What's on the Menu (Speisekarte)?

Major sections of the Speisekarte consist of:

Vorspeisen	appetizers
Suppen	soups
Fleischgerichte	meat dishes
Beilagen	potatoes, rice, noodles, etc.
Gemüse	vegetables
Salate	salads
Nachspeisen	desserts
Getränke	beverages
Tagesmenü	special of the day

Vorspeisen*

die Austern	oysters
der Hummer	lobster
die Krabben	shrimp
die Pilze	mushrooms
der Schinken	ham

Suppen

Bohnensuppe	bean soup
Gulaschsuppe	spicy beef soup
Kartoffelsuppe	potato soup
Nudelsuppe	noodle soup
Tomatensuppe	tomato soup
französische Zwiebelsuppe	French onion soup

Beilagen†

Kartoffeln	potatoes
Bratkartoffeln	hash browns
geröstete Kartoffeln	fried potatoes
der Kartoffelbrei	mashed potatoes
Pommes frites	French fries
Salzkartoffeln	peeled, boiled potatoes
der Reis	rice
die Nudeln	noodles
die Knödel	dumplings

---

*For a more extensive list of **Vorspeisen, Suppen, Fleischspeisen**, etc., see p. 81.

†In some restaurants the **Beilagen** (side dishes) are included in the price; in others they are charged as extras. Check the **Speisekarte** or ask the waiter or waitress.

Fleischgerichte

das (deutsches) Beefsteak	(German) hamburger steak
die Bockwurst	large frankfurter
das Faschierte/Gehackte	minced meat (hamburger)
das Filetsteak	beefsteak
das Gulasch	goulash, stewed beef
der Hackbraten	meat loaf
die Leber	liver
der Schinken	ham
das Schnitzel	cutlet
Naturschnitzel	cutlet, not breaded
Wiener Schnitzel	breaded veal cutlet

Und wie möchten Sie Ihr Fleisch?
How Would You Like Your Meat?

nicht durchgebraten, fast roh	rare
halb durchgebraten	medium
durchgebraten	well-done

Sie haben die Wahl! (You have a choice!):

gebacken	baked
gebraten	fried, roasted
gekocht	boiled
gegrillt	grilled
gedämpft/gedünstet	steamed
gefüllt	stuffed
vom Rost	broiled
geschmort	braised

Gemüse und Salat

der Blumenkohl/Karfiol	cauliflower
die Bohnen, *pl.*	beans
der Broccoli	broccoli
die Erbsen, *pl.*	peas
die Karotten, *pl.*	carrots
der Kohl	cabbage
der Rotkohl, das Blaukraut	red cabbage

Obst

der Apfel, ⁻	apple
die Banane, -n	banana
die Birne, -n	pear
die Erdbeere, -n	strawberry
die Kirsche, -n	cherry
die Melone, -n	melon
die Orange, -n	orange

der Mais	corn, maize	**die Grapefruit, –**	grapefruit
der Salat	salad	**der Pfirsich, -e**	peach
gemischter Salat	mixed salad	**die Traube, -n**	grape
Gurkensalat	cucumber salad	**die Zitrone, -n**	lemon
Kartoffelsalat	potato salad		
der Spargel	asparagus		
der Spinat	spinach		
die Tomaten, *pl.*	tomatoes		

Aktivität B: Im Restaurant—Wünsche und Fragen (Requests and Questions)

Make a suitable choice from the list below. More than one response may be possible.

1. Ich habe Gemüse gern _____.

2. Ich möchte mein Gehacktes _____.

3. Jens möchte sein Steak _____.

4. Sind die Tomaten _____.

5. Servieren Sie den Hackbraten _____ oder _____?

6. Wir möchten die Pilze _____.

gedämpft	gefüllt	gekocht	gebacken
geschmort	vom Rost	gegrillt	gebraten

Aktivität C

Which word doesn't fit? Cross it out.

1. Nudeln   Karotten   Reis   Knödel

2. Erbsen   Pilze   Äpfel   Zwiebeln

3. Schinken   Spargel   Gulasch   Hackbraten

4. Rotkohl   Pfirsiche   Birnen   Erdbeeren

5. Gurken   Trauben   Spinat   Mais

Nachspeisen

der Apfelstrudel	apple strudle
der Käsekuchen	cheesecake
der Pudding	pudding

der Windbeutel	cream puff
die Sachertorte	Viennese chocolate cake (with apricot filling)
die Schwarzwälderkirschtorte	Black Forest cherry cake (chocolate cake with black cherries and whipped cream)
das Kompott	stewed fruit

With dessert you will often hear:

| mit Schlag (Austrian)/mit Sahne | with whipped cream |
| ohne Schlag/ohne Sahne | without whipped cream |

Eis

das Erdbeereis	strawberry ice cream
das Fruchteis	fruit sherbet
das Schokoladeneis	chocolate ice cream
das Vanilleeis	vanilla ice cream
das Zitroneneis	lemon sherbet

Aktivität D

„Man ist, was man isst" (by the German philosopher Feuerbach).

1. Was hat mehr Kalorien?
   a. eine Portion Eis
   b. ein Windbeutel ohne Schlag
   c. ein Stück Sachertorte mit Schlag

2. Wer viel Kuchen isst, soll (should) viel
   a. schlafen   b. laufen   c. zahlen

3. Sie essen gern Obst, aber nicht Gemüse. Was wählen Sie?
   a. Spinat   b. Trauben   c. Äpfel   d. Gurken   e. Kirschen

Other Things You Want to Know or Say at a Restaurant

Wo ist hier ein Telefon?	Where is a telephone, please?
Wo ist die Toilette?	Where is the restroom, please?
Wo ist die Bar?	Where is the bar, please?
Bitte, wo ist der Ober?	Where is the waiter?

Noch ein Glas Milch.	Another glass of milk, please.
Noch ein Glas Bier.	Another glass of beer, please.
Noch eine Tasse Kaffee.	Another cup of coffee, please.
Haben Sie eine Zeitung?	Do you have a newspaper, please?
Haben Sie ein Telefonbuch?	Do you have a telephone book, please?

And before You Leave the Restaurant . . .

Bitte zahlen.	I would like to pay, please.
Die Rechnung, bitte.	The bill, please.

And If You Want to Praise a Little . . .

Es hat geschmeckt.	It tasted good. The meal was good.
Es war sehr gut.	It was very good.
Wir waren zufrieden.	We were satisfied/pleased.
Wir kommen wieder.	We will come again.

Auf Wiedersehen!

Aktivität E: „Ich möchte mich beschweren." (I wish to complain)

Match the German statements with their English equivalents.

1. Ich möchte mich beschweren.
2. Das habe ich nicht bestellt.
3. Die Suppe ist kalt.
4. Das Bier ist warm.
5. Das Fleisch ist zäh.
6. Das schmeckt nicht gut.
7. Das Fleisch ist zu fett.
8. Bitte bringen Sie etwas anderes.
9. Das ist versalzen.
10. Wir warten schon lange.
11. Der Löffel ist schmutzig.
12. Wann kommt das Essen?
13. Das Tischtuch ist nicht sauber.

a. We have been waiting for a long time.
b. I would like to complain.
c. I didn't order that.
d. That doesn't taste good.
e. The meat is tough.
f. The soup is cold.
g. Please bring me something else.
h. That has too much salt.
i. The meat is too fatty.
j. The beer is warm.
k. The tablecloth is not clean.
l. When is the food being served?
m. The spoon is dirty.

GRAMMATIK

1. Giving Orders the Polite Way

Formal commands and requests are very easy in German. Just use the infinitive of the verb + **Sie** (Subject-Verb word order).

Fahren Sie!	go	**Warten Sie!**	wait
Kommen Sie!	come	**Fragen Sie!**	ask
Gehen Sie!	go	**Nehmen Sie!**	take
Bringen Sie!	bring	**Sehen Sie!**	see
Wählen Sie!	choose	**Versuchen Sie!**	try
Essen Sie!	eat	**Suchen Sie!**	seek, look for
Zahlen Sie!	pay	**Bestellen Sie!**	order

As you can see, there is no difference between the "polite" imperative form and the question form (when no question word is used) except for intonation: In commands the voice goes down. Commands are often followed by an exclamation mark.

Command	**Question**
Fahren Sie nach Berlin!	Fahren Sie nach Berlin?
Bestellen Sie jetzt!	Bestellen Sie jetzt?

Übung A

Give a command using the words indicated:

> **BEISPIEL:** Essen/nicht so viel
> Essen Sie nicht so viel!

1. Bringen/ein Glas Wein _____!

2. Versuchen/diese Suppe _____!

3. Kochen/ohne Salz _____!

4. Warten/auf den nächsten Bus _____!

5. Kommen/heute abend _____!

6. Gehen/zur Ecke _____!

7. Wählen/das Steak _____!

8. Fragen/den Ober _____!

9. Nehmen/ein Taxi _____!

10. Fahren/nach Hause _____!

In giving directions, the polite imperative may be used like this:

Gehen Sie . . .		
	geradeaus	straight ahead
	nach rechts	to the right
	nach links	to the left
	bis zur Ecke	to the corner
	bis zum Platz	to the square
	bis zur Ampel	to the traffic light
	bis zur Brücke	to the bridge
	über die Brücke	over the bridge
	bis zum Schild	to the sign
	bis zur Haltestelle	to the bus, streetcar stop

2. The Function of Modals (Modal Auxiliaries)

German, like English, has a small group of verbs that help to express feelings, attitudes, or desires. These verbs are known as *modal auxiliaries* or simply *modals*. They are usually used together with another verb that has to be in the infinitive form.

BEISPIEL: Müssen Sie schon gehen? — Must you go already?
Do you have to go already?

Ich will jetzt bestellen. — I want to order now.
Hier dürfen Sie nicht rauchen. — You are not allowed to smoke here.

Modal + infinitive

dürfen	may, to be allowed (to)
können	can, to be able (to)
✳ mögen	to like (to), to prefer
müssen	must, to have (to)
sollen	ought (to), to be supposed (to)
wollen	to want (to)

pronoun	dürfen	können	müssen	sollen	wollen
ich	darf	kann	muss	soll	will
du	darfst	kannst	musst	sollst	willst
er, sie, es	darf	kann	muss	soll	will
wir	dürfen	können	müssen	sollen	wollen
ihr	dürft	könnt	müsst	sollt	wollt
sie, Sie	dürfen	können	müssen	sollen	wollen

Note: Except for **sollen,** each modal has a stem vowel change in all singular forms. The vowel of the plural forms is the same as that of the infinitive.

Übung B

Complete the sentence with the modal in parentheses.

BEISPIEL: Ich **muss** jetzt essen.   müssen

1. Wir _____ ins Restaurant gehen.   können

2. Der Geschäftsmann _____ nach Amerika fahren.   wollen

3. Wo _____ ich ein billiges Gasthaus finden?   können

4. Man _____ in einem Restaurant ein Trinkgeld geben.   sollen

5. _____ Sie auch das Menü bestellen?   wollen

6. Du _____ jetzt bestellen.   müssen

7. In diesem Restaurant _____ man nicht rauchen.   dürfen

8. Herr Weber, _____ Sie ein Taxi nehmen?   können

9. Was _____ die Kinder trinken?   dürfen

10. Was _____ du jetzt machen?   wollen

Note: Sometimes modals are used without the infinitive. In such cases the infinitive is implied or understood.

Ich kann Deutsch.	(sprechen)
Herr Braun will nach Hause.	(gehen, fahren)
Wir dürfen das nicht.	(tun, machen)
Ich möchte eine Tasse Kaffee.	(trinken, haben)

---

3. *Möchten* Means "Would Like" (an Expression You Will Need)

ich	möchte	I would like
du	möchtest	you would like *(fam. sing.)*
er, sie, es	möchte	he, she, it would like
wir	möchten	we would like
ihr	möchtet	you would like *(fam. pl.)*
Sie	möchten	you would like *(formal)*
sie	möchten	they would like

Übung C

Say the subject would like to do whatever the cue indicates. Use the correct form of **möchten.**

> **BEISPIEL:** Ich _____   einen Tisch bestellen
> Ich **möchte** einen Tisch bestellen.

1. Kurt _____.   heute Tennis spielen
2. Ich _____.   einen Tee trinken
3. Ingrid _____.   jetzt essen
4. Wo _____ Sie _____?   wohnen
5. Er _____.   nach Wien reisen
6. Wir _____.   zahlen bitte
7. Was _____ du _____?   trinken
8. Herr Mayer _____.   einen Tisch bestellen
9. Ihr _____.   ein Gasthaus finden
10. Wohin _____ Sie _____?   fahren

4. Ordinal Numbers

der	erste	elfte	zwanzigste
die	zweite	zwölfte	einundzwanzigste
das	dritte	dreizehnte	zweiundzwanzigste
	vierte	vierzehnte	dreißigste
	fünfte	usw.	vierzigste
	sechste		hundertste
	siebte		tausendste
	achte		zehntausendste
	neunte		millionste
	zehnte		

Ordinal numbers rank an item in a series. The definite article (**der, die, das**) is always used.

from 2 to 19 =
   cardinal number + t + ending = zwei*te*, fünf*te*, dreizehn*te*
from 20 on   =
   cardinal number + st + ending = zwanzig*ste*, achtundreißig*ste*

Note the ending when you use ordinal numbers.
    Heute ist der sech**ste** Mai.
    Morgen ist der dreizehn**te** Oktober.

But if you use **am** (on the) = **-ten, -sten**
    Jens kommt **am** vierundzwanzig**sten*** Juni.
    Inge heiratet **am** dreißig**sten** April.

Ordinal numbers are used to express the date.

	Januar		April
Winter	Februar	**Frühling**	Mai
	März		Juni
	Juli		Oktober
Sommer	August	**Herbst**	November
	September		Dezember

Both the months and the seasons have masculine gender: der Januar, der Februar, der Winter, der Herbst, usw.

How Do You Ask What Day/Date It Is?

Welcher Tag ist heute?	What day is today?
or **Der wievielte (Tag) ist heute?**	What is today's date?

Übung D

Antworten Sie bitte. Use **am** in your answer and add the ending **-ten** to the stem of the ordinal number.

> **BEISPIEL:** Wann ist Ihr Geburtstag?   (*When is your birthday?*)
>   Mein Geburtstag ist am zwölften Juli.

or just . . . am zwölften Juli.

1. Wann ist **Weihnachten** (*Christmas*)?

   _____.

2. Wann ist **der Nationalfeiertag** (*national holiday*) der USA?

   _____.

---

*It is "am vierundzwanzigsten" because ordinals are declined like adjective endings. **Am = an dem** signals the dative case, which requires the -en ending (see chapter 4).

3. Wann ist **Silvester** (*New Year's Eve*)?

   _____.

4. Wann ist **Neujahr**?

   _____.

5. Wann fliegen Sie nach Europa?

   _____.

6. Wann fahren Sie nach Deutschland?

   _____.

7. Wann haben Sie Geburtstag?

   _____.

8. Wann fahren Sie nach Hause?

   _____.

What about fractions?

Fractions in German are treated like neuter nouns. From **Drittel** ($\frac{1}{3}$) on, they are formed by adding the ending -el to the ordinal number.

½ **ein halb*** (*or* **die Hälfte**)	$\frac{1}{10}$ **ein Zehntel**
⅓ **ein Drittel**	1½ **eineinhalb-**
¼ **ein Viertel**	2⅔ **zweizweidrittel**
¾ **Dreiviertel**	$\frac{1}{100}$ **ein Hundertstel**

Übung E

Say: $\frac{5}{8}$; $\frac{3}{5}$; $\frac{1}{9}$; $\frac{2}{3}$; $\frac{1}{5}$; $\frac{1}{2}$; $\frac{1}{4}$; $\frac{3}{4}$; $\frac{1}{10}$. Complete the sentence with the cued fraction.

1. (½) Ein Pfund ist die _____ von einem Kilo.

2. (¼) Ich bleibe noch eine _____ Stunde.

3. (⅛) Er trinkt noch ein _____ Wein.

4. ($\frac{7}{10}$) Liebfrauenmilch kommt in _____ Flaschen.

5. (¾) _____ des Jahres lebe ich in Amerika.

---

*The word **halb-** must take an adjective ending: **eine halbe Stunde, ein halbes Brot, ein halber Apfel.**

Ordinals in action

A:	Wann fliegen Sie nach Wien?	When are you flying to Vienna?
B:	Im Juni.	In June.
A:	Am wievielten?	What date?
B:	Am vierzehnten.	On the 14th.

A:	Wann hat Inge Geburtstag?	When is Inge's birthday?
B:	Ich glaube am fünfundzwanzigsten Mai.	I believe on the 25th of May.
A:	Und Paul?	And Paul's?
B:	Am sechzehnten Juli.	On the 16th of July.

A:	Ist das Ihre erste oder zweite Reise nach Deutschland?	Is this your first or second trip to Germany?
B:	Oh nein, das ist schon meine vierte.	Oh, no. This is already my fourth.
A:	Und wann fahren Sie nach Amerika?	And when are you going to America?
B:	Am siebzehnten Februar.	On the 17th of February.

A:	Herr Ober, ein Glas Wein, bitte.	Waiter, a glass of wine, please.
B:	Ein Viertel oder ein Achtel?	A quarter or an eighth?
A:	Ein Viertel, bitte.	A quarter, please.

Übung F: Sie fragen . . .

BEISPIEL: Is he going to Chicago on the sixth?
Fährt er am sechsten nach Chicago?

1. Is she flying to Berlin on the 20th?

   _____?

2. Is Gregor getting married on the 17th of June?

   _____?

3. Which day is today?

_____?

4. Are you coming on the 14th?

_____?

5. Is the 23rd a Monday?

_____?

Übung G: Sie sagen . . .

BEISPIEL: I am here on the seventh.
Ich bin am siebten hier.

1. She is here on the 21st.

_____.

2. The 5th is a Saturday.

_____.

3. He is coming on the 30th.

_____.

4. We are flying to Austria on the 18th.

_____.

5. I am buying a house on the 10th
of May.

_____.

5. Asking Indirect Questions

When you use question words to introduce *indirect* questions (i.e., I don't know *where* he lives), the verb-last (V-L) word order applies (very much like in English).

BEISPIEL: Wissen Sie, wieviel das kostet?
Do you know how much that costs?
Er weiß nicht, wo das Hotel ist.
He doesn't know where the hotel is.

Übung H

Make *indirect* questions from the direct questions.

BEISPIEL: Wo ist hier das Telefon?
Wissen Sie, *wo hier das Telefon ist?*

1. Wann kommt der Zug?

   Wissen Sie, _____?

2. Wohin fährt die Straßenbahn?

   Wissen Sie, _____?

3. Wo ist hier ein Telefon?

   Wissen Sie, _____?

4. Wie teuer ist das?

   Wissen Sie, _____?

5. Wen frage ich dort?

   Wissen Sie, _____?

6. Warum fährt heute kein Bus?

   Wissen Sie, _____?

7. Wann geht Frau Schmidt nach Hause?

   Wissen Sie, _____?

Übung I

Form questions from these statements.

> **BEISPIEL:** Sie reservieren den Tisch.
> Reservieren Sie den Tisch?

1. Sie suchen eine Milchbar.

   _____?

2. Er bestellt einen Salat.

   _____?

3. Helga nimmt ein Taxi.

   _____?

4. Du kommst ins Hotel.

   _____?

5. Ihr seht die Post.

   _____?

6. Ich finde das Restaurant.

   _____?

7. Sie wartet auf den Zug.

   _____?

8. Er bestellt das Menü.

   _____?

9. Bernd geht zum Schnellimbiss.

   _____?

10. Das Auto steht vor dem Hotel.

   _____?

6. The Conjugation of *wissen* (to know)

As a number of other verbs, **wissen** is an irregular verb and its conjugation must be memorized.

wissen

Singular		Plural	
ich	weiß	wir	wissen
du	weißt	ihr	wisst
er, sie, es,	weiß	Sie, sie	wissen

Übung J

Fill in the blanks with the correct form of *wissen*.

BEISPIEL: _____ Weiß _____ er, wo das Restaurant ist?

1. Ich _____, wann er kommt.

2. Wir _____, wieviel die Zeitung kostet.

3. Martin _____ nicht, wie der Herr heißt.

4. Karin und Bärbel _____, wo eine Bank ist.

5. _____ die Kinder, wo die Eltern sind?

6. Frau Selke _____ alles.

7. Ich _____ nicht, warum er eine Milchbar sucht.

8. _____ du, wer die Rechnung bezahlt?

Übung K: Fragen, nichts als Fragen! (Questions, Nothing but Questions!)

Auf deutsch, bitte.

1. Where is the train station?

   _____?

2. Does Georg know how expensive the restaurant is?

   _____?

3. Do you *(fam. sing.)* know what the policeman is saying?

   _____?

4. Do they know where I live?

   _____?

5. How much is the newspaper?

   _____?

7. More about Word Order

a. Subject-Verb Word Order

You are already familiar with S-V word order. The sentence or clause begins with the subject, and the verb follows.

> BEISPIELE: 1. Ich möchte ein preiswertes Zimmer.
> 2. Wir essen gern Salat.
> 3. Herr Klein bestellt etwas Warmes.

b. Verb-Subject Word Order

You have also learned that in questions V-S word order is used.

> BEISPIELE: Möchten Sie eine Tasse Kaffee?
> Servieren Sie jetzt Abendessen?
> Ist das Menü teuer?

V-S word order is also used for formal commands.

> BEISPIELE: Bringen Sie bitte die Speisekarte!
> Bitte rauchen Sie hier nicht!
> Schreiben Sie bitte eine Postkarte!

c. V-S Word Order

V-S word order is also used when the main verb is preceded by an element that is *not* the subject. This element may consist of a single word, a phrase, or a dependent clause. In questions, it is the question word.

> BEISPIELE: Heute essen wir im Gasthaus.
> Am Wochenende fahre ich nach Nürnberg.
> Wo wohnen Sie in Österreich?

d. Verb-Last Word Order

Verb-last word order is one of the most striking features of German. Mark Twain once quipped that he had read a German novel 257 pages long, yet had no idea what the action was until he came to the last page, where he found all the verbs. Verb-last word order is used in dependent clauses. A dependent clause is one that does not make sense by itself but depends on a main clause for its meaning. Dependent clauses frequently begin with **dass** (that), **weil** (because), or **wenn** (whenever, if). These words are known as **subordinating conjunctions.**

> BEISPIELE: Ich esse viel Salat, **weil** das gesund **ist.**
> I eat a lot of salad because it is healthy.

Christa trinkt nie Alkohol, **wenn** sie Auto **fährt.**
Christa never drinks alcohol when she drives.

Wir wissen nicht, **ob** das Restaurant teuer **ist**
We don't know, whether the restaurant is expensive.

The most common subordinating conjunctions are:*

als	when, as	**obwohl**	although, even though
bevor	before	**seit, seitdem**	since (temporal)
bis	until	**sobald**	as soon as
da	since (casual), because	**solange**	as long as
		während	while, whereas
damit	so that	**weil**	because
dass	that	**wenn**	if, whenever
ob	whether		

Übung L

Complete as suggested by the cue, using V-L word order.

BEISPIEL: (Wir haben Geld)
Wir fliegen nach Deutschland, sobald wir Geld haben.

1. (Die Restaurants sind zu teuer)

Wir essen zu Hause, weil _____.

2. (Er fährt mit einem Taxi)
Ich frage meinen Freund, ob

_____.

3. (Das Essen ist dort billig)
Meine Familie isst gern im Hotel Stern, weil

_____.

4. (Es gibt ein preiswertes Hotel)
Wissen Sie,

wo _____?

---

*These conjunctions are not listed again in the chapter vocabulary, only in the end vocabulary.

5. (Ich habe wenig Geld)

Ich esse im Restaurant, obwohl _____.

6. (Das Wetter ist kalt)
Herr und Frau Braun fahren nach Florida, wenn

_____.

Übung M

Combine the clauses with the German equivalent of the cue conjunction.

    BEISPIEL: Bettina fragt mich. Ich trinke gern Wein.   whether
              Bettina fragt mich, ob ich gern Wein trinke.

1. Ich bin glücklich. Ich bin jetzt in Deutschland.   because

_____.

2. Wir zahlen jetzt. Wir können nach Hause gehen.   so that

_____.

3. Der Kellner empfiehlt das Menü. Es ist nicht gut.   even though

_____.

4. Meine Frau bleibt in Europa. Ich arbeite hier.   while

_____.

5. Ich weiß nicht. Ich kann zur Party kommen.   whether

_____.

6. Die Kellnerin gibt uns einen Tisch am Fenster.   because
Sie kennt uns.

_____.

7. Herr König fährt oft mit dem Auto.   even though
Das Benzin ist teuer.

_____.

8. Wissen Sie . . . Es ist schon sehr spät.   that

_____.

> *Note:* If you start a sentence with the *dependent clause,* the main clause has *verb-subject* word order because the first (dependent) clause is considered the first element in the sentence, and as you know, the *verb* has to be the second grammatical unit.

BEISPIELE: Wenn ich eine Suppe esse, **bestelle** ich keinen Salat.
Sobald ich nach Hause komme, **lese** ich die Zeitung.
Obwohl Dr. Heinze Arzt ist, **raucht** er.

If you use a modal and another verb in a *dependent clause,* the modal must go to the end of the clause.

BEISPIELE: Wissen Sie, dass man hier mit Dollar bezahlen **muss.**
Natalie sagt, dass sie gern einen Tee bestellen **möchte.**
Ich fliege morgen nach England, weil ich meinen Onkel besuchen **will.**

Übung N

Schreiben Sie auf deutsch.

BEISPIELE: Do you know whether Georg has to work today?
Wissen Sie, ob Georg heute arbeiten muss?

1. We are staying at the Hotel Dresden until we buy a house.

   _____.

2. I want to see you *(fam. sing.)* even though I am sick.

   _____.

3. They won't go home until you *(fam. sing.)* come.

   _____.

4. My parents can travel whenever they have time.

   _____.

5. Elke wants to stay here until June 15th.

   _____.

8. Compound Nouns

Many German nouns consist of two or more words joined together, and these compound nouns are written as one word. Although English has similar compound nouns, the parts often continue to be written separately, even though they are pronounced as a single word. In German, compound nouns take their gender from that of the *final* compound.

das Auto + die Bahn = **die** Autobahn

das Auto + die Bahn + das Restaurant = **das** Autobahnrestaurant

Übung O

Sagen oder schreiben Sie "compounds."

1. der Käse + der Kuchen   = _____

2. das Obst + die Torte   = _____

3. das Gulasch + die Suppe = _____

4. die Frucht + das Eis   = _____

5. der Gast + das Haus   = _____

Übung P

Combine and match the words on the left with an appropriate one from the right.

BEISPIEL: <u>der Kaffee</u> + *h.* <u>die Tasse</u> = **die Kaffeetasse**

1. ____ Straßen ____	a. das Haus
2. ____ Gast ____	b. die Bahn
3. ____ Bus ____	c. der Kuchen
4. ____ Käse ____	d. die Haltestelle
5. ____ Stadt ____	e. der Plan
6. ____ Haus ____	f. der Portier
7. ____ Hotel ____	g. die Tür
	h. die Tasse

SPRECHEN LEICHT GEMACHT

Aktivität A: Was möchten Sie?

Der Kellner/die Kellnerin fragt . . .   Sie antworten/sagen

Was möchten Sie trinken?

Ich möchte . . .

einen Orangensaft
ein Mineralwasser
ein Coca Cola
ein Glas Wein
ein kleines/großes Bier
einen Kaffee
einen Tee
einen Apfelsaft
einen Apfelsaft gespritzt
   (mit Mineralwasser)
einen Gespritzten (ein Glas Wein mit
   Mineralwasser)
was noch . . .

Was möchten Sie essen?

Bitte bringen Sie mir . . .

nur eine Suppe
gemischtes Eis
eine Obsttorte
einen Apfelstrudel
einen gemischten Salat
was noch . . .

Aktivität B: Was sucht Mr. Smith?

MR. SMITH:	Entschuldigen Sie, bitte. Wo ist hier ein Hotel oder ein Gasthaus?
PASSERBY A:	Ein Hotel? Ein Gasthaus? Es tut mir leid. Das weiß ich nicht. Ich bin nicht von hier.
MR. SMITH TO PASSERBY B:	Bitte, gibt es hier ein Hotel oder ein Gasthaus?
PASSERBY B:	Was suchen Sie? Ein Hotel? Nein, hier gibt es kein Hotel.
PASSERBY C:	Aber ein Gasthaus. Gut und preiswert. Gar nicht weit von hier.
MR. SMITH:	Wie weit von hier?
PASSERBY C:	Sehen Sie die Ampel dort?
MR. SMITH:	Ja, ich sehe sie.
PASSERBY C:	Gehen Sie bis zur Ampel, und dann rechts um die Ecke.

PASSERBY B:	Und von dort geradeaus bis zum Marktplatz. Dort ist das Gasthaus „Zum Adler."
MR. SMITH:	Und wo finde ich ein Hotel?
PASSERBY D:	Fahren Sie mit dem Bus zur Bahnhofstraße. Dort ist das „Parkhotel."
PASSERBY C:	Oder nehmen Sie ein Taxi.
MR. SMITH:	Wieviel kostet das?
PASSERBY C:	Das weiß ich leider nicht.
MR. SMITH:	Vielen Dank.

Wiederholung

Telling, Asking, Complaining.

A. How would you tell a person . . .

1. to go (drive) . . . straight ahead/to the left/to the right
2. to walk . . . to the corner/to the sign/over the bridge
3. to take . . . the bus/the streetcar/a taxi
4. to bring . . . the menu/the newspaper/the telephone book

B. How would you ask the waiter . . .

1. to have your meat cooked . . . rare/well done
2. to have your vegetables steamed
3. to have your dessert with whipped cream/without cream

C. How would you complain that . . .

1. we have been waiting long
2. the soup is cold
3. the beer is warm
4. this is too salty
5. the table is not clean
6. the meat is tough

D. How would you ask a person . . .

1. whether this place is taken/still free
2. whether they still serve hot meals/lunch/dinner
3. whether they still have the special of the day

E. How would you say . . .

1. you want to pay
2. you were satisfied
3. excuse me, please

F. Was ist das? Indicate whether the following dishes are

a. eine Vorspeise b. ein Getränk c. eine Nachspeise
d. Fleisch e. eine Suppe f. Gemüse g. Obst

1. Pilze _____
2. Erbsen _____
3. Wiener Schnitzel _____
4. Faschiertes _____
5. Gurken _____
6. Sachertorte _____
7. Milch _____
8. Austern _____

9. Bohnen _____
10. Apfelsaft _____
11. Spargel _____
12. Kompott _____
13. Bockwurst _____
14. Kirschen _____
15. Zwiebel _____
16. Windbeutel _____

Wortschatz
Additional Food Vocabulary

Vorspeisen	**Appetizers**
die Fleischpastete	meat-filled pastry
der Hering/Räucherhering	herring/smoked herring
die Russischen Eier	deviled eggs
die Spargelspitzen	asparagus tips
der Thunfisch	tuna
die Wurst/Wurstplatte	sausage/assorted cold cuts

Suppen	**Soups**
Bouillon (mit Ei)	clear bouillon (with egg)
Fischsuppe	fish soup
*Frittatensuppe	broth with pancake strips
Frühlingssuppe	spring vegetable soup
*Grießnockerlsuppe	cream of wheat dumpling soup
Königinsuppe	beef, sour cream, and almond soup
Kraftbrühe (mit Ei)	beef consommé (with egg)

*Leberknödelsuppe	liver-dumpling soup
Linsensuppe	lentil soup

*These soups are typically Austrian.

Fleischspeisen	Meat Dishes
die Bierwurst	beer sausage
die Blutwurst	blood sausage
der Braten	roast
das Eisbein	pig's knuckle
die Frikadelle	croquettes
Kasseler Rippen, die *(pl.)*	smoked pork
das Rippensteak	rib steak
die Roulade	filled, rolled, and braised thin slice of beef
der Schweinebraten	pork roast
der Speck	bacon

Gemüse/Salat	Vegetables/Salad
der Bohnensalat	bean salad
der Kürbis	pumpkin
der Meerrettich	horseradish
das Radieschen	radish
der Rosenkohl	brussels sprouts

Obst	Fruit
die Ananas	pineapple
die Pflaume	plum

Nouns

das Abendessen, –	dinner	das Essen, –	meal
der Adler, –	eagle	das Fenster, –	window
die Ampel, -n	traffic light	das Fleisch	meat
die Autobahn, -en	superhigh-way, inter-state	das Fruchteis	sherbet, fruit ice cream
die Bahn, -en	streetcar, train	der Gastgarten, ⸚	outdoor sitting area of a restaurant
die Beilage, -n	side dish		
das Benzin	gasoline	das Gasthaus, ⸚er	inn
die Betriebsferien	company vacation	die Gaststätte, -n	restaurant
		das Gemüse, –	vegetable
die Brücke, -n	bridge	der Gespritzte, -n	wine with mineral water
die Bushaltestelle, -n	bus stop		
die Ecke, -n	corner		
der Engländer, –	Englishman	das Getränk, -e	beverage

das Hauptgericht, -e	main course	das Postamt, ̈-er	post office
der Hotelportier, -s	desk clerk, concierge	die Raststätte, -n	restaurant (on the Autobahn)
die Jausenstation, -en	snack bar (Austrian)	die Rechnung, -en	bill, invoice
der Kuchen, –	cake	die Renovierung, -en	renovation
der Marktplatz, ̈-e	marketplace	der Ruhetag, -e	day off
das Menü, -s	special of the day	der Salat, -e	salad
		das Salz	salt
die Milchbar, -s	dairy bar	das Schild, -er	sign
das Mineralwasser, –	mineral water	der Schnellimbiss, -sse	snack bar
		der Stadtplan, ̈-e	city map
das Mittagessen, –	lunch	die Straßenbahn-	streetcar stop
die Nachspeise, -n	dessert	haltestelle, -n	
der Ober, –	waiter (head)	das Stück, -e	piece
das Obst	fruit	die Suppe, -n	soup
die Obsttorte, -n	fruit tart	das Tagesmenü, -s	special of the day
der Onkel, –	uncle		
der Parkplatz, ̈-e	parking place	die Tasse, -n	cup
		das Tischtuch, ̈-er	table cloth
der Pfeffer	pepper	die Vorspeise, -n	appetizer
der Platz, ̈-e	place, seat, spot, public square	die Weinstube, -n	wine tavern
		das Wochenende, –	weekend

Verbs

sich beschweren	to complain	rauchen	to smoke
bestellen	to order	reservieren	to reserve
bringen	to bring	schlafen (schläft)	to sleep
dämpfen	to steam	schmecken (*dat.*)	to taste
dürfen (darf)	may, to be allowed (to)	sollen	ought (to), to be supposed (to)
empfehlen (empfiehlt)	to recommend	stehen	to stand
		versuchen	to choose, to try
essen (isst)	to eat		
kochen	to cook	wählen	to choose, to select
können (kann)	can, to be able (to)		
		warten	to wait
laufen (läuft)	to run	wissen (weiß)	to know
möchten	would like	wollen (will)	to want (to)
mögen (mag)	to like	zahlen	to pay
müssen	must, have to		

Other Words

aber	but	geschmort	braised
alles	everything	glücklich	happy
als	when	hinter	behind
ander-	other	hungrig	hungry
ausgezeichnet	excellent	oder	or
bald	soon	preiswert	low-priced,
durchgebraten	well done		reasonably
halb durchgebraten	medium		priced
nicht durchgebraten	rare	roh	rare, raw
fett	fat, fatty	sauber	clean
frei	free	schattig	shady
gar nicht	not at all	schmutzig	dirty
gebacken	baked	schön	beautiful,
gebraten	fried,		pretty
	roasted	sehr	very
gedämpft	steamed	versalzen	oversalted
gefüllt	filled, stuffed	vom Rost	broiled
gegrillt	grilled	von . . . bis	from . . .
gekocht	cooked		until (to)
geöffnet	open	was noch	what else?
geradeaus	straight	wegen	because
	ahead	wen	whom
geräuchert	smoked	zäh	tough
geschlossen	closed		

Idiomatic Expressions

Alles in Ordnung?	Everything okay?
Es tut mir leid.	I am sorry.
mit Schlag/Sahne	with whipped cream
ohne Schlag/Sahne	without whipped cream
um 11 Uhr	at 11 o'clock

Cognates

das Hotel, -s
der Hunger
die Kalorie, -n
die Postkarte, -n

Lodging, Hotels, and Overnight Accommodations

CULTURE NOTES

You are traveling in a German-speaking country and need a place to stay overnight. Since you haven't made any reservations in advance, you might look for a:

(das) Hotel	hotel
(der) Gasthof	inn (restaurant and rooms)
(das) Gasthaus	restaurant, often with rooms
(die) Pension	boarding house
(das) Fremdenzimmer	room for rent
(die) Jugendherberge	youth hostel
(das) Studentenheim	dormitory

If you arrive by plane or train, most larger cities have a counter at the airport or train station called **Zimmernachweis, Hotelnachweis, oder Information** *(i)*—room information, hotel information, or general information.

If you are traveling by car, the same help may be available at the outskirts of a city, especially on the **Autobahn.**

Hotel prices differ according to the category under which they are listed: A, B, C, or D or I., II., and so on. Better hotels are also identified as three-, four-, or five- star hotels. Prices are usually higher in metropolitan areas.

Zimmer mit Bad means a room with a bath tub, sink, and toilet (W.C.). **Zimmer mit Dusche** may include a shower and W.C. or just a shower with a W.C. across or down the hall. A **Zimmer ohne Bad und Dusche** may still be a nice, clean room, but bath, shower and W.C. are somewhere else.

Note that the price of a double room is often listed as **pro Person.** If it says €50,00 **pro Person,** that double room will cost €100 for two.

The price for lodging usually includes a standard Continental breakfast consisting of coffee, tea, or hot chocolate and rolls or bread with butter, cheese, jam, or honey. Buffet breakfasts are also offered at many hotels. The term **Vollpension** means that all meals are included, and **Halbpension** that breakfast and dinner are included.

Telephone calls from your hotel room cost 30 to 100 percent more than a call from a pay phone or the post office. Nowadays most people have cell phones (**Handys**).

Tips for the maid are included in the price, but you may leave additional money in the room before departure. Tip the person who carries your luggage to your room.

All travelers must register, even if staying only one night. This is the law.

Hotels near railroad stations are often more expensive than hotels in the city center or in the suburbs. Traveling by car gives you an advantage to find less expensive and often charming overnight accommodations outside the city.

European (Eurocheck) and American credit cards are accepted in most higher-priced hotels. Smaller establishments, especially in the countryside, may not be familiar with "plastic money." Not yet!

An alternative to hotels is lodging in a place with the sign **Zimmer frei.** This is the German equivalent of a bed-and-breakfast. These are private homes (or farms) that rent out rooms. It is an economical way to stay overnight, and most of these places are nice and clean and often provide contact with a family.

Then there is the inexpensive **Jugendherberge,** the youth hostel, which is popular with young people. Families can use them, too. **Jugendherbergen** have mostly **Schlafsäle** (large rooms with several single beds) and no private bath, shower, etc. Some also stick to a **Sperrstunde**—that is, you must be in at a stated hour. **Jugendherbergen** differ in quality and location. There you can also meet interesting people from all over the world.

DIALOGE

Read the following three dialogues aloud in German and check the English translation:

GAST:	Haben Sie noch ein Zimmer frei?	Do you still have a vacant room?
PORTIER:	Nein, es tut mir leid, wir sind besetzt.	No, I am sorry. We have no vacancy.
GAST:	Und morgen?	And tomorrow?
PORTIER:	Einen Augenblick, ich sehe nach. Ja, morgen können Sie ein Einzel- oder Doppelzimmer mit Dusche bekommen (haben).	Just a moment, I will see. Yes, tomorrow you can have a single or double with shower.
GAST:	Wieviel kostet es?	How much does it cost?
PORTIER:	Das Einzelzimmer kostet 75 Euro, das Doppelzimmer 110.	The single is 75 euros and the double is 110.
GAST:	Gut, ich nehme das Doppelzimmer.	Good. I will take the double.

PORTIER:	Entschuldigen Sie, gehört Ihnen dieser Koffer?	Excuse me, is this your suitcase?
GAST:	Ja, er gehört mir, und diese Tasche auch.	Yes, that's mine, and this bag belongs to me too.
PORTIER:	Peter, bitte helfen Sie der Dame mit dem Gepäck.	Peter, please help the lady with her luggage.
PETER:	Bitte folgen Sie mir.	Please follow me.

HERR S.:	Wohin fahren Sie in Urlaub?	Where are you going for your vacation?
HERR H.:	Diesmal in die Schweiz, nach Grindelwald.	This time we are going to Switzerland, to Grindelwald.
HERR S.:	Und wer fährt mit?	And who all is going?
HERR H.:	Die ganze Familie, meine Frau, unser Sohn und unsere Tochter.	The whole family, my wife, our son and our daughter.
HERR S.:	Wie schön. Haben Sie schon Quartier?	How nice. Do you already have a place?

HERR H.:	Ja, wir mieten eine Ferien-wohnung. Drei Zimmer mit Küche und Balkon.	Yes, we are renting a vacation home. Three rooms with kitchen and balcony.
HERR S.:	Und wie kommen Sie hin?	And how are you getting there?
HERR H.:	Wir fliegen bis Zürich und von dort fahren wir mit dem Zug bis Grindelwald.	We are flying to Zurich and from there we are going by train to Grindelwald.

KOMMUNIKATION

Before doing the Aktivitäten, read the dialogues again carefully.

Aktivität A: Was ist ein/eine/das . . ./was heißt . . . ?

Match each term correctly.

1. ein Einzelzimmer
2. ein Studentenheim
3. ein Doppelzimmer
4. eine Jugendherberge
5. ein Gasthaus
6. (ein) Urlaub
7. das Gepäck
8. „Zimmer frei"
9. „Wir sind besetzt"
10. eine Ferienwohnung

a. Man hat Ferien, hat freie Zeit.
b. Es ist ein bed-and-breakfast, bei einer Familie oder auf einer Farm.
c. Ein Zimmer für eine Person.
d. Ein billiges Quartier für junge Leute.
e. Ein Heim, wo Studenten wohnen.
f. Ein Koffer oder eine Tasche.
g. Ein Restaurant, wo man essen kann.
h. Ein Zimmer für zwei Personen.
i. Man mietet sie für die Ferien.
j. Es gibt keine freien Zimmer.

Aktivität B: Wir reisen!

Which response is *not* a correct one? Cross out the one that doesn't fit.

1. Bitte, was haben Sie noch frei?
   Wir haben noch . . .   . . . ein Einzelzimmer
                             . . . einen Koffer
                             . . . ein Doppelzimmer
                             . . . ein Zimmer mit Dusche

2. Wem gehört dieser Koffer?
   Er gehört . . .   . . . der Dame
                                        . . . mir
                                        . . . dem Doppelzimmer
                                        . . . dem Touristen

3. Wohin fahren Sie?
   Ich fahre . . .   . . . in die Dusche
                                        . . . in die Schweiz
                                        . . . nach Österreich
                                        . . . bis Zürich

4. Was mieten Sie?
   Wir mieten . . .   . . . ein Auto
                                        . . . ein Gepäck
                                        . . . eine Ferienwohnung
                                        . . . ein Zimmer

GRAMMATIK

1. The Dative Case

The dative is the case of the **indirect object,** answering the question **wem?** (to whom? *or* for whom?). Basically, the dative case is used to identify the person or thing for whom an action is carried out.

Wem gehört das Haus?	To whom does the house belong?
Es gehört dem Mann dort.	It belongs to the man over there.
Wem geben Sie das Geld?	To whom are you giving the money?
Ich gebe es der Kellnerin.	I am giving it to the waitress.
Wem erzählst du die Geschichte?	To whom are you telling the story?
Ich erzähle sie den Kindern.	I am telling it to the children.

Case	Masculine	Feminine	Neuter	Plural
Nominative	der	die	das	die
	ein	eine	ein	keine
Dative	dem	der	dem	den
	einem	einer	einem	keinen
Accusative	den	die	das	die
	einen	eine	ein	keine

BEISPIELE:

Wir schreiben den Kindern.	We are writing to the children.
Sagen Sie es der Ärztin.	Tell (it to) the doctor. *(f.)*
Geben Sie dem Kellner die Rechnung.	Give the bill to the waiter.
Ich zeige den Touristen die Stadt.	I am showing the tourists the city
Die Mutter kauft dem Kind eine Limonade.	The mother is buying the child a lemonade.

Übung A

In each of the following sentences an indirect object is used. The dative case is in boldface. Restate the sentence with the cued noun in the dative.

> **BEISPIEL:** Ich zeige **dem Mann** das Buch.   die Frau
> Ich zeige **der Frau** das Buch.

1. Ich zeige _____ das Buch.   die Freunde

2. Ich zeige _____ das Buch.   der Arzt

3. Ich zeige _____ das Buch.   das Kind

4. Ich zeige _____ das Buch.   der Professor

5. Ich zeige _____ das Buch.   das Mädchen

6. Ich zeige _____ das Buch.   die Managerin

2. Dative Ending for a Few Masculine Nouns in the Singular

Whereas most German nouns do not change their form in the dative case singular, a few add -**en** (or -**n**) in all cases except the nominative. Here are some of the nouns.

Nominative	Dative	Accusative
der Tourist	dem Touristen	den Touristen
der Junge	dem Jungen	den Jungen
der Student	dem Studenten	den Studenten
der Soldat	dem Soldaten	den Soldaten
der Herr	dem Herrn	den Herren

3. Dative Endings for Nouns in the Plural

Almost all nouns end in -(e)n in the dative plural.

Wir geben den Kindern das Geld.	We give the money to the children.
Ich zeige den Gästen die Wohnung.	I am showing the guests the apartment.

There are also some exceptions. Words that form their plurals by adding -**s** (mostly foreign words) keep that -**s** in the dative case.

Wir sprechen von den Hotels.*	We are speaking about the hotels.
Mit den Fotos habe ich viel Spaß.	I have a lot of fun with the pictures.

Übung B

Complete using the cued expression.

> **BEISPIEL:** Geben Sie . . . das Geld.   die Kinder
> Geben Sie **den Kindern** das Geld.

der den dem
die die der
das das dem
die die den

1. Sagen Sie es _dem_ Herrn.   der Herr
2. Erzählen Sie es _der_ Amerikaner.   die Amerikaner
3. Geben Sie es _der_ Studenten.   die Studenten
4. Zeigen Sie es _dem_ Freund.   der Freund
5. Sagen Sie es _den_ Freunde.   die Freunde
6. Zeigen Sie es _dem_ Touristen.   der Tourist
7. Zeigen Sie es _der_ Touristen   die Touristen

Übung C

Übersetzen Sie.

> **BEISPIEL:** Say it to the student *(male)*.
> Sagen Sie es dem Studenten.

1. Give it to the tourists.   2. We show it to Mother.

   _____.   _____.

*****mit** and **von** are dative prepositions (see p. 92).

3. I am saying it to the teacher.   5. I am telling it to the people.

_____.   _____.

4. Karl writes to the businessman.

_____.

4. Dative Prepositions*

The following prepositions always require the use of the dative case.

aus	out of, from	**nach**	after, toward, according to
außer	except for	**seit**	since, for (referring to time)
bei	near, at	**von**	from
mit	with	**zu**	to, at

BEISPIEL: **Toni wohnt bei seinen Eltern.**   Toni lives with his parents.
Gabi kommt aus der Bibliothek.   Gabi is coming out of the library.

Übung D

Complete the sentence as suggested, using the dative.

BEISPIEL: Wir fahren jetzt zu . . .   der Bahnhof
Wir fahren jetzt **zu dem (zum)** Bahnhof.

1. Ich fahre nicht gern mit _____.   der Bus

2. Michael kommt aus _____.   das Geschäft

3. Was hörst du von _____.   die Kollegin

4. Seit _____ rauche ich nicht mehr.   ein Monat

5. Nach _____ gehe ich nach Hause.   das Konzert

5. The Dative Case of Personal Pronouns

Case	Singular					Plural			
Nominative	ich	du	er	sie	es	wir	ihr	Sie	sie
	I	you	he	she	it	we	you	you	they
Dative	mir	dir	ihm	ihr	ihm	uns	euch	Ihnen	ihnen
	me	you	him	her	it	us	you	you	them
Accusative	mich	dich	ihn	sie	es	uns	euch	Sie	sie
	me	you	him	her	it	us	you	you	them

*The prepositions listed in this chapter are given in the end vocabulary.

Here are a few examples in which only the dative of personal pronouns are used:

Nein, dieser Koffer gehört uns nicht.	This suitcase does not belong to us.
Bitte schreiben Sie mir.	Please write to me.
Was soll ich ihr geben?	What should I give her?
Ich kaufe ihm nichts.	I am not buying him anything.

And here are dative pronouns and a direct object:

Sie gibt ihm das Geld.	She gives him the money.
Wir kaufen ihr einen Stadtplan.	We are buying her a city map.
Ein Freund zeigt uns die Stadt.	A friend is showing us the city.
Er verkauft ihnen den Computer.	He is selling the computer to them.

Übung E

Apply the personal pronoun of the *dative* case in context. Complete the command with the appropriate pronoun.

BEISPIEL: Ich brauche ein Taxi. Bitte rufen Sie mir ein Taxi.

1. Thomas sucht eine Wohnung. Finden Sie _____ eine Wohnung.

2. Wir haben kein Zimmer. Geben Sie _____ ein Zimmer.

3. Maria möchte die Zeitung. Bringen Sie _____ die Zeitung.

4. Ich habe keine Euro. Bitte geben Sie _____ Euro.

5. Die Touristen möchten die Stadt sehen. Bitte zeigen Sie

   _____ die Stadt.

6. Was, du hast keinen Regenschirm, Martin? Ich kaufe _____ einen Regenschirm.

6. Verbs That Require the Dative Case

If you use these verbs, you must always use the **dative** case:

antworten	to answer	**helfen (hilft)**	to help
danken	to thank	**leid tun**	to be sorry
gefallen (gefällt)	to like	**passen**	to suit, fit
gehören	to belong	**scheinen**	to seem
glauben	to believe	**schmecken**	to taste
passieren	to happen		

Dieser Gasthof gefällt meinem Vater.	My father likes this hotel.
Ich danke der Frau.	I thank the woman.
Bitte antworten Sie mir.	Please answer me.
Es tut ihr leid.	She is sorry.
Gehört das Ihnen?	Does that belong to you?
Wir glauben Ihnen nicht!	We don't believe you.
Christopher hilft dem alten Mann.	Christopher is helping the old man.
Wie schmeckt dir das?	How does this taste (to you)?
Freitag abend? Ja, das passt uns.	Friday night? Yes, that suits us.

Übung F

Restate the sentence, contracting the preposition and the definite article.

> **BEISPIEL** Wann ziehen Sie in das Haus?
> Wann ziehen Sie **ins** Haus?

1. Wir sprechen über das Wetter.

   _____.

2. Bitte gehen Sie an das Fenster.

   _____.

3. Das Fahrrad steht vor dem Geschäft.

   _____.

4. Fahren Sie heute in das Büro?

   _____.

5. Mein Pass ist in dem Koffer.

   _____.

6. Die Katze liegt unter dem Tisch.

   _____.

Übung G

Restate the sentence with the cue verb.

> **BEISPIEL:** Christian wohnt in der Stadt.   fahren
> Christian fährt in die Stadt.

1. Wir fahren ins Hotel.   wohnen

   _____.

2. Schreiben Sie den Brief im Büro?   bringen

   _____.

3. Ich gehe jetzt ins Geschäft.   arbeiten

   _____.

4. Frau Müller lebt in der Schweiz.   reisen

   _____.

5. Karin steht vor dem Gasthaus.   fahren

   _____.

Übung H

Restate each sentence replacing the italicized noun with a suitable pronoun.

> **BEISPIEL:** Das Wienerschnitzel schmeckt *dem Jungen.*
> Das Wienerschnitzel schmeckt **ihm.**

1. Das tut *der Amerikanerin* leid.
2. Antworten Sie *dem Mann.*
3. Ich glaube *den Leuten.*
4. Das passt *den Kindern.*
5. Wie gefällt *dem Vater* das Hotel?
6. Die Wohnung gehört *Frau Müller.*
7. Wir danken *dem Schweizer.*
8. Können Sie *Ingrid* helfen?

Übung I

Now restate each sentence, replacing the dative pronoun with the dative case of the noun in parentheses.

> **BEISPIEL:** Das Eis schmeckt ihm.   der Junge
> Das Eis schmeckt **dem Jungen.**

1. Bitte helfen Sie ihr.   die Frau

   _____.

2. Glaubt er ihm nicht?   der Amerikaner

   _____.

3. Das passt uns nicht.   die Österreicher

   _____.

4. Wir danken ihnen.   die Deutschen

   _____.

5. Diese Wohnung gefällt mir.   die Studentin

   _____.

6. Das Haus gehört uns.   die Firma

   _____.

7. Schmeckt es Ihnen?   die Gäste

   _____.

8. Leider kann ich ihm nicht helfen.   das Kind

   _____.

7. Separable-Prefix Verbs

Many German (and English) verbs consist of two parts: a *prefix* and a *stem*.

BEISPIELE:

Prefix	Stem		
an	kommen	ankommen	to arrive
ab	fahren	abfahren	to depart

an·fangen*	to begin	zurück·fliegen	to fly back
an·rufen	to call	an·schauen	to look at
ein·ziehen	to move in	ein·steigen	to board, get in
um·ziehen	to move	aus·steigen	to get off
aus·ziehen	to move out	zu·machen	to close
mit·nehmen	to take along	auf·machen	to open
auf·stehen	to get up	mit·gehen	to go (come) along

*Separable-prefix verbs are listed in dictionaries in this manner: ab·fahren, an·rufen, mit·nehmen.

> *Note:* In separable-prefix verbs, the *stress* is on the prefix. The *prefix* is separated from the verb.

a. In a main clause (present and past tense):
   Der Bus *kommt* um 9 Uhr *an*.   The bus arrives at 9 o'clock.
b. In a command:
   ***Rufen* Sie mich morgen *an*!**   Call me tomorrow!
c. In a question
   ***Ziehen* Sie im Sommer *um*?**   Are you moving in the summer?

Übung J

Complete the statement or question with the correct German equivalent of the English verb.

> **BEISPIEL:** Wann _____ der Zug _____? to arrive
>   Wann **kommt** der Zug **an**?

1. Wann _____ Lisa in die neue Wohnung _____.   to move

2. Bitte _____ Sie das Buch _____.   to take along

3. Herr Emmerich, _____ Sie morgen _____.   to call

4. Bitte _____ Sie das Fenster _____.   to close

5. Wann _____ Sie nach Amerika _____?   to fly back

6. Der Zug _____ um 16 Uhr 40 _____.   to depart

7. Herr Richter _____ am Freitag _____.   to arrive

8. Wann _____ das Konzert _____?   to begin

A separable prefix does *not* separate:

a. when it is used with an infinitive:
   Ich muss um 7 Uhr aufstehen.   I have to get up at 7 o'clock.
b. when used in a dependent clause:
   Ich weiß nicht, ob Philipp anruft.   I don't know if Philipp is going to call.

Übung K

Complete the sentence with the cue statement.

BEISPIEL: Laura fährt morgen ab.
Ich weiß nicht, ob . . .
Ich weiß nicht, ob Laura morgen abfährt.

1. Tina fliegt am Mittwoch zurück.
Ich glaube, dass . . .

   _____.

2. Ernst zieht im Sommer um.
Ich möchte wissen, warum . . .

   _____.

3. Das Spiel fängt um 19 Uhr an.
Wissen Sie, ob . . .

   _____.

4. Ingrid kommt nach Österreich mit.
Ich freue mich, wenn . . .

   _____.

5. Er fährt am Sonntag ab.
Wir besuchen Fritz heute, weil . . .

   _____.

6. Karin steigt dort immer aus.
Fragen Sie Karin, warum sie . . .

   _____.

8. Word Order of Direct and Indirect Objects

What are the rules for word order when you encounter both a direct and an indirect object in the same sentence or clause?

a. The indirect object usually precedes the direct object.

	Indirect Object	**Direct Object**
Ich gebe	der Frau	den Schlüssel.
I give	the woman	the key.

Sie zeigt	**dem Mann**	**die Wohnung.**
She shows	the man	the apartment.
Wir kaufen	**den Kindern**	**die Bücher.**
We buy	the children	the books.

b. All pronouns precede nouns.

	Indirect Object	**Direct Object**
Ich gebe	ihr	**den Schlüssel.**
I give	her	the key.
Sie zeigt	ihm	**die Wohnung.**
She shows	him	the apartment.
Wir kaufen	ihnen	**die Bücher.**
We buy	them	the books.

	Direct Object	**Indirect Object**
Ich gebe	ihn	**der Frau.**
I give	it	to the woman.
Sie zeigt	sie	**dem Mann.**
She shows	it	to the man.
Wir kaufen	sie	**den Kindern.**
We buy	them	for the children.

c. But when both the direct and the indirect objects are pronouns, the direct object *precedes* the indirect object. Needless to say, such sentences make sense only in context.

	Direct Object	**Indirect Object**
Ich gebe	ihn	ihr.
I give	it	to her.
Sie zeigt	sie	ihm.
She shows	it	to him.
Wir kaufen	sie	ihnen.
We buy	them	for them.

Übung L

Restate, replacing the boldface word(s) with the appropriate direct or indirect object pronoun. Watch word order.

BEISPIEL: a. Der Ober gibt **dem Gast** die Rechnung.
Der Ober gibt **ihm** die Rechnung.

b. Der Ober gibt dem Gast **die Rechnung.**
Der Ober gibt **sie** dem Gast.

c. Der Ober gibt **dem Gast die Rechnung.**
Der Ober gibt **sie ihm.**

1. a. Helmut bringt **Elke** den Koffer.

   _____.

   b. Helmut bringt Elke **den Koffer.**

   _____.

   c. Helmut bringt **Elke den Koffer.**

   _____.

2. a. Wir verkaufen **den Amerikanern** einen Fernseher.

   _____.

   b. Wir verkaufen den Amerikanern **einen Fernseher.**

   _____.

   c. Wir verkaufen **den Amerikanern einen Fernseher.**

   _____.

3. a. Ich zeige **den Freunden** das Geschäft.

   _____.

   b. Ich zeige den Freunden **das Geschäft.**

   _____.

   c. Ich zeige **den Freunden das Geschäft.**

   _____.

Übung M

Form three sentences of your choice using any of the direct and indirect objects listed.

BEISPIEL: Wir verkaufen den Studenten einen Volkswagen.

Wir zeigen . . .	sie
Ich bringe . . .	den Deutschen
Er kauft . . .	ihnen
	ein Auto
	dem Studenten
	ihr
	einen Koffer
	es
	ihm
	den Österreichern

---

den 17. Mai 2006

KURZER GESCHÄFTSBRIEF

Sehr geehrter Herr Müller!*

Mein Kollege John Tyler und ich kommen am 23. Juni um 15 Uhr 30 mit Lufthansaflug 79 aus Hamburg in Düsseldorf an. Holen Sie uns am Flughafen ab, oder sollen wir direkt zum Hotel fahren? Wir freuen uns, wenn Sie uns abholen, aber es ist nicht nötig.

Bitte schreiben Sie uns, bevor wir hier abreisen.

Mit freundlichen Grüßen
Ihr . . .

---

9. Two-Way Prepositions

These nine prepositions require either the **accusative** or the **dative** case.

an	at the side of, at, on, to		**über**	over, above, about
auf	on top of, on, to		**unter**	under, among
hinter	in back of, behind		**vor**	in front of, before
in	inside of, in, into		**zwischen**	between
neben	next to, beside			

---

*Do you understand this letter? If not, consult answers on p. 233.

These nine prepositions take the *accusative* if there is motion from one place to another (in other words, if there is a change in location). They usually answer the question **wohin?** (where to?).

Wohin fahren Sie?	Where are you going (to)?
Ich fahre in die Stadt.	I am driving into the city.

But the same nine prepositions take the *dative* case when they express position in a place and when they answer the question **wo?** (where?).

Wo wohnen Sie?	Where do you live?
Ich wohne in der Stadt.	I live in the city.

These prepositions also take the dative case when the verb indicates action or motion within a place and thus also answers the question **wo?** (where?).

Wo arbeiten Sie?	Where do you work?
Ich arbeite in einem Büro.	I work in an office.

Contractions of the definite articles **dem, das,** and some of the two-way prepositions are commonly used in everyday speech.

an + dem = **am**	über + dem = **überm**
hinter + dem = **hinterm**	unter + dem = **unterm**
in + dem = **im**	vor + dem = **vorm**

Übung N

Dative or accusative? Complete using the cue in the *accusative* or the *dative* as appropriate. (Hint: Do you ask **wohin?** or **wo?**)

BEISPIEL: Wir ziehen morgen in _____.   *die Wohnung*
Wir ziehen morgen in die Wohnung.

1. Ich ziehe jetzt in _____.	die Stadt
2. Wir warten vor _____ auf Sie.	das Hotel
3. Die Kinder laufen hinter _____.	das Haus
4. Sie sitzt neben _____.	ein Österreicher
5. Die Rechnung liegt auf _____.	der Tisch
6. Wir gehen heute auf _____.	ein Berg
7. Ich bleibe oft in _____.	ein Gasthof

8. Wir essen oft in _____. das Gasthaus

9. Der Hund liegt vor _____. das Sofa

10. Der Tourist geht an _____. die Ecke

SPRECHEN LEICHT GEMACHT

Aktivität A: Was zeigen/kaufen/geben Sie?

Wem . . . ? We are talking about showing/buying/giving/selling things to other people. Complete the answer to each question. Replace the bold-faced noun(s) with a pronoun.

> **BEISPIELE:** Was zeigen Sie der Studentin?   *die Jugendherberge*
> Ich zeige *ihr* die Jugendherberge.
> oder:
> Ich zeige *ihr* das Museum.
> usw.

1. Was kaufen Sie **den Kindern?** *Kuchen*

   Ich kaufe . . .

2. Was zeigen Sie **der Managerin?** *das Einzelzimmer*

   Ich zeige . . .

3. Was gebt ihr **der Kellnerin?** *ein Trinkgeld*

   Wir geben . . .

4. Was schenken Sie **ihrem Bruder?** *ein Buch*

   Ich schenke . . .

5. Was kaufst du **dem Kind?** *eine Limonade*

   Ich kaufe . . .

6. Was gebt ihr **dem Gast?** *das Gepäck*

   Wir geben . . .

Aktivität B: Wo wohnen Sie gern?

Tell us where you live. Choose from the places listed below and provide the correct definite or indefinite article. Include one of the following adverbs in your answers: *oft, nie, immer,* or *jetzt.*

BEISPIEL: Ich wohne jetzt in der Stadt.

Ich wohne . . .

in _____ Schweiz/in _____ Hotel/in _____ Jugendherberge/

in _____ Gasthof/in _____ Studentenheim/in _____ Ferienwohnung/

in _____ Haus/in _____ Wohnung

Wo noch . . . ?

Aktivität C: Wohin fahren Sie?

You like to travel. Select your choice of destination from the list below and provide the correct definite or indefinite article. Also include one of these adverbs: **oft, gern, nie,** or **immer.**

BEISPIEL: Ich fahre oft in die Stadt.

Ich fahre . . .

in _____ Büro/in _____ Schweiz/in _____ Theater/

in _____ Geschäft/in _____ Berge

Wohin noch . . . ?

Aktivität D: Im Hotel

You are in the lobby of a hotel (Gasthof). Complete each sentence in a meaningful way that pertains to lodging.

Guten Abend. Haben Sie noch . . . ?   Wo ist . . . ?

Wieviel kostet . . . ?   Soll ich jetzt zahlen
          oder . . . ?

Ich nehme . . .

Aktivität E: Wohin gehen Sie, wenn Sie Zeit haben?

Respond by choosing from the choices below. Complete with the correct definite or indefinite article.

BEISPIEL: Ich gehe gern ins (in das) Theater.

in ____ Oper/in ____ Geschäft/in ____ Büro/in ____ Hotel/in ____
Restaurant/auf ____ Universität/auf ____ Zimmer/in ____ Konzert

---

Wiederholung

Complete the review on a separate piece of paper. Answers are located in the back of the book.

A. Ask someone in German . . .

1. if there is still a room available
2. whether it is a single room or a double room
3. if you can see the apartment
4. when you can move in
5. how many rooms the apartment has

B. Tell someone that . . .

1. you are moving to Zürich this summer
2. they like to stay in New York
3. you *(pl.)* are traveling to Germany

C. Give it . . . to whom?

   Beispiel: Geben Sie es _____ (to me)
   Geben Sie es mir.

1. Geben Sie es (to them)
2. Geben Sie es (to her)
3. Geben Sie es (to him)
4. Geben Sie es (to us)

D. Delete the modal auxiliary in the following sentences.
   All the verbs used have separable prefixes. Check your English translation.

   BEISPIEL: Ich muss um 6 Uhr aufstehen.   I must get up at 6 o'clock.
   Ich stehe um 6 Uhr auf.   I get up at 6 o'clock.

1. Wir wollen Tina am Wochenende abholen.
2. Ich soll am Sonntag anrufen.
3. Ich möchte ihn auf der Party kennenlernen.

4. Er kann den Koffer nicht mitnehmen.

5. Wo müssen wir aussteigen?

6. Wann darf ich dort einziehen?

7. Elfe will am Freitag ankommen.

8. Das Konzert soll um 19 Uhr anfangen.

E. Auf deutsch bitte!

1. The bicycle belongs to her.

2. When do you arrive in Frankfurt?

3. We are not pleased with the house. (use **gefallen**)

4. She is coming back on Wednesday.

5. The guest would like a room with a shower.

6. I must get up at 7 o'clock.

Wortschatz

Nouns

die Anzeige,-n	advertise-ment, ad	**die Jugendherberge, -n**	youth hostel
der Augenblick, -e	moment	**die Katze, -n**	cat
das Bad, ̈er	bath	**die Küche, -n**	kitchen
der Balkon, -e	balcony	**der Lufthansaflug, ̈e**	Lufthansa-flight
die Beförderung, -en	promotion	**der Name, -n**	name
der Berg, -e	mountain	**die Pension, -en**	boarding house
das Büro, -s	office		
das Doppelzimmer, –	double room	**das Quartier, -e**	quarters, room
die Dusche, -n	shower		
das Einzelzimmer, –	single room	**der Schlüssel, –**	key
das Fahrrad, ̈er	bicycle	**der Schweizer, –**	Swiss, *m.*
die Ferienwohnung, -en	vacation apartment	**die Schweizerin, -nen**	Swiss, *f.*
		der Soldat, -en	soldier
die Firma, die Firmen	firm, com-pany	**der Spaß, ̈sse**	fun
		die Sperrstunde, -n	closing hour
das Foto, -s	photo	**das Spiel, -e**	game
der Gast, ̈e	guest	**die Tasche, -n**	bag, purse
der Gasthof, ̈e	inn	**der Urlaub, -e**	vacation
der Geschäftsbrief, -e	business letter	**der Zimmer-nachweis**	room reser-vation ser-vice
die Geschichte, -n	story		
der Gruß, ̈e	greetings	**die Zweizimmer-wohnung, -en**	two-room apartment
der Hauptplatz	main square		
der Hund, -e	dog		

Verbs

ab·fahren (fährt ab)	to depart	**hin·kommen**	to get there
ab·holen	to pick up	**hoffen**	to hope
ab·reisen	to depart	**kennen·lernen**	to meet, to
an·fangen (fängt an)	to begin,		become ac-
	to start		quainted
an·kommen	to arrive	**leben**	to live,
an·rufen	to phone,		to reside
	to call	**leid·tun** *(dat.)*	*to* be sorry,
an·schauen	to look at		to regret
auf·machen	to open	**liegen**	to lie
auf·stehen	to get up	**mieten**	to rent
aus·steigen	to get off	**mit·fahren (fährt mit)**	to drive
aus·ziehen	to move out		along,
danken *(dat.)*	to thank		to come
ein·steigen	to get in,		along
	to board	**mit·nehmen (nimmt mit)**	to take along
ein·ziehen	to move in	**nach·schauen**	to look up,
erlauben	to allow,		to inquire
	to permit	**passen** *(dat.)*	to suit well,
erzählen	to tell,		to fit
	to narrate	**rufen**	to call
folgen *(dat.)*	to follow	**sagen**	to say
sich freuen	to enjoy,	**scheinen**	to seem
	to be glad	**um·ziehen**	to move
gefallen (gefällt) *(dat.)*	to be	**verkaufen**	to sell
	pleased,	**vermieten**	to rent
	to like	**zeigen**	to show
gehören *(dat.)*	to belong	**zu·machen**	to close
glauben *(dat.)*	to believe	**zurück·kommen**	to return,
helfen *(dat.)*	to help		to come
hier·bleiben	to remain,		back
	to stay		

Other Words

auch	also	**ganz**	whole, entire
besetzt	occupied	**nicht mehr**	no more
diesmal	this time	**nötig**	necessary

Idiomatic Expression

Wie schön!	how nice!

Cognates

die Limonade, -n   **das Theater, –**
die Party, -s   **der Tourist, -en**
direkt

KAPITEL 5

Telling Time

Germans use two sets of time systems side by side. One is for everyday use and conversations, comparable to our A.M. and P.M. system. Another is for "official" purposes, the 24-hour system.

The 24-hour time system is always used for official business, by radio and television stations, and by the armed forces. Bus, train, airline, movie, and theater schedules are also listed in the 0–24 format. Using this system, 1:30 P.M. is expressed as 13:30.

For most other communications referring to time, the 0–12 hour system will suffice. Our A.M. and P.M. hours are mostly implied through context. If someone tells you **Kommen Sie um 3 Uhr,** it will rarely mean 3 A.M. but 3 P.M. If ambiguity could exist, the addition of **früh, vormittags, nachmittags,** or **abends** will settle the matter. For instance, **9 Uhr vormittags** is distinguished from **9 Uhr abends.**

While 0:00 is midnight in the official 24-hour system, Germans would say **um Mitternacht** (midnight) instead of **null Uhr** (zero hour). However, **ein Uhr** must become clear through context because it could mean 1 A.M. or 1 P.M. in colloquial German.

If you want to be sure of the local time, call a certain number listed in the phone book under **Zeitangabe.**

Sie sehen . . .	Sie sagen . . .
0:40	null Uhr vierzig
5:25	fünf Uhr fünfundzwanzig
11:17	elf Uhr siebzehn
13:50	dreizehn Uhr fünfzig
20:15	zwanzig Uhr fünfzehn
23:04	dreiundzwanzig Uhr vier

When expressing time, we have a number of options. For conversational use, the "quarter-and-half-hour" method is a common way to specify time.

> 3:00 or 15:00 = Es ist drei Uhr.
> 3:15 or 15:15 = Es ist viertel nach drei (or viertel vier).*
> 3:30 or 15:30 = Es ist halb vier.
> 3:45 or 15:45 = Es ist viertel vor vier (or dreiviertel vier).
> 4:00 or 16:00 = Es ist vier Uhr.

If you want to be precise, use the "minute" method.

> 4:05 or 16:05 = Es ist fünf nach vier (or vier Uhr fünf or sechzehn Uhr fünf).
> 4:25 or 16:25 = Es ist fünf vor halb fünf (or vier Uhr fünfundzwanzig or sechzehn Uhr fünfundzwanzig).

DIALOGE

Timetables govern the lives of people everywhere. Here are a few situations in a German setting, using time expressions.

	Im Hotel	At the Hotel
PORTIER:	*(ruft an)*: Guten Morgen, Herr Jones. Es ist halb sieben.	*(calls)*: Good morning, Mr. Jones. It is half past six.
JONES:	Danke. Ab wann gibt es bei Ihnen Frühstück?	Thank you. When do you start serving breakfast?
PORTIER:	Ab sieben Uhr. Im Frühstückssaal.	From seven o'clock on. In the breakfast room.
JONES:	Vielen Dank.	Thank you very much.

*The expressions used in parentheses are often used in southern Germany and Austria.

	Bei der Bahnhofs-Information	**At the Train Station Information Desk**
FRAU R.:	Guten Tag. Bitte, wann fährt ein Schnellzug von Wien nach Salzburg?	Hello. When does an express train go from Vienna to Salzburg?
AUSKUNFT:	Wann wollen Sie fahren—morgens, mittags, oder abends?	When do you want to go—in the morning, afternoon, or evening?
FRAU R.:	Am Vormittag.	In the late morning.
HERR K.:	Es gibt einen Schnellzug, Abfahrt um 10 Uhr 17 vom Westbahnhof.	There is an express train, departure at 10:17 from the West train station.
FRAU R.:	Und wann kommt dieser Zug in Salzburg an?	And when does this train arrive in Salzburg?
HERR K.:	Um vierzehn Uhr.	At 2:00 P.M.
FRAU R.:	Fährt dieser Zug auch am Wochenende?	Does this train run on weekends as well?
HERR K.:	Ja, er fährt täglich. Ich wünsche gute Fahrt.	Yes, it runs daily. Have a nice trip.
FRAU R.:	Danke schön.	Thank you.

	Eine Verabredung	**A Meeting**
HERR T.:	Können wir uns heute nachmittag treffen?	Could we meet this afternoon?
FRAU S.:	Ja, vielleicht. Um wieviel Uhr?	Yes, perhaps. At what time?
HERR T.:	Um halb fünf.	At four thirty.
FRAU S.:	Das ist zu früh für mich. Unser Büro schließt erst um viertel nach fünf.	That's too early for me. Our office doesn't close until quarter after five.
HERR T.:	Sie arbeiten aber lange!	You sure work long hours.
FRAU S.:	Ja, am Freitag sind es immer acht einhalb Stunden. Da komme ich schon um viertel vor neun ins Büro.	Yes, on Friday I work eight and a half hours. (Then) I arrive at the office at fifteen before nine.

| HERR T.: | Sie sind sehr fleißig. Passt Ihnen sechs Uhr? Ich warte vor dem Büro. | You are very busy. Is six o'clock okay? I'll be waiting for you in front of the office. |
| FRAU S.: | Ja, das geht. | Yes, that's fine. |

An der Universität / At the University

RICK:	Sag, weißt du, wann Professor Wilhelm sein Seminar hält?	Say, do you know when Professor Wilhelm holds his seminar?
UDO:	Ich glaube, Montag und Donnerstag von 16 bis 18 Uhr.	I believe on Monday and Thursday from 4 till 6 P.M.
RICK:	Fängt er pünktlich an?	Does he start on time?
UDO:	Nein, es beginnt immer erst um viertel nach vier.	No, it (the seminar) never starts until a quarter after four.
RICK:	Prima, dann komme ich nicht zu spät. Ich habe bis halb vier eine Tennisstunde.	Great, then I won't be late. I have a tennis lesson until three thirty.

Auf einer Party: Sie danken der Gastgeberin und wollen nach Hause gehen / At a Party: You Thank the Hostess and Want to Go Home

FRAU K.:	Vielen Dank für die Einladung. Es war wirklich nett bei Ihnen.	Thank you for the invitation. It was really nice here.
HERR P.:	Was, Sie wollen schon gehen? Es ist doch erst elf.	What? You want to go already! It is only eleven o'clock.
HERR K.:	Ja, wir müssen noch packen. Wir fliegen morgen nach Zürich.	Yes, we still have to pack. We are flying to Zurich tomorrow.
FRAU P.:	Wann geht Ihr Flug?	When does your flight leave?
FRAU K.:	Leider schon um 6 Uhr 45. Und man muss eine halbe Stunde vor Abflug dort sein.	Unfortunately, already at 6:45. And one has to be there a half hour before departure.

FRAU P.:	**Ja, ich weiß. Guten Flug.**	Yes, I know. Have a good flight.
FRAU K.:	**Danke. Auf Wiedersehen.**	Thank you. Good-bye.
HERR P.:	**Auf Wiedersehen.**	Good-bye.

KOMMUNIKATION

Aktivität A: What's Your Timetable?

Fill in the appropriate time expression.

> **BEISPIEL:** Ich gehe um _____ ins Kino. at half past seven
> Ich gehe um halb acht ins Kino.

1. Ich stehe um _____ auf. quarter past six

2. Mein Freund und ich laufen eine _____ im Park. half an hour

3. Wir kommen um _____ an der Uni an. at 9:35

4. Um _____ holt mich mein Kollege in der Bibliothek ab. quarter of twelve

5. Um _____ essen wir in der Mensa. one o'clock

6. Um _____ gehe ich nach Hause. quarter past five

7. Ich gehe um _____ ins Bett. half past ten

Aktivität B

Answer these questions with the given time cue. Provide only the time element in your answer.

> **BEISPIEL:** Wann kommen Sie zurück? 3:30
> Um drei Uhr dreißig *or*
> um halb vier.

1. Wann fährt der Zug ab? at 16:45

_____

2. Wie spät ist es? 11:15

_____

3. Um wieviel Uhr beginnt das Konzert?   at 20:00

   _____

4. Wie lange arbeiten Sie morgen?   until 5:45 P.M.

   _____

5. Wie viele Stunden in der Woche
   arbeiten Sie?   42 hours

   _____

6. Wann spielt Inge Golf?   at 4:30

   _____

GRAMMATIK: Present Perfect Tense—an Overview

Present Perfect Tense: An Overview

Any time we wish to describe an event in the past, we must use one of the past tenses.

Simple past tense:	**Ich ging nach Hause.**	I went home.
Present perfect:	**Ich bin nach Hause gegangen.**	I have gone home. (I went home)
Past perfect:	**Ich war nach Hause gegangen.**	I had gone home.

In everyday life, Germans usually use the present perfect, especially in conversation. The present perfect in German, as in English, is a compound tense, formed with an *auxiliary verb* plus the *past participle of the verb*. The auxiliary verb can be either **haben** or **sein**. The auxiliary verb is the second element in a clause or sentence, and the past participle goes to the end.

	auxiliary	+	participle
Wir	**haben**	Tennis	**gespielt.**
Er	**hat**	bis 6 Uhr	**gearbeitet.**
Erika	**hat**	heute zu Hause	**gegessen.**

Whereas most German verbs use **haben** as the auxiliary in the present perfect, **sein** is used to denote either a change of place or a change in condition. Such verbs must also be intransitive; that is, such verbs never take a direct object.

" motion "
verb

motion

Ich	**bin**	nach Hause	**gefahren.**
Sie	**sind**	zu uns	**gekommen.**

Compare: **Ich bin mit dem Zug gefahren.** I went by train.
Ich habe den Porsche gefahren. I drove the Porsche.

Here is how to form a past participle in German:

1. Regular (Weak) Verbs

Prefix ge + *stem* + *ending* -t (-et)   *same every time*

Infinitive	Past Participle	
spielen	gespielt	Ich habe Tennis gespielt.
lernen	gelernt	John hat Deutsch gelernt.
hören	gehört	Wir haben gute Musik gehört.
arbeiten	gearbeitet	Gisela hat am Wochenende gear-beitet.

Übung A

Complete with the past participle of the cue verb.

> **BEISPIEL:** Frau Rielke hat ein Haus __gekauft.__

1. John hat ein Jahr in der Schweiz _____.   wohnen

2. Er hat dort sehr gut Deutsch _____.   lernen

3. Zuerst hat er viele Fehler _____.   machen

4. Am Wochenende hat er viel _____   arbeiten

5. Natürlich hat er Schweizer Uhren _____.   kaufen

2. Irregular (Strong) Verbs

Prefix ge + *stem* + *ending* -en

Infinitive	Past Participle	
kommen	gekommen	Ist Ulli gestern gekommen?
finden	gefunden	Wir haben die Adresse gefunden.
schreiben	geschrieben	Ich habe einen Brief geschrieben.
essen	gegessen	Gestern haben wir zu viel gegessen.

Note: A vowel change occurs in the past participle of many verbs. This vowel change cannot be predicted. It must be learned by heart—just as those who learn English must memorize verbs like: *go, went, gone; write, wrote, written,* and so on.

Übung B

Complete the following sentences with the past participle of the cue verb. Note the vowel change—i.e., **nehmen, o.**

BEISPIEL: Haben Sie ein Zimmer _____?   nehmen, o
Haben Sie ein Zimmer genommen?

1. Ich habe Lisa eine Karte _____.   schreiben, ie

2. Sie ist vor drei Wochen nach Wien _____.   fahren, a

3. Dort ist sie manchmal in die Oper _____   gehen, a

4. Sie hat auch sehr gute Restaurants _____   finden, u

5. Natürlich hat sie auch Sachertorte _____   essen, e

3. Separable-Prefix Verbs

Separable prefix **ge** + *stem* + *ending*

Infinitive	Past Participle	
mit·spielen	mitgespielt	Haben Sie mitgespielt?
an·rufen	angerufen	Jens hat angerufen.
ab·fahren	abgefahren	Der Zug ist abgefahren.

Übung C

Complete with the past participle of the cue verb. For irregular verbs, the vowel change is indicated—i.e., **ankommen, o.**

BEISPIEL: Elke ist um 9 Uhr   angekommen.   ankommen

1. Herr Müller hat um 8 Uhr _____.   anrufen, u

2. Um 10 Uhr sind wir nach Berlin _____.   abfliegen, o

3. Unsere Verabredung mit Frau Jung hat um   anfangen, a

     14:00 Uhr _____.

4. Um 16:00 Uhr haben wir _____.   aufhören

5. Um 17 Uhr ist noch ein Freund _____.   vorbeikommen, o

6. Wir sind erst sehr spät wieder _____.   zurückkommen, o

Present Perfect: Separable Prefixes in Action

Dialog A: Anruf beim Flughafen

HERR BIEBER: Guten Abend. Bitte ist der Lufthansaflug 312 aus Köln schon angekommen?

INFORMATION: Nein, Lufthansaflug 312 hat Verspätung. Er ist noch nicht von Köln abgeflogen.

HERR BIEBER: Und wann kommt er hier an?

INFORMATION: Das kann ich Ihnen leider noch nicht sagen. Bitte rufen Sie in einer Stunde bei uns an.

(Eine Stunde später)

HERR BIEBER: Guten Abend, ich habe vor einer Stunde mit Ihnen gesprochen. Wissen Sie jetzt schon, wann Lufthansaflug 312 hier ankommt?

INFORMATION: Einen Augenblick, ich schaue mal auf unserem Computer nach. Ja, Lufthansaflug 312 ist um 17 Uhr 35 in Köln abgeflogen.

HERR BIEBER: Und ist die Maschine schon gelandet?

INFORMATION: Nein, noch nicht. Voraussichtliche Landezeit ist hier 19 Uhr 25.

HERR BIEBER: Vielen Dank.

4. Inseparable-Prefix Verbs

German verbs with *inseparable* prefixes (**be-, emp-, ent-, er-, ver-, zer-**) don't use **-ge** in forming their past participle.

verkaufen	verkauft	Wir haben das Haus verkauft.
besuchen	besucht	Warum hast du mich nicht besucht?
gefallen	gefallen	Das Konzert hat mir sehr gefallen.

The same is true for verbs whose infinitive ends in **-ieren**.

studieren	studiert	Inge hat Biologie studiert.
reservieren	reserviert	Ich habe keine Karten reserviert.
reparieren	repariert	Wer hat mein Auto repariert?

Übung D

Complete the following sentences with the past participle of the cue verb. Watch out—not all verbs are either inseparable-prefix or **-ieren** verbs.

1. Haben Sie ein Zimmer _____.   reservieren

2. Wo haben Judy und Michael _____?   studieren

3. Wann habt ihr heute _____?   essen, e

4. Haben Sie diesen Regenschirm _____?   vergessen, e

5. Hast du das Konzert auch _____?   besuchen

6. Wann hat deine Mutter _____?   anrufen, u

Present Perfect: Inseparable Prefixes in Action

Dialog B: Im Hotel beim Portier

FRAU MILLER: Guten Tag, ich bin Frau Miller, Elisabeth Miller. Ich habe letzte Woche ein Zimmer bestellt.

PORTIER: Haben Sie uns geschrieben oder haben Sie telefoniert?

FRAU MILLER: Ich habe eine Postkarte aus Hamburg geschickt.

PORTIER: Einen Augenblick, ich sehe gleich nach. Ja, wir haben Ihre Karte bekommen.

FRAU MILLER: Und haben Sie ein Zimmer für mich reserviert?

PORTIER: Ja, ein Einbettzimmer für zwei Nächte. Zimmer 7 im ersten Stock.

5. Irregular Verbs Using *haben* as Auxiliary Verb

Ich habe mit ihm gesprochen.	I spoke with him.
Du hast mit ihm gesprochen.	You *(fam. sing.)* spoke with him.
Er/sie hat mit ihm gesprochen.	He/she spoke with him.
Wir haben mit ihm gesprochen.	We spoke with him.
Ihr habt mit ihm gesprochen.	You *(fam. pl.)* spoke with him.
Sie haben mit ihm gesprochen.	You spoke with him.
Sie haben mit ihm gesprochen.	They spoke with him.

6. Regular Verbs Using *sein* as Auxiliary Verb

Sein is used only for those verbs that denote either a *change of place* or a *change in condition*. It is also the auxiliary verb for the verbs **sein**, **werden**, and **bleiben**.

Ich bin viel gereist.	I traveled a lot.
Du bist viel gereist.	You *(fam. sing.)* traveled a lot.

Er/sie ist viel gereist.	He/she traveled a lot.
Wir sind viel gereist.	We traveled a lot.
Ihr seid viel gereist.	You *(fam. pl.)* traveled a lot.
Sie sind viel gereist.	You traveled a lot.
Sie sind viel gereist.	They traveled a lot.

7. Irregular Verbs Using *sein* as Auxiliary Verb

Ich bin in die Stadt gefahren.	I went downtown.
Du bist in die Stadt gefahren.	You *(fam. sing.)* went downtown.
Er/sie ist in die Stadt gefahren.	He/she went downtown.
Wir sind in die Stadt gefahren.	We went downtown.
Ihr seid in die Stadt gefahren.	You *(fam. pl.)* went downtown.
Sie sind in die Stadt gefahren.	You went downtown.
Sie sind in die Stadt gefahren.	They went downtown.

Present Perfect in Action

Dialog C: In einem Studentenheim

KARL: Guten Morgen, John! Hast du gut geschlafen?

JOHN: Danke, sehr gut—und lange.

KARL: Wann bist du heute aufgestanden?

JOHN: Erst um halb neun. Ich bin gestern sehr spät ins Bett gegangen.

KARL: Bist du auf einer Party gewesen?

JOHN: Nein, ich bin nur sehr müde gewesen. Am Nachmittag habe ich Tennis gespielt und abends habe ich dann noch lange in der Bibliothek gelesen.

8. Mixed Verbs

Finally, German has a small group of mixed verbs that combine both the characteristic irregular vowel change and the regular ending.

Ich habe das nicht gewusst.	I didn't know that.
Du hast das nicht gewusst.	You *(fam. sing.)* didn't know that.
Er/sie hat das nicht gewusst.	He/she didn't know that.
Wir haben das nicht gewusst.	We didn't know that.
Ihr habt das nicht gewusst.	You *(fam. pl.)* didn't know that.
Sie haben das nicht gewusst.	You didn't know that.
Sie haben das nicht gewusst.	They didn't know that.

Other verbs that follow this pattern are:

denken	gedacht	to think
bringen	gebracht	to bring
rennen	gerannt	to run
brennen	gebrannt	to burn

One More Time: Present Perfect— Mixed Verbs in Action

Dialog D: Gespräch auf einer Party

KARIN: Hab' ich richtig gehört? Sie haben den letzten Sommer in Amerika verbracht?

KLAUS: Ja, das stimmt. Wir haben unsere Verwandten in Chicago besucht.

KARIN: Wie lange sind Sie in den USA geblieben?

KLAUS: Fünf Wochen. Ich habe leider nicht mehr Urlaub gehabt.

CHRIS: Haben Sie außer Chicago noch anderes gesehen?

KLAUS: Ja, ein bisschen von New York. Dort sind wir beim Hinflug angekommen.

FRITZ: Und wie hat Ihnen Amerika gefallen?

KLAUS: Recht gut. Wir möchten wieder hin.

Übung E

Complete each sentence with an appropriate verb. Choose one from the list below. More than one choice may be possible.

BEISPIEL: Wir haben ihn gestern auf der Party <u>gesehen, getroffen, gesprochen</u>.

1. Jedes Wochenende sind wir in die Berge _____.

2. Haben Sie heute schon die Zeitung _____?

3. Wann ist der Bus _____?

4. Wo haben Sie das _____?

5. Warum ist Franz nach Schweden _____?

6. Wie hat Ihnen die Ausstellung _____?

7. Wir haben uns vor dem Bahnhof _____.

8. Wie lange ist Frau Ebner in Österreich _____?

9. Ich bin heute vormittag in die Stadt _____.

10. Wo haben Sie Ihren Freund _____?

fahren	finden	treffen
ab·fahren	gefallen	bleiben
an·kommen	reisen	lesen
gehen	laufen	sehen
kaufen	hören	sein

9. The Genitive Case

The last German case is the genitive, which usually expresses possession.

BEISPIELE: **Georgs Vater ist krank.**
George's father is sick.

Ich verstehe die Reaktion des Präsidenten nicht.
I don't understand the reaction of the President.

Lisa kommt am Ende des Monats.
Lisa is coming at the end of the month.

Look at the chart and notice the genitive endings for the definite and indefinite articles.

	Masculine	Feminine	Neuter	Plural
Nominative	der	die	das	die
	ein	eine	ein	keine
Genitive	des	der	des	der
	eines	einer	eines	keiner

Also note that masculine and neuter nouns take an **-s** in the singular (but **-es** if the noun has only one syllable).

BEISPIELE: das Auto des Vaters/des Freundes/des Onkels
der Hund des Kindes/des Lehrers/des Mannes

As in English, proper nouns add an **-s**, but not an apostrophe. However, if the name already ends in an **-s**, then an apostrophe is added.

BEISPIELE: **Gerlindes Haus ist neu.**
Gerlinde's house is new.

Achims Kinder sind noch klein.
Achim's children are still small.

Thomas' Mutter kommt heute.
Thomas's mother is coming today.

Übung F

Express in German.

> **BEISPIEL:** I don't know the name of the town
> Ich weiß den Namen der Stadt nicht.

1. Where is Karin's father?
2. Is this Karl's room?
3. Do you know the professor's name?
4. I don't have the address of the restaurant.
5. The children's parents have left.
6. Would you like to see Heidi's photos?
7. We can't buy John's car.

SPRECHEN LEICHT GEMACHT

Aktivität A: Was haben sie gemacht?

Respond with an answer of your choice.

> **BEISPIEL;** Was haben Sie gestern abend gemacht?
> Ich habe einen Freund besucht.

Was haben Sie gestern
abend gemacht?

Karten gespielt.
Tennis gespielt.
Freunde besucht.
ein gutes Buch gelesen.
fern gesehen.
meine Eltern angerufen.

Ich habe . . . im Restaurant gegessen.
Radio gehört.
fleißig gearbeitet.
die Zeitung gelesen.
ein Auto gekauft.

in den Supermarkt gegangen.
ins Kino gegangen.

Ich bin . . . zu Hause geblieben.
früh ins Bett gegangen.
auf einer Party gewesen.
zu den Eltern gefahren.

Was hat Inge heute morgen gemacht?	Sie ist . . .	um 6 Uhr aufgestanden. zwei Meilen gelaufen. um 8 Uhr 30 ins Büro gegangen. bis 7 Uhr im Bett geblieben.
	Sie hat . . .	um 7 Uhr gefrühstückt. um Viertel nach 10 telefoniert. keinen Parkplatz bekommen. die Zeitung gelesen. einen Ausflug gemacht. eine Ausstellung gesehen. Golf gespielt.
Was habt ihr am Wochenende gemacht?	Wir haben . . .	lange geschlafen. zu viel gegessen. Freunde besucht.
	Wir sind . . .	in die Berge gefahren. nach Berlin geflogen. zu Hause geblieben. in die Stadt gegangen. bei Freunden gewesen.

Aktivität B: Urlaub in der Schweiz

Your German friend asks you about your recent trip to Switzerland. You respond to his or her questions using the present perfect tense. Make use of the suggested vocabulary. To complete the sentences, use a suitable verb.

FREUND:	Bist du im Urlaub zu Hause geblieben?	
SIE:	Nein. Ich bin . . .	. . . in die Schweiz, nach Deutschland, Österreich, Frankreich, usw. fahren
FREUND:	Allein?	
SIE:	Nein, ich bin mit . . .	. . . einem Freund, meinen Eltern, usw. reisen
FREUND:	Seid ihr mit dem Auto gefahren?	
SIE:	Wir sind . . .	. . . mit dem Zug, Autobus, Camper, Motorrad

FREUND: Wie lange hast du Urlaub gemacht?

SIE: Ich habe . . .   . . . ein paar Tage, _____ Wochen, _____ Monat, usw.

FREUND: Und welche Länder habt ihr besucht?

SIE: Wir haben . . .   . . . die Schweiz, Frankreich, Italien, usw.

FREUND: Reisen ist schön, aber ist das Gepäck nicht oft ein Problem?

SIE: Ich habe diesmal nicht viel . . .   . . . packen, mitnehmen

FREUND: Und wie habt ihr eure Rechnungen bezahlt?

SIE: Wir haben mit Euro . . .   . . . Kreditkarte, Scheck, Bargeld, Franken, usw.

FREUND: Wie viele Währungen hast du mitgenommen?

SIE: Ich habe Euro . . .   . . . Schweizer Franken, keine . . .

FREUND: Bist du auch in Genf gewesen?

SIE: Ja, aber ich bin nur . . . dort . . .   . . . drei Tage, eine Woche, usw.

FREUND: In welchen anderen Städten seid ihr noch geblieben?

SIE: In Zürich. Dort hat es mir gut . . .   . . . gefallen
Leider hat es nur wenige Parkplätze . . .   . . . geben

FREUND: Hast du die Schweizer gut verstanden?

SIE: Nein, ich habe fast nichts . . .   . . . verstehen
Sie haben zu viel Schweizerdeutsch . . .   . . . sprechen
Aber für den nächsten Sommer habe ich schon in Grindelwald ein Zimmer . . .   . . . reservieren

FREUND: Prima, vielleicht fahre ich mit!

Wiederholung

A. Was machen Sie um diese Zeit?
What are you doing at that time? Make use of the expressions below.

BEISPIEL: 6:00 Ich stehe um sechs Uhr auf. *oder*
Um sechs Uhr stehe ich auf.

7:00	10:30	16:30	19:00
7:45	12:30	17:15	20:00
8:15	13:45	17:45	21:00
9:30	l5:00	18:00	22:30

frühstücken	zur Arbeit fahren	im Büro ankommen
mit Kunden sprechen	Briefe lesen und beantworten	auf die Post gehen
Mittagessen gehen	in den Park gehen	ins Büro zurückgehen
einen Kaffee trinken	mit dem Chef sprechen	zu Hause ankommen
nach Hause gehen	die Zeitung lesen	Abendessen kochen
fern·sehen	die Nachrichten hören	einen Nachbarn
ein Buch lesen	Klavier spielen	besuchen
ins Bett gehen	im Garten arbeiten	mit Kollegen
		diskutieren

B. One more time, but this time use the present perfect tense.

C. Ein Brief
You are on a trip in Europe and you are writing a letter to a German friend.
See if you can complete it by providing the correct auxiliaries (**haben** or **sein**)
and verb forms. (present perfect tense) The infinitives of the verbs are listed in
order below.

Berlin, den 2. Juli

Lieber Stefan!

Am 8. Mai _____ ich um 18:15 in Berlin _____. Vom Flughafen

_____ ich ein Taxi _____ und _____ sofort zum Hotel _____. Ich _____

den Portier _____, ob er ein Zimmer für mich _____ _____. Ja, ich

_____ Glück _____. Ich _____ ein Zimmer für drei Tage _____. Ich

_____ drei Tage in Berlin _____. Ich _____ einige deutsche Firmen _____ und ich _____ auch öfters bei deutschen Kollegen _____. Herr Müller von der Firma Siemens _____ mir auch eine neue Fabrik _____. Am Wochenende _____ wir einen Ausflug in den Grunewald _____. An einem Abend _____ ich ins Konzert _____. Es _____ mir sehr gut _____. Die Berliner Philharmoniker _____ Beethoven und Mozart _____.

Herzliche Grüße

Dein Michael

ankommen	nehmen	fahren	fragen
reservieren	haben	bekommen	sein
besuchen	sein	zeigen	machen
gehen	gefallen	spielen	

Wortschatz

Nouns

der Abend, -e	evening	**das Frühstück, -e**	breakfast
am Abend	in the evening	**die Gastgeberin, -nen**	hostess
		das Gespräch, -e	conversation
die Abfahrt, -en	departure	**der Hinflug, ̈e**	flight to
der Abflug, ̈e	flight departure	**der Kunde, -n**	customer
		die Landezeit, -en	landing time, arrival time
der Anruf, -e	telephone call		
der Ausflug, ̈e	outing, trip	**der Mittag, -e**	noon
die Ausstellung, -en	exhibit	**am Mittag**	at noon
der Brief, -e	letter	**der Nachmittag, -e**	afternoon
der Chef, -s	boss	**am Nachmittag**	in the afternoon
das Einbettzimmer, –	single room		
die Einladung, -en	invitation	**der Nachbar, -n**	neighbor
die Fahrt, -en	trip, journey	**die Nachricht, -en**	news
der Flug, ̈e	flight	**die Nacht, ̈e**	night

der Schnellzug, ¨-e	express train	der Vormittag, -e	time before noon
Schweden	Sweden		
der Stock, die Stockwerke	floor	am Vormittag	in the morning
im 1. Stock	on the second floor	die Verspätung, -en	delay
		der Verwandte, -n	relative
die Tennisstunde, -n	tennis lesson	die Währung, -en	currency (foreign)
die Verabredung, -en	appointment, date	der Westbahnhof	West railway station

Verbs

Note: Verbs with an asterisk (*) take **sein** as an auxiliary.

ab·fliegen*, ist abgeflogen	to depart by plane, to fly off	packen	to pack
		reparieren	to repair
an·fangen (fängt an), angefangen	to begin, to start	schicken	to send, to mail
auf·hören	to stop, to discontinue	schließen, geschlossen	to close, to shut
		telefonieren	to telephone
auf·stehen*, ist aufgestanden	to get up	treffen (trifft), getroffen	to meet
beantworten	to answer	verbringen, verbracht	to spend (time)
fern·sehen (sieht fern) ferngesehen	to watch television	vergessen (vergisst), vergessen	to forget
frühstücken	to have breakfast	vorbei·kommen,* ist vorbeigekommen	to stop by, to come by
landen*	to land		
mit·spielen	to play, to take part in	wünschen	to wish
		zurück·kommen,* ist zurückgekommen	to return, to come back
nach·sehen (sieht nach), nachgesehen	to check out, to look for		

Other Words

abends	in the evening	halb	half
		heute nachmittag	this afternoon
bisschen	a little bit		
dann	then	hin	to (there)
erst (um)	not until	letzt-	last
früh	early	mittags	at noon
gleich	right away, at once	morgens	in the morning

recht	quite	voraussichtlich	probably,
recht gut	quite well		approxi-
viertel	quarter		mately

Idiomatic Expressions

Ab wann?	From what time on?
Das stimmt.	That's correct.
Um wieviel Uhr?	At what time?

Cognates

| der Portier, -s | das Seminar, -e |

KAPITEL **6** Health Care

CULTURE NOTES

If you are in a German-speaking country for a long period of time, you will probably choose your physicians the same way you do at home: through recommendations from friends or business associates and through referrals.

But for emergencies abroad, keep in mind that one does not have to go to a hospital. Many German, Swiss, and Austrian cities maintain a medical emergency service at night, on weekends, and on holidays. Participating physicians take turns performing this service in their offices, in the patient's home, or even in hotels. These **Notdienst** (emergency) physicians who are on call are listed in the local newspapers. Their telephone numbers can also be obtained through special **Notruf** numbers listed in the phone book under **Notdienst, Notruf,** or **Erste Hilfe.**

Because most Germans, Austrians, and Swiss must carry health insurance, physicians and dentists receive payments from health insurance companies. Thus, doctors and their office staff are well versed in the ensuing **Papierkrieg** (the battle with paperwork and bureaucracy). Advice to the traveler: Take your insurance forms along. In case of a health emergency, these forms will probably be accepted and filled out by physicians in these countries.

If hospitalization is required, several **Klassen** (categories) of rooms are available. **Erste Klasse** or **Sonderklasse** means a private room. **Zweite Klasse** means that you share the room with another person. **Dritte Klasse** could be a larger room with several people.

Learn to distinguish between a **Drogerie** (drugstore) and an **Apotheke** (pharmacy). You can buy prescription drugs only in an **Apotheke**. If you need medicine during the night, you can usually find a **Nachtapotheke** open.

DIALOGE

Read the dialogues aloud in German and check the English translations:

KLAUS:	**Gehst du ins Museum mit?**	Are you coming along to the museum?
KURT:	**Nein, ich fühle mich leider nicht wohl.**	No, unfortunately, I don't feel well.
KLAUS:	**Was fehlt dir denn?**	What is wrong with you?
KURT:	**Ich habe furchtbare Halsschmerzen.**	I have a terrible sore throat.
KLAUS:	**Warst du schon beim Arzt?**	Have you been to the doctor yet?
KURT:	**Nein, noch nicht. Ich wollte noch ein bisschen warten.**	No, not yet. I wanted to wait a bit.
KLAUS:	**Komm, ich fahre dich lieber zu Dr. Jung. Er ist unser Hausarzt.**	Come, I'll take you to Dr. Jung. He is our family doctor.

FRAU S.:	**Waren Sie schon einmal im Krankenhaus?**	Have you ever been in a hospital?
FRAU K.:	**Ja, als Kind. Warum fragen Sie?**	Yes, as a child. Why are you asking?
FRAU S.:	**Mein Blinddarm muss raus.**	I have to have my appendix removed.
FRAU K.:	**Wann?**	When?
FRAU S.:	**Noch diese Woche.**	This coming week.
FRAU K.:	**Hatten Sie wenigstens Zeit, ein gutes Krankenhaus auszusuchen?**	Did you at least have time to look for a good hospital?
FRAU S.:	**Mein Arzt empfahl mir das Universitätskrankenhaus.**	My doctor recommended the university hospital.

FRAU K.:	Da war meine Mutter, als sie ihren Herzanfall hatte.	That's where my mother was when she had a heart attack.
FRAU S.:	Wirklich? Das wusste ich nicht.	Really? I didn't know that.
FRAU K.:	Ja, sie war sehr mit dem Krankenhaus zufrieden.	Yes, she was very satisfied with the hospital.
FRAU S.:	Gut —dann gehe ich also dorthin.	Good, then I will go there.

KARIN:	Du siehst aber blass aus.	You look really pale.
ELKE:	Mir ist ganz schwindelig, und ich habe auch Fieber.	I am very dizzy, and I also have a temperature.
KARIN:	Vielleicht hast du die Grippe.	Perhaps you have the flu.
ELKE:	Ich glaube auch.	I believe so, too.
KARIN:	Hast du schon Aspirin genommen?	Did you already take aspirin?
ELKE:	Ja, ich nahm vor einer Stunde wieder zwei.	Yes, I took another two an hour ago.
KARIN:	Hast du auch genug ge- trunken?	Did you drink enough?
ELKE:	Natürlich. Ich trank seit gestern bestimmt zwei Liter Mineralwasser.	Of course. I probably drank two liters of mineral water since yesterday.
KARIN:	Ich muss jetzt gehen. Hoffentlich fühlst du dich bald besser.	I have to go now. I hope you will feel better soon.

ARZT:	Wo tut's denn weh?	Where does it hurt?
PATIENT:	Ich habe schreckliche Ohrenschmerzen.	I have a terrible earache.
ARZT:	Lassen Sie mich mal sehen. Ja, Sie haben eine schlimme Entzündung.	Let me see. Yes, you have a bad infection.
PATIENT:	Der Hals tut mir auch weh.	My throat hurts, too.

ARZT:	**Machen Sie den Mund weit auf. Sagen Sie „ah."**	Open your mouth wide. Say "ah."
PATIENT:	**Ah.**	Ah.
ARZT:	**Die Mandeln sind auch geschwollen.**	Your tonsils are swollen, too.
PATIENT:	**Was soll ich dagegen nehmen?**	What should I take for it?
ARZT:	**Ich verschreibe Ihnen Penicillin-tabletten. Nehmen Sie die Tabletten wie vorgeschrieben.**	I will prescribe some penicillin tablets for you. Take the tablets as prescribed.

KOMMUNIKATION

Aktivität A: Was stimmt? Was stimmt nicht?

Mark with an *R* (richtig) those responses that are correct. Cross out the ones that are not.

1. Sie fühlen sich nicht wohl.
   Sie gehen . . .

   . . . zum Arzt.
   . . . ins Museum.
   . . . ins Krankenhaus.
   . . . in die Bibliothek.
   . . . ins Kino.

2. Wenn man Fieber hat,
   soll man . . .

   . . . viel trinken.
   . . . Aspirin nehmen.
   . . . ins Wasser springen.

3. Sie sind beim Arzt, weil Sie
   Halsschmerzen haben.
   Er fragt sie . . .

   . . . „Ist Ihnen schwindelig?"
   . . . „Wo tut's weh?"
   . . . „Wie fühlen Sie sich?"
   . . . „Warum fahren Sie nicht in Urlaub?"
   . . . „Haben Sie Fieber?"

4. Ihr Arzt verschreibt Ihnen
   Tabletten, weil Sie . . .

   . . . im Krankenhaus waren.
   . . . hohen Blutdruck haben.
   . . . wieder gesund sind.
   . . . Ohrenschmerzen haben.

Krankheitsvokabular

sich an·stecken	to catch an illness
bewusstlos werden	to become unconscious, to faint
geimpft werden	to get immunized
sich untersuchen lassen	to have a physical examination
sich verletzen	to hurt oneself
sich einen Arm oder ein Bein brechen	to break an arm or a leg
den Blutdruck messen	to take one's blood pressure
einen Herzanfall haben	to have a heart attack
sich operieren lassen	to have an operation
den Puls fühlen	to feel one's pulse
Fieber messen	to take one's temperature

Krankheiten (Illnesses)

das Asthma	asthma
die Blindarmentzündung	appendicitis
die Erkältung	cold
das Fieber	fever
die Grippe	flu
der Husten	cough
der Krebs	cancer
die Lungenentzündung	pneumonia
die Bauch- (Magen-), Kopf-, Hals, Ohren-, Rücken-, Herz-, schmerzen	stomach-, head-, throat-, ear-, back-, heartaches or pain

Fachärzte (Specialists)

der/die Augenarzt,	⟩ ¨e, ¨-in, ¨-innen	eye doctor, ophthalmologist
der/die Hautarzt,		dermatologist
der/die Kinderarzt,		pediatrician
der/die Frauenarzt		gynecologist
Praktischer Arzt		family doctor (general practitioner)
der Chirurg, -en		surgeon
der Internist, -en		internist
die Krankenschwester, -n		nurse, *f.*
der Krankenpfleger, –		nurse, *m.*
die Sprechstundenhilfe, -n		(doctor's) receptionist
der Optiker, –		optician

Aktivität B: Was machten Sie in diesen Situationen?

Choose from the answers below and mark *a, b,* or *c.* More than one answer may be correct. Check Krankheitsvokabular if necessary.

> **BEISPIEL:** Sie brauchten eine Operation.
> Antwort *c:* Ich musste ins Krankenhaus.

1. Sie wachten mit Kopfschmerzen auf.   Antwort _____

2. Ihre Mandeln mussten raus.   Antwort _____

3. Sie hatten furchtbare Bauchschmerzen.   Antwort _____

4. Sie hatten die Grippe.   Antwort _____

5. Was machten Sie, als Sie eine Erkältung hatten?   Antwort _____

6. Ihr Arzt wollte Ihren Blutdruck messen.   Antwort _____

7. Sie hatten Lungenentzündung.   Antwort _____

ANTWORTEN:

a. Ich machte nichts.
b. Ich musste ins Krankenhaus.

c. Ich ging zum Arzt.
d. Ich blieb zu Hause und legte mich ins Bett.

GRAMMATIK

1. The Simple Past Tense

So far, you have learned the preferred way of expressing past time situations in the conversational past (or present perfect tense). Another way of expressing past time in German is the simple past tense (also known as the narrative past), which is used primarily when reporting past events.

> Mein Arzt **empfahl** mir das Universitätskrankenhaus.
> My doctor *recommended* the university hospital to me.
>
> Ich **nahm** ein Aspirin.
> I *took* an aspirin.
>
> Felix **hatte** die Grippe.
> Felix *had* the flu.
>
> Tina **war** gestern krank.
> Tina **was** sick yesterday.

German *regular* verbs form their past tense by adding a -**t** plus ending to the stem.

Present Tense	Past Tense	English Meaning
ich sag **e**	ich sag **te**	I said
du sag **st**	du sag **test**	you said
er/sie sag **t**	er/sie sag **te**	he/she said
wir sag **en**	wir sag **ten**	we said
ihr sag **t**	ihr sag **tet**	you said
Sie sag **en**	Sie sag **ten**	you said
sie sag **en**	sie sag **ten**	they said

When the stem of a regular verb ends in a -**d** or -**t**, a linking -**e** is inserted between the stem and the ending.

arbeiten = ich arbei<u>t</u>ete   antworten = er antwor<u>t</u>ete

Übung A: Ich bin (war) krank

Restate, changing the present tense to the *past tense.*

> **BEISPIEL:** Ich brauche Tabletten.
> Ich **brauchte** Tabletten.

1. Ich fühle mich nicht wohl.

   _____.

2. Wir holen den Arzt.

   _____.

3. Ich antworte auf seine Fragen.

   _____.

4. Er sagt nicht viel.

   _____.

5. Ich kaufe mir Tabletten.

   _____.

6. Bald bin ich wieder gesund.

   _____.

Irregular verbs form their past tense by changing the stem vowel. The personal endings are slightly different. There is no ending in the **ich** and **er/sie** forms and no -**e** in the **du** and **ihr** forms.

Regular Verbs

glaube	to believe
ich glaubte	I believed
du glaubtest	you believed
er/sie glaubte	he/she believed
wir glaubten	we believed
ihr glaubtet	you believed
Sie glaubten	you believed
sie glaubten	they believed

Irregular Verbs

fahren	to drive	
ich	**fuhr**	I drove
du	**fuhrst**	you drove
er/sie	**fuhr**	he/she drove
wir	**fuhren**	we drove
ihr	**fuhrt**	you drove
Sie	**fuhren**	you drove
sie	**fuhren**	they drove

A few irregular verbs change not only the stem vowel, but also the stem:

gehen	to go	**er ging**	he went
tun	to do	**er tat**	he did
stehen	to stand	**er stand**	he stood

Also, when the stem ends in -d or -t, a linking -e is inserted between the stem and the ending in the **du** and **ihr** forms: **finden, du fandest.** As in English, the best way to learn the past tense of irregular verbs is to *memorize* them. Here is a list of a few. Check the appendix for more.

Infinitive	Past	Past Participle	
fahren	fuhr	ist gefahren	to drive
kommen	kam	ist gekommen	to come
sehen	sah	gesehen	to see
trinken	trank	getrunken	to drink
essen	aß	gegessen	to eat
sein	war	ist gewesen	to be
haben	hatte	gehabt	to have
nehmen	nahm	genommen	to take
tun	tat	getan	to do
schreiben	schrieb	geschrieben	to write
empfehlen	empfahl	empfohlen	to recommend
gehen	ging	ist gegangen	to go
anrufen	rief an	angerufen	to call
lesen	las	gelesen	to read

Übung B: Sarah fühlt (fühlte) sich nicht wohl

Restate the sentences in the past tense. Then translate them into English.

> **BEISPIEL:** Die Ärztin hilft Sarah.
> Die Ärztin **half** Sarah.
> The doctor helped Sarah.

1. Sarah ist krank.

   _____.

2. Sie ruft die Ärztin an.

   _____.

3. Sie kommt und verschreibt Tabletten.

   _____.

4. Sarah trinkt viel Tee und Saft.

   _____.

5. Sie isst nur Suppe.

   _____.

6. Bald geht es ihr besser.

   _____.

German *modals* have the same personal endings as regular verbs. Note that they do not have an *umlaut* in the past tense.

Pronoun	dürfen	können	müssen	sollen	wollen
ich	durfte	konnte	musste	sollte	wollte
du	durftest	konntest	musstest	solltest	wolltest
er/sie/es	durfte	konnte	musste	sollte	wollte
wir	durften	konnten	mussten	sollten	wollten
ihr	durftet	konntet	musstet	solltet	wolltet
Sie	durften	konnten	mussten	sollten	wollten
sie	durften	konnten	mussten	sollten	wollten

Übung C: Ihr wolltet doch kommen!

Fill in the blanks with the correct form of the modal in the simple past tense.

1. JUTTA: Wo wart ihr gestern? Ihr _____ doch kommen.   wollen

    JENS: Ja, aber ich hatte keine Zeit.

    JUTTA: Warum nicht?

2. JENS: Ich _____ arbeiten,   müssen

3.   und Karin und Martin _____ ohne mich nicht kommen.   können

    JUTTA: Warum hast du mich nicht angerufen?

4. JENS: Ich _____ das Telefon bei der   dürfen

    Arbeit nicht benutzen.

5. JUTTA: Ich _____ leider zu Hause bleiben.   müssen

6. JENS: Das _____ wir nicht wissen.   können

    JUTTA: Macht nichts. Sollen wir jetzt ins Kino gehen.

    JENS: Warum nicht?

Übung D: *Fragen, nichts als Fragen*

Hier sind einige Fragen zu den Dialogen. Beantworten Sie sie. Use only simple past tense. You may want to read the dialogues on pages 129–131 again.

BEISPIEL: Wer empfahl das Krankenhaus?
   Der Arzt empfahl es.

Dialog 1

1. Was tat Kurt weh?

   _____.

2. Warum war er noch nicht beim Arzt?

   _____.

3. Wie hieß der Hausarzt?

   _____.

4. Wer fuhr Kurt zum Arzt?

   _____.

Dialog 2

1. Warum musste Frau S. ins Krankenhaus gehen?

   _____.

2. Welches Krankenhaus empfahl der Arzt?

   _____.

3. Wer war auch im Universitätskrankenhaus?

   _____.

Dialog 3

1. Warum sah Elke blass aus?

   _____.

2. Wer besuchte sie?

   _____.

3. Wann hat sie Aspirin genommen?

   _____.

4. Wieviel Mineralwasser hat sie getrunken?

   _____.

5. Was sagte Elke, als sie wegging?

   _____.

Dialog 4

1. Warum ging der Patient zum Arzt?

   _____.

2. Hatte er nur Ohrenschmerzen?

   _____.

3. Was verschrieb der Arzt?

   _____.

2. Reflexive Pronouns

Reflexive pronouns are used when the *subject* and the *object* are the same. Note that sometimes the object can be *dative*, sometimes *accusative*.

Peter rasiert sich.	Peter is shaving (himself).
Ich fühle mich gut.	I feel fine.
Du kämmst dir das Haar.	You are combing your hair.

In the accusative and dative, reflexive pronouns take the same forms as personal pronouns, *except* in the third-person singular and plural. (The reflexive pronoun in the third person is **sich.**)

Reflexive Pronouns		Personal Pronouns				
Accusative	**Dative**	**Nominative**	**Accusative**		**Dative**	
mich	mir	ich	mich	(me)	mir	(to me)
dich	dir	du	dich	(you)	dir	(to you)
sich	**sich**	er	ihn	(him)	ihm	(to him)
sich	**sich**	sie	sie	(her)	ihr	(to her)
sich	**sich**	es	es	(it)	ihm	(to it)
uns	uns	wir	uns	(us)	uns	(to us)
euch	euch	ihr	euch	(you)	euch	(to you)
sich	**sich**	Sie	Sie	(you)	Ihnen	(to you)
sich	**sich**	sie	sie	(them)	ihnen	(to them)

Also, note how the **ich** and **du** forms of the reflexive pronouns are different in the accusative (**mich, dich**) and the dative (**mir, dir**). Therefore, you need to know when to use the accusative or the dative. If there is just one reflexive pronoun object referring back to the subject, use the *accusative*. But if there is a direct object plus a reflexive pronoun, use the *dative*.

Jens fühlt *sich* nicht wohl.	Jens doesn't feel well.
Ich habe *mich* erkältet.	I have caught a cold.
Du kaufst *dir* ein Auto.	You are buying yourself a car.
Ich putze *mir* die Zähne.	I am brushing my teeth.

German has many verbs that can be used either reflexively or nonreflexively. Their English equivalent often is nonreflexive.

Ich interessiere mich für Sport.   (reflexive)
I am interested in sports.

Der Sport interessiert ihn.   (nonreflexive)
Sports interest him.

Die Mutter zieht das Kind an.   (nonreflexive)
The mother is dressing the child.

Die Mutter zieht sich an.   (reflexive)
The mother is dressing herself.

Übung E

Fill in the blanks with the appropriate reflexive pronoun.

BEISPIEL: Ich habe _____ mich _____ erkältet.

1. Peter duscht _____ jeden Abend.

2. Karl rasiert _____ nur morgens.

3. Marie kämmt _____ oft.

4. Der Junge zieht _____ die Schuhe an.

5. Ich kaufe _____ ein neues Kleid.

6. Wir interessieren _____ für Musik.

7. Aber Herr Schmidt interessiert _____ für Sport.

8. Heute muss ich _____ beeilen.

9. Ich kaufe _____ einen Mantel.

10. Frau Braun, wie fühlen Sie _____?

More Reflexive Verbs

Learn these useful expressions.

sich duschen	to take a shower
sich rasieren	to shave
sich anziehen, zog an, angezogen	to get dressed
sich die Zähne putzen	to brush one's teeth
sich das Haar kämmen	to comb one's hair

sich fühlen (wohl/schlecht)	to feel (well or poorly)
sich erkälten	to catch a cold
sich beeilen	to hurry
sich bewerben um (a, o)	to apply for
sich erinnern an + Akk.	to remember something/someone
sich freuen auf + Akk.	to look forward to
sich interessieren für	to be interested in

The Reflexive in Conversation

HERR B.: Möchten Sie ins Museum gehen?

HERR K.: Ja gerne. Ich interessiere mich sehr für Kunst.

HERR B.: Wir müssen uns aber beeilen.

HERR K.: Wir können gleich gehen. Ich ziehe mir nur noch einen Pullover an.

MARTIN: Warum hast du dich verspätet?

CHRIS: Mein Wecker hat nicht geklingelt.

MARTIN: Deshalb hast du dich nicht rasiert?

CHRIS: Ja, ich habe mich nur schnell geduscht.

MARTIN: Gehen wir jetzt.

CHRIS: Ich kann mich nicht erinnern, wann wir uns mit Herrn König treffen.

Übung F: Bei Biebers zu Hause

Schreiben Sie auf deutsch.

BEISPIEL: I am interested in Computers.
Ich interessiere mich für Computers.

1. MUTTER: Children, we have to hurry.

2. PETER: I must shower first.

3. KRISTA: Dad (Vati) is still shaving.

4. MUTTER: Who is getting the baby (das Baby) dressed?

5. KRISTA: I don't know.

6. VATER: Paul, why haven't you combed your hair?

7. PAUL: I did comb my hair.

8. KRISTA: Mom (**Mutti**), Paul and Peter didn't brush their teeth.

9. PETER: I'm staying home, I don't feel well.

10. MUTTER: We're all going to the restaurant.

11. VATER: Aren't you looking forward to eating at (**bei**) . . .

12. PETER: No, I'm really sick.

13. VATER/   Then we'll all stay home.
    MUTTER:

3. The Use of als, wenn, wann

Als (when) describes or tells something about the past.

> *Als* ich krank war, konnte ich dich nicht besuchen.
> When I was sick, I couldn't visit you.

> *Als* wir in Hamburg waren, hatten wir das schönste Wetter.
> When we were in Hamburg, we had the nicest weather.

Wenn (whenever, if) usually signals an *if* situation or a repeated event (whenever).

> *Immer wenn* Sophie die Grippe hatte, trank sie viel Orangensaft.
> Whenever Sophie had the flu, she drank a lot of orange juice.

> *Wenn* ich in Deutschland bin, spreche ich immer Deutsch.
> Whenever I am in Germany, I always speak German.

> *Wenn* es morgen regnet, bleibe ich zu Hause.
> If it rains tomorrow, I will stay home.

Wann (when) is always a question word. It can also be used in indirect statements.

> *Wann* gehen wir ins Kino?
> When are we going to the movie?

> *Wann* musst du ins Krankenhaus gehen?
> When do you have to go to the hospital?

> Ich weiß nicht, *wann* ich ins Krankenhaus gehen muss.
> I don't know when I have to go to the hospital.

Übung G

Complete the sentence or question with **als, wenn,** or **wann.**

> BEISPIEL: _____ haben Sie Geburtstag?
> **Wann** haben Sie Geburtstag?

1. _____ wir in der Schweiz waren, sind wir oft gewandert.

2. Herr Braun fragt, _____ die Post kommt?

3. Wissen Sie, _____ der Zug ankommt?

4. _____ Frau Schmidt krank ist, nimmt sie immer Aspirin.

5. _____ ich viel Zeit habe, lese ich meistens.

6. Spielst du auch Tennis, _____ es kalt ist?

7. _____ Martin studierte, war er sehr arm.

8. _____ kommen Sie nach Amerika?

9. Jennifer fragte mich, _____ ich nach Hause fahre.

10. Sind Sie oft ins Ausland geflogen, _____ Sie für Lufthansa arbeiteten?

SPRECHEN LEICHT GEMACHT

Aktivität A: Was machten Sie heute?

Use simple past tense.

1. **Um sieben Uhr . . .**	I got up
2. **Dann . . .**	ate breakfast
3. **Um 9 Uhr . . .**	I read a book
4. **Um 10 Uhr . . .**	I went shopping
5. **Später . . .**	I visited a friend
6. **Um 12 Uhr . . .**	we ate again
7. **Um 1 Uhr . . .**	I went home
8. **Am Nachmittag . . .**	I worked in the garden
9. **Abends . . .**	I saw a movie
10. **Um Mitternacht . . .**	I went to bed

Aktivität B: Beantworten Sie die Fragen

Several answers are possible.

> BEISPIEL: Wie oft gehen Sie zum Arzt?
> Ich gehe nur, wenn ich krank bin.

1. Was machten Sie, als Sie die Grippe hatten?

2. Was tat Ihnen weh?

3. Wann muss man ins Krankenhaus gehen?

4. Wann verschreibt ein Arzt Medikamente?

5. Was machten Sie, als Sie eine Erkältung hatten?

6. Haben Sie einen Hausarzt?

7. Warum haben so viele Menschen Lungenkrebs?

8. Wie oft gehen Sie in die Apotheke?

9. Schlafen Sie genug?

10. Wie bleibt man gesund? (Was sollte man tun/nicht tun?)

Wiederholung

Complete the review on a separate piece of paper. Answers are located in the back of the book.

A. Norbert ist krank.

Report or write this paragraph about Norbert's illness in the *simple past tense*. Put all boldface verbs into the simple past.

Norbert **bleibt** heute zu Hause. Er **hat** Hals- und Kopfschmerzen und **fühlt** sich nicht wohl. Auch **sieht** er sehr blass **aus**. Am Nachmittag **geht** er zum Arzt, denn sein Fieber **ist** sehr hoch. Er **ist** wohl wirklich krank. Er **muss** sich untersuchen lassen. Der Arzt **glaubt**, dass er eine schwere Erkältung oder vielleicht sogar eine Grippe **hat**. Er **gibt** ihm Penicillintabletten. Bald **geht** es ihm besser.

B. Write a question replacing the boldface word(s).

BEISPIEL: Jutta hat hohes Fieber.
   Wer hat hohes Fieber?   (Jutta hat hohes Fieber.)

1. **Gestern** war Kim nicht im Büro.

2. **Mein Kollege** hat sich ein neues Auto gekauft.

3. Kurt hat sich gestern **krank** gefühlt.

4. **Wir** schlafen nicht genug.

5. Letzte Woche fuhr Herr Schwarz **nach** Köln.

Wortschatz

Nouns

der Anzug, ‒e	suit	die Tablette, -n	tablet, pill
das Ausland	abroad	das Universitäts-	university
im Ausland	foreign	krankenhaus, ‒er	hospital
	country	der Wecker,–	alarm clock
der Ausländer, –	foreigner, *m.*	das Wetter	weather
die Ausländerin, -nen	foreigner, *f.*	der Zahn, ‒e	tooth
der Autoschlüssel, –	car key		
der Blindarm, -e	appendix		
der Blutdruck	blood	**Verbs**	
	pressure		
die Entzündung, -en	inflamma-	(sich) an·stecken	to catch an
	tion		illness
das Fieber, –	fever	sich an·ziehen, zog an,	to get
die Grippe, -n	flu	angezogen	dressed
das Haar, -e	hair	auf·wachen*	to wake up
der Hals, ‒e	throat	aus·sehen, (sieht aus),	to look like
die Halsschmerzen	sore throat	sah aus, ausgesehen	
der Hausarzt, ‒e	family	aus·suchen	to choose
	doctor	sich beeilen	to hurry
das Kleid, -er	dress	benutzen	to use
der Krebs, –	cancer	sich bewerben um	to apply for
die Kunst, ‒e	art	brechen, (i) a, o	to break
die Lungenent-	pneumonia	sich duschen	to take a
zündung, -en			shower
die Mandeln	tonsils	sich erkälten	to catch a
der Mantel, ‒	coat		cold
das Medikament, -e	medicine	sich erinnern	to remember
der Mund, ‒er	mouth	fehlen	to miss,
der Ohrenschmerz, -en	earache		to lack
das Rezept, -e	prescription	(sich) fühlen	to feel
der Schirm, -e	umbrella	impfen	to immunize,
der Schmerz, -en	pain, ache		to vacci-
der Schuh, -e	shoe		nate
die Sprechstunde, -n	office hour	(sich) kämmen	to comb
die Sprechstunden-	receptionist	klingeln	to ring
hilfe, -n	(in a		(a bell)
	doctor's	lassen (lässt), ließ,	to let,
	office)	gelassen	to permit
		(sich) putzen	to clean,
			to brush

---

*Indicates that the verb uses **sein** as the auxiliary. See the discussion in the Wortschatz in Kapitel 5.

(sich) rasieren	to shave	**Other Words**	
raus·müssen,	*here:* to have		
muss raus,	removed	also	therefore,
rausgemusst			well, so
regnen	to rain	best	best
schwellen, o, o	to swell	bestimmt	certain(ly)
springen*, a, u	to jump	blass	pale
stehen, stand,	to get up	deshalb	therefore,
gestanden			that's why
tun (tut), tat, getan	to do,	furchtbar	terrible
	to make	genug	enough
untersuchen	to examine	gestern	yesterday
verschreiben, ie, ie	to prescribe	gesund	healthy
sich verspäten	to be late, to	hoffentlich	hopefully
	be delayed	interessant	interesting
		jeder, jede, jedes	each
weh·tun (tut weh),	to hurt	schlimm	bad
tat weh, wehgetan		schwindelig	dizzy
		wenigstens	at least
		zufrieden	satisfied

Idiomatic Expressions

Was fehlt Ihnen?	What's wrong with you?
sich untersuchen	to be examined by a physician
lassen	

Cognates

der Liter, –	die Musik
das Museum, die	der Patient, -en
Museen	der Sport

KAPITEL 7 Television and Radio

---------------------------------- CULTURE NOTES ----------------------------------

Television and radio stations in Germany, Austria, and Switzerland are owned by their respective federal governments. The law states that TV and radio must be politically neutral. Independent boards, made up of people from all walks of life, are in charge of programming. Several television networks called **Programme**, as well as local radio stations, offer news, educational programs, entertainment, and sports. Cable stations have been available since 1982, but cable service remains expensive.

Although television and radio is government supported in these countries, all owners of TV and radio sets must pay a flat monthly fee.

There are few interruptions of programs by commercial advertisements. Instead, a block of television ads is presented for about five to fifteen minutes two or three times daily.

Television broadcasts usually begin early in the morning and end at midnight or shortly thereafter. Some radio stations broadcast around the clock.

DIALOGE

Read the dialogues aloud in German and check the English translations.

FRAU M.:	**Siehst du immer noch fern?**	Are you still watching TV?
HERR M.:	**Ja, das Fußballspiel ist noch nicht vorbei.**	Yes, the soccer game isn't over yet.

FRAU M.:	Ich möchte mir aber die Nachrichten ansehen.	But I would like to see the news.
HERR M.:	Das geht nicht. Ich schalte jetzt noch nicht um.	That's not possible. I am not going to change the channel yet.
FRAU M.:	Immer diese verrückten Sportprogramme!	Always these crazy sports programs!
HERR M.:	Naja. Ich habe meine verrückten Sportprogramme und du deine langweiligen Quiz-Shows.	Oh, well. I have my crazy sports programs and you your boring quiz shows.

KARIN:	Was gibt's heute abend im Fernsehen?	What's on TV tonight?
ELKE:	*(liest das Fernsehprogramm)* Nichts Besonderes. Im ersten Programm gibt es einen bekannten Krimi, im zweiten Programm eine alberne Unterhaltungssendung, und im dritten Programm einen langweiligen Dokumentarfilm über Brasilien.	*(reads the TV guide)* Nothing special. On channel 1 they're showing a well-known detective film, on channel 2 a silly entertainment show, and on channel 3 a boring documentary about Brazil.
KARIN:	Was sollen wir uns ansehen?	What should we watch?
ELKE:	Nichts. Ich lese lieber den neuen *Spiegel** und höre mir etwas Schönes im Radio an.	Nothing. I would rather read the new *Spiegel* and listen to something nice on the radio.

HERR S.:	Was halten Sie vom amerikanischen Fernsehen?	What do you think of American television?
HERR J.:	Ich finde es ganz gut, nur stören mich die dummen Werbungen.	I think it's pretty good, only the stupid commercials bother me.

---

*The most important weekly newsmagazine in Germany, similar to *Newsweek* or *Time* magazine.

HERR S.:	Ja, Sie haben recht. In Deutschland gibt es nicht so viele Werbungen im Fernsehen.	Yes, you're right. In Germany there aren't as many commercials on television.
HERR J.:	Doch. Aber nur zu bestimmten Zeiten zwei- oder dreimal am Tag.	Yes, there are. But only at certain times two or three times a day.
HERR S.:	Aber nur selten während einer Sendung.	But only rarely (seldom) during a program.
HERR J.:	Das stimmt nicht ganz. Zum Beispiel bei Sportsendungen gibt es schon Werbungen.	That's not totally correct. For example, during sports programs there are (already) commercials.

KOMMUNIKATION

Aktivität A

Was stimmt? Was stimmt nicht? (What fits? What doesn't?) Cross out the completions or responses that do *not* fit or do not make sense.

1. Wie können Fernsehprogramme sein?

                          . . . interessant.
                          . . . gut durchgebraten.
   Einige sind . . .   . . . verrückt.
                          . . . langweilig.

2. Im Fernsehen gibt es . . .

                          . . . Bibliotheken.
                          . . . Dokumentarfilme.
                          . . . Werbungen.
                          . . . Sportprogramme.
                          . . . Nachrichten.

3. Wenn ich den Fernseher einschalte, . . .

                          . . . sehe ich nichts.
                          . . . verpasse ich alle Programme.
                          . . . höre ich das Radio.
                          . . . kann ich Nachrichten sehen.

4. Wer in Deutschland
   fernsieht, . . .

. . . muss nichts bezahlen.
. . . sieht auch Werbungen.
. . . bekommt monatlich eine
   Rechnung.
. . . kann auch politische
   Debatten hören.

Aktivität B: Kleiner Fernsehquiz*

Mark the answers that apply to you.

1. Ich habe einen
   a. schwarz-weiß Fernseher.
   b. Farbfernseher.
   Was noch?

2. Ich sehe gern
   a. Unterhaltungssendungen.
   b. Dokumentarfilme.
   c. Nachrichten.
   d. Sportübertragungen.
   Was noch?

3. Ich sehe
   a. so oft wie möglich fern.
   b. selten fern.
   c. fast nie fern.
   Was noch?

4. Ich sehe gerne Programme, die
   a. mich unterhalten.
   b. mich informieren.
   Was noch?

5. Am Wochenende
   a. gehe ich meistens ins Kino.
   b. sehe ich meistens fern.
   c. besuche ich Freunde.
   Was noch?

---

*If you don't know a word, look it up in the Wortschatz.

6. Ich finde die amerikanischen Werbungen
   a. albern.
   b. interessant.
   c. störend.
   d. langweilig.
   Was noch?

7. Das amerikanische Fernsehen zeigt zu viele
   a. Sportübertragungen.
   b. Unterhaltungssendungen.
   c. Dokumentarfilme.
   d. Nachrichten.
   Was noch?

8. Ich finde das amerikanische Fernsehen
   a. interessant.
   b. langweilig.
   c. informativ.
   Was noch?

9. Ich finde die amerikanischen Nachrichten
   a. objektiv.
   b. subjektiv.
   c. sachlich.
   Was noch?

10. Was sind Sie?
    a. Ich bin vor allem Zeitungsleser.
    b. Ich bin vor allem Radiohörer.
    c. Ich sehe vor allem viel fern.
    Was noch?

GRAMMATIK

1. Possessive Adjectives (Pronouns)

Possessive adjectives—**mein** (my), **dein** (your), **sein** (his), and so on—are also called ein words because they take the same ending as the indefinite article **ein** and **kein**. Look at these examples.

Ich sehe einen Hund.	I see a dog.
Ich sehe *meinen* Hund.	I see my dog.
Ich sehe eine Katze.	I see a cat.
Ich sehe *meine* Katze.	I see my cat.

Ich gebe einem Kind das Buch.	I give a child the book.
Ich gebe *meinem* Kind das Buch.	I give my child the book.

As you can see, the ending of the possessive adjective, like that of **ein** and **kein**, is determined by the gender and case of the noun that follows it. Look at this chart and learn the possessive adjectives.

POSSESSIVE ADJECTIVES

Singular		Plural		
ich = **mein**	my	wir = **unser**	our
du = **dein**	your	ihr = **euer**	your
er = **sein**	his	sie = **ihr**	their
sie = **ihr**	her		
es = **sein**	its		
Sie = **Ihr**	your *(polite, sing., pl.)*		

Remember that these *possessive adjectives* have the same endings as **ein** or **kein**.

Übung A

Fill in the blanks with the correct German equivalent of the English possessive adjectives in parentheses.

> **BEISPIEL:** Geben Sie mir bitte _____Ihre_____ Zeitung.   *your*

1. Ich möchte mit _____ Eltern sprechen.   your *(fam. sing.)*

2. Herr Braun braucht _____ Tabletten.   his

3. Wir haben _____ Freunde lange nicht gesehen.   our

4. Frau Meyer konnte _____ Geld nicht finden.   her

5. Erich wollte _____ Fernseher anschalten.   my

6. Ich finde _____ Sportprogramme langweilig.   your *(fam. pl.)*

7. Ich kann _____ Deutsch gut verstehen.   your *(formal)*

8. Ich sehe _____ Kollegen jeden Tag.   their

Übung B

You are looking for an object and you ask who has it.

> **BEISPIEL:** (his radio) = Wer hat sein Radio?
> (my watch) = Wer hat meine Uhr?

1. (our car keys) _____?

2. (my umbrella) _____?

3. (his suitcase) _____?

4. (their car) _____?

5. (her theater ticket) _____?

6. (your book, *formal*) _____?

7. (your CDs, *fam. sing.*) _____?

2. The *der* Words

German has a group of **der** words or **dieser** words that change their endings exactly like **der, die,** and **das.** An example is **dieser** (this). The ending to these words (see below) depends on the gender, number, and case of the noun it modifies.

der Tisch	→	**dieser** Tisch	die Tür	→	**diese** Tür
das Kind	→	**dieses** Kind	die Leute	→	**diese** Leute

Learn these so-called **der** words:

dies- = this, that, these, the latter

jed- = each, every (only used in the singular)

jen- = that, those, the former

manch- = many a, several, some

solch- = such, such a

welch- = which

Übung C

Replace the boldface definite article with the appropriate form of the cue **der** word.

1. Ich habe **den** Sprecher noch nie gehört.   jen . . .
2. Frau Braun kauft immer **das** Fernsehprogramm.   dies . . .
3. **Die** Kinder besuchen mich.   welch . . .
4. **Die** Platten kaufe ich nicht mehr.   solch . . .
5. In **den** Fragen hat sie recht.   manch . . .
6. Der Journalist spricht über **dieses** Thema.   jed . . .

3. Adjectives Used as Predicate Adjectives

When adjectives follow nouns or pronouns, they have no ending and remain unchanged. They are called *predicate adjectives* and often complete statements introduced by verbs like **sein** (to be), **werden** (to become), or **bleiben** (to remain).

Das Programm ist *langweilig*.	The program is boring.
Meine Eltern bleiben *aktiv*.	My parents remain active.
Das Wetter wird *schön*.	The weather is getting nice.

Note: German adverbs also have no endings:

Du sprichst zu schnell.	You talk too fast.
Sie singt schön.	She sings beautifully.

Übung D

Let's review some adjectives. Give the opposites.

BEISPIEL: Hamburg ist groß, Siegburg ist _____klein_____.

1. Meine Freundin ist gesund, ich bin ____.

2. Meine Kinder sind faul, Ihre sind ____.

3. Julia steht immer früh auf, Lisa immer ____.

4. Die Demokratie in Deutschland ist jung, in Amerika ist sie ____.

5. Vater sagt: „Ich werde alt, aber Mutter bleibt immer ____.“

6. Das Essen in eurem Hotel war gut, aber in unserem war es ____.

7. Dieses Jahr war der Sommer sehr heiß, aber letztes Jahr war er

   ____.

8. Dein Urlaub war sehr lang, meiner war leider zu ____.

9. Ältere Leute spielen ihr Radio ziemlich leise, aber Teenagers

   spielen es meistens zu ____.

10. Die Mathematikprüfung war schwer, aber die Englischprüfung

    war ____.

4. Adjectival Endings

Attributive (descriptive) adjectives describe the noun they modify. They almost always add an ending to show the noun's number, gender, and case.

A. Adjective Endings after der Words and ein Words

The choice of adjective endings is determined by the words (or lack of them) that precede adjectives. The chart below tells you which adjective ending is used after **der** words and **ein** words.

	Masculine	Feminine	Neuter	Plural
Nominative	(der) **-e**	(die) **-e**	(das) **-e**	(die) **-en**
	(ein) **-er**	(eine) **-e**	(ein) **-es**	(keine) **-en**
Accusative	(den) **-en**	(die) **-e**	(das) **-e**	(die) **-en**
	(einen) **-en**	(eine) **-e**	(ein) **-es**	(keine) **-en**
Dative	(dem) **-en**	(der) **-en**	(dem) **-en**	(den) **-en**
	(einem) **-en**	(einer) **-en**	(einem) **-en**	(keinen) **-en**
Genitive	(des) **-en**	(der) **-en**	(des) **-en**	(der) **-en**
	(eines) **-en**	(einer) **-en**	(eines) **-en**	(keiner) **-en**

Note: All datives, all genitives, and all plurals end in **-en**

Adjectives that follow definite articles (**der, die, das, dieser, solcher, jeder**) or interrogatives (**welcher**) have these endings:

Case	Masculine	Feminine	Neuter	Plural
Nominative	der klein**e** Ball	die klein**e** Stadt	das klein**e** Auto	die klein**en** Kinder
Accusative	den klein**en** Ball	die klein**e** Stadt	das klein**e** Auto	die klein**en** Kinder
Dative	dem klein**en** Ball	der klein**en** Stadt	dem klein**en** Auto	den klein**en** Kindern

Ich nehme dieses preiswert*e* Zimmer	I'll take this reasonable room.
Wo haben Sie diesen billig*en* Flug bekommen?	Where did you get this cheap flight?
Diese interessant*e* Sendung gefällt mir.	I like this interesting program.

B. Adjectives after ein words

Adjectives that follow indefinite articles (**ein, eine**), the negative **kein(e)**, or the possessives (**mein, dein, sein,** etc.) take slightly different endings.

Case	Masculine	Feminine	Neuter	Plural
Nominative	ein klein**er** Ball	eine klein**e** Stadt	ein klein**es** Auto	keine klein**en** Kinder
Accusative	einen klein**en** Ball	eine klein**e** Stadt	ein klein**es** Auto	keine klein**en** Kinder
Dative	einem klein**en** Ball	einer klein**en** Stadt	einem klein**en** Auto	keinen klein**en** Kindern

Ich konnte kein billig*es* Restaurant finden.	I couldn't find a cheap restaurant.
Wir sahen gestern einen ausländisch*en* Film.	We saw a foreign film yesterday.
Kennen Sie meine deutsch*en* Verwandten?	Do you know my German relatives?

C. Unpreceded Adjectives

Finally, unpreceded adjectives (no **ein** or **der** word) in most cases take the same ending as the *definite articles.*

Case	Masculine	Feminine	Neuter	Plural
Nominative	kalt**er** Wein	kalt**e** Milch	kalt**es** Wasser	kalt**e** Getränke
Accusative	kalt**en** Wein	kalt**e** Milch	kalt**es** Wasser	kalt**e** Getränke
Dative	kalt**em** Wein	kalt**er** Milch	kalt**em** Wasser	kalt**en** Getränken

Kalt*e* Milch schmeckt gut.	(nominative feminine **die** = -e)
Ich esse gern weiß*es* Brot.	(accusative neuter **das** = -es)
Wir servieren nur frisch*en* Fisch.	(accusative masculine **den** = -en)

Note: Adjective endings are important, but you should remember that it takes time to learn them correctly. Even Germans sometimes make mistakes with adjective endings!

Übung E: Ja, das Wetter . . .

Add the correct adjective endings. Watch whether the adjective is preceded by a **der** word or an **ein** word, or is unpreceded.

1. Februar ist ein kurz_____ Monat.

2. Ich warte auf den warm_____ Frühling.

3. Der heiß_____ Sommer gefällt mir nicht.

4. In meinem Sommerurlaub mache ich eine lang_____ und teur_____ Reise.

5. Dann sehe ich keine langweilig_____ Fernsehprogramme.

6. Im September freuen wir uns alle auf die kühl_____ Herbstage.

7. Der November hat aber schon kurz_____ Tage.

8. Dann kommt der schön_____, weiß_____ Schnee im Dezember.

9. Natürlich haben nicht alle Leute das kalt_____ Winterwetter gern.

10. Die kalt_____ Wintermonate dauern nicht sehr lang_____.

Übung F

Auf deutsch, bitte.

> **BEISPIEL:** German TV is supposed to be very good.
> Das deutsche Fernsehen soll sehr gut sein.

1. They do not have many advertisements.

   _____.

2. I am not interested in foreign TV.

   _____.

3. Elke listens only to classical music.

   _____.

4. Paul likes American Jazz.

   _____.

5. Do you want to see this crazy program?

   _____.

6. Yes, because it is very interesting.

   _____.

7. I did not like this boring movie. (use **gefallen**)

   _____.

8. My father gave my little brother a new TV set.

   _____.

5. Adjectives Used as Nouns

In German many adjectives are used as nouns. When used as nouns, they are always *capitalized* and *declined*—they have endings.

> **BEISPIELE:** ein reicher Mann   ein Reicher
> der reiche Mann   der Reiche

ein armes Kind   ein Armes
das arme Kind   das Arme
reiche Leute   die Reichen
die reichen Leute   die Reichen

Übung G

Change the sentence by replacing the adjective with the appropriate noun.

> **BEISPIEL:** Der fremde Mann spricht kein Deutsch.
> <u>Der Fremde spricht kein Deutsch.</u>

1. Mein ältester Sohn bekommt ein neues Auto.

   _____ bekommt ein neues Auto.

2. Der große Junge ist mein Sohn.

   _____ ist mein Sohn.

3. Ich kenne den neuen Kollegen nicht.

   Ich kenne _____ nicht.

4. Meine jüngste Tochter ist Ärztin.

   _____ ist Ärztin.

5. Helfen Sie doch der kranken Frau.

   Helfen sie doch _____.

6. In Amerika gibt es viele arme Menschen.

   In Amerika gibt es viele _____.

7. Pelé war der beste Fußballspieler in der Welt.

   Pelé war _____ in der Welt.

6. Indefinite Adjectives

einige	some	ähnliche	similar
viele	many	folgende	the following
wenige	a few	mehrere	several
andere	others	verschiedene	different

Nominative	viele kleine Kinder	diese vielen kleinen Kinder
Accusative	viele kleine Kinder	diese vielen kleinen Kinder
Dative	vielen kleinen Kindern	diesen vielen kleinen Kindern

These *indefinite adjectives* are in the plural and are treated like descriptive adjectives. Note that their endings are the same as those of *unpreceded* adjectives.

Ich habe viele gute Freunde.
Kennen Sie **meine** vielen guten Freunde?
Elke hilft folgenden amerikanischen Touristen.
Elke hat **den** folgenden amerikanischen Touristen geholfen.

Lesestück: Familie—Haus—Wetter (Adjektive angewandt)

Read this Lesestück and notice how adjectives are used almost excessively. Underline all adjectives and notice their endings. The vocabulary is house, family, and weather oriented.

Das Wetter ist mild und warm; es ist ein schöner Sommertag, und die Sonne brennt nicht zu heiß. Die Familie (der Vater, die Mutter, und Onkel Christian) sitzt gemütlich im Garten. Der Vater trinkt starken schwarzen Kaffee, die Mutter Eistee, und der Onkel kalte Limonade. Sie essen frisches Brot mit Butter und Marmelade. Das noch warme Brot duftet so stark, dass der Nachbar hungrig wird!

Die Eltern sprechen von dem Sohn; er ist ein lebendiges und manchmal lautes Kind. Er heißt Tobias und ist acht Jahre alt. Tobias ist nicht dumm, er ist intelligent. „In der Schule sollte er der Beste sein," sagt der Vater. „Ja, ja . . ." antwortet Onkel Christian, gähnt ein bisschen und beißt wieder ins frische, duftende Brot.

Tobias spielt im großen, frischgemähten Garten. Im nassen Gras findet er unter einem blühenden Rosenbusch einen roten Ball. Onkel Christian sagt zu ihm: „Gib' deiner kleinen Schwester den Ball!" Tobias gibt ihr den roten Ball—aber nicht gern. Anna, seine Schwester, ist ein liebes, kleines Mädchen—vor allem wenn sie den Ball bekommt.

Die Eltern gehen ins saubere, zweistöckige Haus. Im Wohnzimmer sehen sie Michael, den Sohn des Onkels. Michael ist ein junger Mann und studiert fleißig an der Universität. Er sitzt auf dem bequemen Sofa und denkt an seine blonde Freundin. Sie heißt Hilde und ist achtzehn Jahre alt. Sie hat langes, blondes Haar und studiert auch. Michael telefoniert mit ihr und sagt: „Es ist heute so heiß, wir sollten schwimmen gehen."

Michael und Hilde fahren in Hildes neuem Sportwagen an den Strand. Der Himmel ist blau, der Sand ist warm, aber das Wasser ist kühl. Michael und Hilde sind gute Schwimmer. Zuerst schwimmen sie, dann liegen sie im warmen Sand. Am Abend sind sie braun von der Sonne.

Alle sind sich einig, der heutige Tag war nicht aufregend, aber angenehm und entspannend. Diese Adjektive beschreiben ihn gut . . .

Übung H

Without looking at the text, try to complete the statements with the correct words from the list scrambled below.

> **BEISPIEL:** Der Vater trinkt ____schwarzen Kaffee.____ .

1. Tobias hat einen _____ .

2. Er finden den Ball unter einem _____ .

3. Die Erwachsenen essen Brot mit _____ .

4. Michael ist ein _____ .

5. Seine Freundin hat _____ .

6. Das Wasser ist _____ .

7. Hildes Sportwagen ist _____ .

8. Hilde und Michael sind _____ .

guter Marmelade/neu/junger Mann/langes, blondes Haar/roten Ball/ kühl/großen Rosenbusch/gute Schwimmer

SPRECHEN LEICHT GEMACHT

Aktivität A: Ja, das Fernsehen!

Choose a fitting positive or negative response from the right column. More than one can be suitable. Say both the statement (or question) and the response aloud.

> **BEISPIEL:** Was gibt's heute abend im Fernsehen?
> *i.* Ich muss im Programm nachsehen.

1. Ich höre gern Radio.
2. Wir verbringen zu viel Zeit vor dem Fernseher.
3. Ich kann ohne Fernsehen nicht mehr leben.
4. Warum müssen wir so viele Werbungen haben?
5. Wir kaufen einen neuen Fernseher.
6. Radio und Fernsehen informieren uns.
7. Die Werbungen im Fernsehen sind schrecklich.

a. Sie bezahlen das Fernsehen.
b. Ja, das sagt man.
c. Das ist nicht nötig.
d. Das kostet zu viel.
e. Ich brauche kein Fernsehen, ich lese viel.
f. Ich auch.
g. Man kann immer umschalten.
h. Das glaube (finde) ich nicht.
i. Ich muss im Programm nachsehen.

Aktivität B: Was paßt? (What Fits?)

Incorporate fitting adjectives, adverbs, and nouns into your responses. Choose from the words below and complete the phrase or sentence. More than one word may be suitable.

> **BEISPIEL:** Was trinken Sie gern?
> Ich trinke gern heißen/kalten/warmen Tee.
> (kalte Milch, Limonade, usw.)

1. Wo esst ihr oft? Wir essen oft . . .

2. Wie fühlen Sie sich, wenn Sie nicht genug essen? Ich werde . . .

3. Wie denken Sie über Karin? Sie ist . . .

4. Wo wohnten Sie in Österreich? Wir wohnten . . .

5. Wo arbeiten Sie gern? Ich arbeite gern . . .

6. Wie sieht Ihre Schwester/Ihr Bruder aus? Sie/er hat . . .

7. Was für ein Auto hat er/sie? Er/sie hat ein . . .

8. Wohin bist du in Urlaub gefahren? Ich bin . . .

in einer kleinen Stadt/an einer lauten Straße/in Innsbruck/teures/ billiges/schönes Auto/heißen /kalten/warmen Tee/kalte Milch/ Limonade/schwindelig/krank/in einem österreichischen Restaurant/ in einem eleganten Hotel/in einem modernen Büro/bei einer kleinen Firma/an einem sauberen Strand/in meinem schönen Garten/eine nette Frau/eine gute Freundin/in die hohen Berge/in die schöne Schweiz/ blondes Haar/braune Augen

Wiederholung

A. Write sentences using all the words given. Be sure to use the correct articles. Also watch adjective endings.

> **BEISPIEL:** im/deutsch/Fernsehen/es/geben/viele/langweilig/Werbungen
> Im deutschen Fernsehen gibt es viele langweilige Werbungen.

1. ich/hören/jeden/Abend/Nachrichten
2. heute/wir/kaufen/ein/neu/Auto
3. d—/Arzt/können/d—/Krank-/nicht/helfen
4. trinken/Sie/gerne/schwarz-/Kaffee?
5. weil/d—/Wetter/heiß/sein/,/gehen/wir/heute/schwimmen

B. Adjectives and Adverbs Review
Match the adjectives on the left with their opposites on the right.

1. langweilig	a. weiß	11. intelligent	l. heiß
2. bekannt	b. oft	12. groß	m. wenig
3. neu	c. alt	13. faul	n. froh
4. gut	e. klein	14. kurz	o. lang
5. schwarz	f. subjektiv	15. gesund	p. nah
6. selten	g. immer	16. arm	q. dort
7. nie	h. dumm	17. hier	r. krank
8. objektiv	i. unbekannt	18. weit	s. fleißig
9. warm	j. schlecht	19. viel	t. reich
10. kalt	k. kühl	20. traurig	u. interessant

Wortschatz

Nouns

das Brot, -e	bread	**die Sportübertragung,**	sports
der Dokumentarfilm, -e	documentary	**-en**	broadcast
der Eistee, -s	ice tea	**der Sportwagen, –**	sports car
der Erwachsene, -n	adult, grown-up	**der Sprecher, –**	announcer, speaker
der Farbfernseher,–	color television set	**das Thema, die Themen**	theme, topic
die Kirche, -n	church	**die Unterhaltungs-**	entertainment
der Krimi, -s	detective story	**sendung, -en**	show
		die Welt, -en	world
die Opernübertragung, -en	opera broadcast	**die Werbung, -en**	advertisement, commercial
der Rosenbusch, ⁓e	rosebush	**das Wohnzimmer, –**	living room
die Sendung, -en	broadcast		

Verbs

sich an·hören	to listen to	halten von, (hält), hielt, gehalten	to think of
sich an·sehen, (sieht an), sah an, angesehen	to look at	(sich) informieren	to inform
		klopfen	to knock
beißen, biss, gebissen	to bite	stören	to disturb, to bother
besteigen, bestieg, bestiegen	to climb	um·schalten	to switch over, to change the channel
brennen, brannte, gebrannt	to burn; *here:* to tan		
duften	to smell pleasantly	(sich) unterhalten, (unterhält), unter-hielt, unterhalten	to enjoy one self
fern·sehen, (sieht fern), sah fern, ferngesehen	to watch television	verpassen	to miss
gähnen	to yawn		

Other Words

albern	silly	langweilig	boring
angenehm	pleasant	leise	quiet, softly
aufregend	exciting	möglich	possible
ausländisch	foreign	nass	wet
bekannt	known	politisch	political
bequem	comfortable	rot	red
beschäftigt	busy, occu-pied	sachlich	factual
		schwarz-weiß	black and white
blau	blue		
entspannt	relaxing	schwierig	difficult
fast	almost	traurig	sad
frisch	fresh	unbekannt	unknown
frischgemäht	just mowed	verrückt	crazy
froh	glad	vor allem	above all
gemütlich	cozy, com-fortable	ziemlich	rather
		zweimal	twice
hübsch	pretty	zweistöckig	two-story

Idiomatic Expressions

Das geht nicht.	That doesn't work.
nichts Besonderes	nothing special
Es ist noch nicht vorbei.	It isn't over yet.
schade	too bad
sich einig sein	to be in agreement

Cognates

die Debatte, -n	das Radiopro-gramm, -e
der Fisch, -e	blond
das Gras, ¨er	objektiv
die Marmelade, -n	subjektiv
das Programm, -e	

Sports, Physical Education, and Recreation

German-speaking people are sports and recreation minded, and the huge number of sports clubs and recreation associations bear witness to this. Even small villages often have their own sports club, usually a **Fußball-club** (soccer club) or a **Turnverein** (gymnastics club). If one had to identify one or two national sports in the German-speaking countries, soccer and skiing would win that poll, the latter being especially popular in Austria, Switzerland, and southern Germany. But people engage in many other sports, too.

Physical education is a required and important part of the school curriculum at all age levels. Intramurals are stressed more than interschool rivalries, however. Top-level competitors use clubs, not school, as their home base for training and competition. Universities are not engaged in big-time sports competition.

Hiking has always been a favorite pastime for young and old in all German-speaking countries. Gentle walks through city parks, short and long hikes through the countryside, and ever-demanding climbs in the high mountains—all these activities can be considered a part of their lifestyle. There is no shortage of hiking paths *anywhere*. Maps of hiking routes are available in every bookstore and often at newspaper stands. In the mountains of Austria and Switzerland, many lodges are maintained by different Alpine clubs. They enable hikers and climbers to explore the serenity and beauty of the Alps.

Swimming pools can be found in almost any community, large or small. But don't look for public tennis courts in parks or high schools. There aren't any. For this sport, one has to belong to a club or rent a court by the hour.

DIALOGE

Read the dialogues aloud in German and check the English translations.

	Laufen	**Jogging**
FRAU K.:	Frau Rieger, laufen Sie mit?	Mrs. Rieger, will you jog along?
FRAU R.:	Ich glaube nicht, Sie laufen so viel schneller als ich.	I don't believe so. You run so much faster than I do.
FRAU K.:	Oh, das stimmt gar nicht. Gestern bin ich mit einem älteren Ehepaar nach Fürberg* gelaufen. Da war ich die Langsamste.	Oh, that's not true. Yesterday I ran with an older couple to Fürberg. At that time I was the slowest.
FRAU R.:	Na gut, ich laufe mit. Aber bitte warten Sie nicht auf mich, wenn ich langsamer werde. Das wäre mir peinlich.	OK then. I will jog along. But please don't wait for me if I run slower. That would be embarrassing for me.
FRAU K.:	Einverstanden.	Agreed.

	Schilaufen	**Skiing**
ANDREA:	Brrr. Heute ist es viel kälter als gestern, nicht wahr?	Brrr. Today it is much colder than yesterday. Isn't it?
TRUDE:	Ja, aber die Luft ist trockener. Und es ist auch nicht so windig wie gestern.	Yes, but the air is drier (less humid). And it isn't as windy as yesterday.
ANDREA:	Hoffentlich kommt bald die Sonne heraus.	I hope the sun will come out soon.

*a small village on the Wolfgangsee, a lake in Austria

| TRUDE: | Ja, das hoffe ich auch. Aber der Schnee ist herrlich. Reiner Pulver! Heute ist keine Abfahrt vereist. | Yes, I hope so, too. But the snow is wonderful. Pure powder! Not one slope is icy today. |
| ANDREA: | Prima, dann könnten wir ja ein bisschen schussen. | Great, then we can go straight down. |

	Wandern und Bergsteigen	**Hiking and Mountain Climbing**
HERR A.:	Herr Wagner, machen Sie morgen einen Ausflug?	Mr. Wagner, are you going on a hiking trip tomorrow?
HERR W.:	Ja, wenn das Wetter schön bleibt, würden wir gern auf den Dachstein gehen.	Yes, if the weather stays nice, we would like to go to the Dachstein.
HERR A.:	Dachstein? Das ist doch der höchste Berg in dieser Gegend. Der ist ja noch höher als die Lammspitze. Dort wollen Sie hinauf?	Dachstein? Isn't that the highest mountain in this area? It's even higher than the Lammspitze. Do you want to go up there?
HERR W.:	Stimmt, aber wir lassen uns Zeit. Wir sollten es in fünf Stunden schaffen.	That's correct. But we'll take our time. We should make it in five hours.

KOMMUNIKATION

Aktivität A

Was kann nicht stimmen? What's not right? Cross out the one statement that doesn't make sense.

1. Frau K. . . . . . . macht einen Ausflug.
. . . ist verreist.
. . . läuft schneller als Frau R.

2. Die Luft . . . . . . ist heute herrlich.
. . . ist heute trocken.
. . . kommt bald heraus.

3. Der Schnee . . . . . . ist heute peinlich.
. . . ist heute trocken.
. . . ist heute reiner Pulver.

4. Morgen . . .   . . . machen wir das Wetter.
                                          . . . bleibt das Wetter schön.
                                          . . . gehen wir auf einen Berg.

5. Beim Wandern wünscht man sich . . . . . . reinen Pulverschnee.
                                          . . . bequeme Schuhe.

Aktivität B: Sportvokabular

Verstehen Sie das deutsche Sportvokabular? Was stimmt: *a, b,* oder *c?*

1. Jogging ist eine Form von   a. Schilaufen.
                                      b. Laufen.
                                      c. Tennisspielen.

2. Das Wort *schussen* gehört zum   a. Bergsteigen
                                      b. Golfspielen.
                                      c. Schilaufen.

3. Auf englisch ist ein Turnverein ein   a. soccer club.
                                           b. gymnastic club.
                                           c. hiking club.

GRAMMATIK

1. The Comparative of Adjectives and Adverbs

Life and language are full of comparisons. That's why we need a

Positive:	schnell	fast
Comparative:	schneller	faster
Superlative:	am schnellsten	the fastest
	der, die, das Schnellste	

The Positive

> When things and persons are the same, use *so . . . wie*

Seine Wohnung ist so groß wie mein Haus.
His apartment is as large as my house.

Rudi ist so alt wie Ingrid.
Rudi is as old as Ingrid.

Der BMW fährt so schnell wie ein Mercedes.
The BMW drives as fast as a Mercedes.

Übung A

Respond as indicated in this example.

> **BEISPIEL:** Ich arbeite viel. Und Gerda?
> Sie arbeitet so viel wie du.

1. Brigitte ist 25 Jahre alt. Und Herbert? Er ist . . .

   _____.

2. Peter läuft schnell. Und Karin? Sie läuft . . .

   _____.

3. Heute ist es heiß. Und gestern? Gestern war es . . .

   _____.

4. Du hast wenig Zeit. Und die Nachbarn? Sie haben . . .

   _____.

5. Mary versteht gut Deutsch. Und John? John versteht Deutsch . . .

   _____.

6. Robert bezahlt viel für seine Wohnung. Und Sie? Ich bezahle . . .

   _____.

The Comparative

The comparative is formed in German by adding **-er** to the stem of the adjective or adverb.

weit	**weiter**	far	farther
billig	**billiger**	cheap	cheaper
klein	**kleiner**	small	smaller
schön	**schöner**	beautiful	more beautiful

One-syllable adjectives and adverbs usually add an umlaut to the stem vowel (except with the diphthong **-au**).

jung	**jünger**	young	younger
groß	**größer**	big	bigger
alt	**älter**	old	older

Übung B

Respond using **noch** + comparative.

> **BEISPIEL:** **Meine Wohnung ist ziemlich klein.**
> My apartment is rather small.
>
> **Ist Ihre Wohnung auch so klein?**
> Is your apartment that small too?
>
> **Meine Wohnung ist noch kleiner.**
> My apartment is even smaller.

1. Ist Texas so groß wie die Bundesrepublik? Ich glaube, Texas ist . . .

2. Ist die Fahrt von München nach Salzburg so weit wie die Fahrt von Würzburg nach Nürnberg? Nein, die Fahrt von München nach Salzburg ist. . .

3. Dauert der Flug von Frankfurt nach Wien so lange wie der Flug nach Köln? Nein, der Flug nach Wien . . .

4. Ist euer Hotelzimmer so billig wie unseres? Unser Zimmer ist . . .

5. Ist Mainz so alt wie Hamburg? Nein, Mainz ist . . .

6. Sind die Berge in Alaska so hoch wie in Österreich? Nein, die Berge in Alaska sind . . .

7. War dieser Sommer so warm wie der letzte? Ich finde, er war . . .

Note: Dissimilarities are often expressed by comparison + **als.**
   Ich bin größer als er.

The Superlative

The German superlative is formed by adding **-st** to the stem of the adjective. One-syllable adjectives often add an umlaut.

> **schnell**   der, die, das **Schnellste**

Der BMW fährt schnell.
Dieser Mercedes ist der **schnellste** Wagen.
oder: Dieser Mercedes fährt **am schnellsten.**

Ist dieses Geschäft **billig?**
Ja, es ist das **billigste** Geschäft in der Stadt.

Kauft man dort **billig?**
Ja, dort kauft man **am billigsten.**

The superlative construction with **am** + *adjective/adverb* + *ending* is just an alternative form of the superlative and is usually used when the superlative modifies a verb. If the stem of the adjective ends in **-d, -t,** or **-z,** a linking **-e** is inserted between the stem and the ending to facilitate pronunciation.

Der Februar ist kurz.	Er ist der **kürzeste** Monat.
Diese Stadt ist alt.	Sie ist die **älteste** Stadt.
Wo gibt es ein gesundes Klima?	Wo gibt es das **gesündeste** Klima?

Übung C

Complete with the superlative. Remember to use the correct endings.

> **BEISPIEL:** Michael ist mein ältest ____ Bruder.
>
> Michael ist mein ältest**er** Bruder.

1. Ilse ist seine jüng____ Schwester.

2. Jens kauft immer das schnell____ Auto.

3. Das ist die größ____ Firma in dieser Gegend.

4. Gestern hatten wir das schön____ Wetter.

5. Mainz ist die ält____ Stadt.

Irregular Comparisons

German has a number of common comparatives and superlatives that are irregular just as they are in English: *good, better,* and *best.* They must be memorized.

gut	**besser**	**best-**	good	better	best
viel	**mehr**	**meist-**	much	more	most
gern	**lieber**	**liebst-**	gladly	rather	best
hoch*	**höher**	**höchst-**	high	higher	highest
nahe	**näher**	**nächst-**	near	nearer	nearest

---

*When **hoch** is used before a noun, it becomes **hoh** (zum Beispiel: Der Groß-glockner ist ein sehr hoher Berg).

Übung D

Restate each sentence in the comparative and superlative.

> **BEISPIEL:** Ich esse Huhn gern. Fisch esse ich noch lieber.
> Aber Kuchen esse ich am liebsten.

1. In München regnet es viel. In Wien noch _____, und in

   Salzburg am _____.

2. Dieser Orangensaft schmeckt gut. Tomatensaft schmeckt

   noch _____. Aber Apfelsaft schmeckt am _____.

3. Die Zugspitze ist hoch. Der Dachstein ist noch _____.

   Aber der Großglockner ist am _____.

4. Wir wandern gern, aber noch _____ fahren wir Schi, und

   Tennis spielen wir am _____.

The comparative and superlative play a prominent role in the world of advertising. Here are a few samples of the German **Werbung,** the language of advertising.

Für die Schönheit nur das Beste.	Only the best for beauty.
Das beste Persil, das es je gab.	The best Persil (a brand of detergent) there ever was.
Es gibt nichts Schöneres als reine Seide.	There is nothing more beautiful than pure silk.
Bei uns ist das Beste gerade noch gut genug.	At our place the best is barely good enough.

2. The Subjunctive Mood

Every language finds ways to distinguish between reality and unreality. It is the subjunctive that deals with contrary-to-fact conditions and with wishes, conjectures, and suppositions.

Compare: *indicative* **When I have time, I read a lot.**
Wenn ich Zeit habe, lese ich viel.

subjunctive **If I had time, I would read a lot.**
Wenn ich Zeit hätte, würde ich viel lesen.

The present and future tense forms of the general subjunctive are derived from the past tense of the verb.

Regular Verbs			Irregular Verbs		
Infinitive	**Past**	**Subjunctive**	**Infinitive**	**Past**	**Subjunctive**
kaufen	kaufte	**kaufte**	bleiben	blieb	**bliebe**
ich	kaufte	**-e**	ich	blieb	**-e**
du	kauftest	**-est**	du	bliebst	**-est**
er/sie/es	kaufte	**-e**	er/sie/es	blieb	**-e**
wir	kauften	**-en**	wir	blieben	**-en**
ihr	kauftet	**-et**	ihr	bliebt	**-et**
Sie	kauften	**-en**	Sie	blieben	**-en**
sie	kauften	**-en**	sie	blieben	**-en**

A. The endings **-e**, **-est**, and **-en** are used for all types of verbs in the *subjunctive*. Irregular verbs add an umlaut to the stem vowels **a, o, u,** or **au:**

> **BEISPIELE:** ich äße, du gingest, er hörte, wir wären, Sie hätten

> *Indicative:* Ich **bleibe** heute bei dir, denn ich **habe** Zeit.
> I am staying with you today since I have time.

> *Subjunctive:* Ich **bliebe** heute bei dir, wenn ich Zeit **hätte**.
> I would stay with you today if I had time.

B. Present and future subjunctive of regular ("weak") verbs cannot be distinguished from those of the past indicative. Therefore, recognition of the present/future subjunctive mood is possible only within context. There is also a tendency to substitute an alternate subjunctive construction with **würden** (subjunctive of **werden**) + *infinitive of the main verb.*

> *Indicative:* Wir **freuen** uns, wenn wir **reisen**.
> We are happy when we travel.

> *Subjunctive:* Wir **freuten** uns, wenn wir zusammen **reisten**.
> *oder*
> Wir **würden** uns **freuen**, wenn wir zusammen **reisten**.
> We'd be happy if we traveled together.

C. The subjunctive mood in the present and future time frame can be expressed through **würde** + *infinitive of the verb.* It is this **würde** construction that is primarily used in modern German, especially in conversation.

Indicative	**Subjunctive**
Ich gehe gern ins Museum.	**Ich würde gern ins Museum gehen.**
I like to go to the museum.	I would like to go to the museum.

Inge besucht ihre Verwandten.	**Inge würde ihre Verwandten besuchen.**
Inge visits her relatives.	Inge would visit her relatives.
Mieten Sie dieses Auto?	**Würden Sie dieses Auto mieten?**
Are you renting this car?	Would you rent this car?

The **würde** + *infinitive* construction of the present subjunctive is simple and uncomplicated. Use it often.

Urlaub

Vacation

FRAU J.: **Stimmt's, dass Sie letzten Winter in Österreich waren?**

Is it correct that you were in Austria last winter?

FRAU L.: **Leider nicht. Wir wären gern nach St. Christof am Arlberg gefahren, aber wir konnten kein Quartier finden.**

Unfortunately not. We would have liked to have gone to St. Christof am Arlberg, but we couldn't find any lodging.

FRAU J.: **Fahren Sie dieses Jahr?**

Are you going this year?

FRAU L.: **Schön wär' es! Wir würden gern fahren, aber diesen Winter haben wir keinen Urlaub.**

It would be nice. We would love to go, but this winter we don't have any vacation.

Übung E

Restate each sentence as an unreal condition. Use the **würde** construction in the concluding clause.

> **BEISPIEL:** Wenn das Fahrrad noch gut ist, kaufe ich es.
> Wenn das Fahrrad noch gut wäre, würde ich es kaufen.

1. Wenn Christopher nicht krank ist, läuft er täglich vier Kilometer.

2. Was machen Sie, wenn Sie Kopfschmerzen haben?

3. Wenn wir Urlaub haben, reisen wir ins Ausland.

4. Lernen Sie Deutsch?

5. Ich wandere gern, wenn es warm ist.

6. Wir fahren mit Ihnen, wenn es Ihnen recht ist.

D. Mixed verbs such as **bringen**, **brennen**, **wissen**, etc., form their sub-junctive forms from the simple past tense and usually add an umlaut. They are seldom heard in spoken German and, with the exception of **wis-sen (wüsste)**, are usually replaced by **würde** plus the infinitive of the verb.

Mixed Verbs		
Infinitive	**Past**	**Subjunctive**
bringen	brachte	**brächte**
ich	brachte	**-e**
du	brachtest	**-est**
er, sie, es	brachte	**-e**
wir	brachten	**-en**
ihr	brachtet	**-et**
Sie	brachten	**-en**
sie	brachten	**-en**

Indicative: Erika bringt die Karten. Erika is bringing the tickets.

Subjunctive: Erika **brächte** die Karten.
Erika **würde** die Karten **bringen.** } Erika would bring the tickets.

E. Modals in the Subjunctive
The present tense subjunctive of modals is also used frequently, and often to express politeness. Modals with an umlaut in the infinitive also have an umlaut in the subjunctive.

Modals		
Infinitive	**Past**	**Subjunctive**
dürfen	durfte	**dürfte**
können	konnte	**könnte**
müssen	musste	**müsste**
sollen	sollte	**sollte**
wollen	wollte	**wollte**

Könnten Sie mir sagen, wann der Bus nach Tölz fährt?
Could you tell me when the bus for Tölz is leaving?

Dürfte ich Sie bitten, mir zu helfen?
May I ask you to help me?

Wir sollten das nicht tun.
We shouldn't do that.

Er müsste nicht kommen.
He wouldn't have to come.

Beim Wandern	Going Hiking
(vor der Wanderung in einem Geschäft)	*(before the hike in a store)*
HERR A.: **Könnten Sie uns eine Wanderkarte dieser Gegend zeigen? Wir möchten morgen den . . . besteigen.**	Could you show us a hiking map for this area? We would like to climb . . . tomorrow.
VERKÄUFER: **Wie wär's mit dieser? Sie hat Maßstab . . . und ist billiger als die größere.**	How about this one? It has the scale of . . . and is cheaper than the bigger one.
HERR A.: **Bill, sollten wir noch etwas mitnehmen?**	Bill, should we take anything else?
BILL: **Mir fällt nichts mehr ein.**	I can't think of anything.

Übung F: Wünsche für den Alltag—mit *hätte* und *wäre*

Choose any of the completion to the phrase: **Ich wünschte . . .** Say each sentence out loud.

Ich wünschte . . .

. . . das Wetter wäre besser.
. . . ich hätte länger Urlaub.
. . . wir hätten mehr Geld.
. . . die Preise wären nicht so hoch.
. . . du hättest mehr Zeit.

Ich wünschte . . .

. . . ihr wäret schon hier.
. . . Sie wären toleranter.
. . . Sie hätten mehr Spaß.
. . . ich wäre nicht immer so müde.
. . . er wäre höflicher.
. . . sie wären nicht so unfreundlich.
. . . wir wären schon dort.
. . . ich wäre nicht so oft krank.

. . . du wärest Nichtraucher.

. . . der See wäre wärmer.

. . . es wäre nicht so kalt.

. . . es wäre nicht so laut hier.

. . . er hätte nette Freunde.

Ich wünschte . . .   sie wäre . . .

Sie wären . . .

er wäre . . .

Übung G: Things We Ought to Do but Don't Want To

Complete the phrase **Ich müsste** . . . according to your choice. Give several answers.

Ich müsste/sollte/   . . . die Wohnung putzen.

aber ich will es   . . . die Wäsche waschen.

nicht . . .   . . . den Rasen mähen.

. . . einkaufen gehen.

. . . Rechnungen bezahlen.

. . . mit meinem Rechtsanwalt sprechen.

. . . mit meiner Chefin telefonieren.

. . . schon zurückfahren.

. . . ins Büro gehen.

. . . meine Steuerabrechnungen machen.

. . . die Garage sauber machen.

. . . die Fenster putzen.

. . . Briefe schreiben.

Übung H: Was würden sie machen, wenn . . .

Complete the phrase **Was würden Sie tun, wenn** . . . with appropriate responses.

Was würden Sie tun,   . . . das Wetter besser wäre?

wenn . . .   . . . Sie mehr Energie hätten?

. . . Sie viel Geld hätten?

. . . Sie viel Zeit hätten?

. . . Sie in Europa wären?

. . . Sie längere Ferien hätten?

. . . Sie Politiker wären?

. . . Sie eine Erkältung hätten?

. . . Sie eine Einladung ins Weiße Haus hätten?

3. The Past Subjunctive

There is only *one* past-tense subjunctive for all past tenses of the indicative. It is formed with:

hätt-
wär- } + *past participle**

Ich **hätte** dich **angerufen.**

Wir **wären** nach Hause **gegangen.**

ich	hätte	/	wäre
du	hättest	/	wärest
er/sie/es	hätte	/	wäre
wir	hätten	/	wären
ihr	hättet	/	wäret
Sie	hätten	/	wären
sie	hätten	/	wären

BEISPIEL: I would have given him the book if he had asked me.
Ich **hätte** ihm das Buch **gegeben,** wenn er mich **gefragt hätte.**

We would have driven to Berlin if we had a car.
Wir **wären** nach Berlin **gefahren,** wenn wir ein Auto **hätten.**

Note: When a modal is added in the past subjunctive, the following construction is used:

hätt- + double infinitive, with modal last
Das **hätten** Sie nicht **tun** *sollen.*
You shouldn't have done that.

Subjunctive in Action

	Wandern und Bergsteigen	**Hiking and Mountain Climbing**
KARL:	Wie weit ist es noch bis zum Gipfel?	How far is it still to the top?
JENS:	Ich glaube etwa zwei Stunden.	I believe about two hours.
KARL:	Zwei Stunden! Wenn ich das gewusst hätte, wäre ich vielleicht nicht mitgekommen. Wie wär' es mit einer kurzen Rast und einer Flasche Bier?	Two hours! If I had known that, I may not have come along. How about a short rest and a bottle of beer?
JENS:	Ich würde kein Bier trinken. Alkohol macht müde.	I wouldn't drink beer. Alcohol makes you tired.
KARL:	. . . und meine Schuhe drücken mich auch.	And my shoes hurt, too.

---

*Consult Kapitel 5 for the use of **haben** or **sein** as an auxiliary.

JENS:	**Neue Schuhe? Das kenne ich. Damit hätte ich auch Schwierigkeiten. Neue Schuhe sollte man immer vor einer Tour ein bisschen eingehen.**	New shoes? I know how that is. I'd have difficulties with them, too. One should always break in new shoes a little before a tour.
KARL:	**Ja, das hätte ich tun sollen.**	Yes, I should have done that.
JENS:	**Gehen wir weiter. Wir schaffen es schon.**	Let's continue. We'll make it.

Übung I

Supply the proper form of **haben** or **sein** in the subjunctive to complete the sentence.

BEISPIEL: Ich <u>wäre</u> nach Hause gefahren, wenn ich Zeit gehabt <u>hätte</u>.

1. Wir _____ das Tennismatch gewonnen, wenn wir besser gespielt _____.

2. Wenn Tim das gewusst _____ , _____ er es mir gesagt.

3. Chris und Bettina _____ hier geblieben, wenn das Wetter besser gewesen _____.

4. Wir _____ das Haus verkauft, wenn wir einen guten Preis bekommen _____.

5. Unser Freund _____ am Wochenende gekommen, wenn er Zeit gehabt _____.

Übung J

Express these brief sentences   a. in the present subjunctive
                                      b. in the past subjunctive

BEISPIEL: **If I only had the time!**
         Wenn ich nur Zeit hätte!
         Wenn ich nur Zeit gehabt hätte!

1. If I only knew that.

    a.

    b.

2. If it only were warmer.

    a.

    b.

3. If we only would find the dog.

    a.

    b.

4. If we only had more vacation.

    a.

    b.

5. If he only had the money.

    a.

    b.

You have noticed that many hypothetical statements begin with **wenn.**

> **Wenn ich heute nicht so müde wäre, würde ich mitkommen.**
> If I weren't so tired today, I would come along.

> **Wenn meine Mutter nicht arbeitete, würde sie mich besuchen.**
> If my mother didn't work, she would visit me.

But you can also omit the **wenn** without changing the meaning of the sentence. Just begin the sentence with the verb and apply *V-S* word order.

> **Wäre ich heute nicht so müde, würde ich mitkommen**
> If I weren't so tired, I would come along.

SPRECHEN LEICHT GEMACHT

Aktivität A: Sie geben Rat (You Are Giving Advice)

You are telling a friend what you would do if you were he or she. Choose from the statements below. Use the **würde** + *infinitive* form in your response.

> **BEISPIEL:** (Freund)   Ich esse zuviel.
> *Response:* (Sie)   Ich würde nicht soviel essen.
>   *oder*
>   Ich würde weniger essen.

1. Ich trinke zuviel!

2. Ich sitze so oft vor dem Fernseher!

3. Ich kaufe zuviel!

4. Ich schlafe zuviel!

5. Ich treibe nicht genug Sport!

6. Ich habe nicht genug Zeit für meine Familie.

7. Ich rauche zuviel!

8. Ich spiele zuviel Golf!

9. Ich kaufe zuviel ein!

10. Ich telefoniere zu lange!

Aktivität B: „Ach, wenn . . .‟

Tell us—with a deep sigh, of course—what you or others wish. But it isn't possible! Refer to the items listed below in the indicative form (the reality form). You should respond in the subjunctive mood (the contrary-to-fact form).

> **BEISPIEL:**   Ich habe keine Zeit.
> *Response:*   Ach, wenn ich nur (mehr) Zeit hätte.
>
> Wir können uns kein Auto leisten.
> Ach, wenn wir uns nur ein Auto leisten könnten.
>
> Er sagt es mir nicht.
> Ach, wenn er es mir nur sagen würde.*

1. Ich habe keinen Job.

2. Das Wetter ist heute schlecht.

3. Meine Eltern haben kein Geld.

4. Du hilfst mir nicht.

5. Mein Freund schreibt keine Briefe.

6. Sie wandern nicht mit uns.

7. Unsere Freunde bleiben nicht lange bei uns.

8. Elfe hat im Sommer keinen Urlaub.

9. Ich darf keinen Kaffee trinken.

10. Wir wissen es nicht.

---

*Strict grammarians argue for the use of the subjunctive form here—**sagte** in a **wenn** clause. However, in colloquial German, this rule is often ignored in favor of the **würde** + *infinitive* form.

Aktivität C: Ich hätte . . . / ich wäre . . .

You think about the past or a past event and you are wishing you had done things differently. Choose from the statements below and use the past subjunctive form in your response.

BEISPIEL: mehr Sport getrieben
Ich wünschte, ich hätte mehr Sport getrieben.
in Deutschland geblieben
Ich wünschte, ich wäre in Deutschland geblieben.

1. toleranter gewesen
2. ihm/ihr geglaubt
3. (nicht) geheiratet
4. nicht so schwer gearbeitet
5. ihn/sie kennengelernt
6. nicht so oft umgezogen
7. das Wienerschnitzel bestellt
8. gesünder gegessen
9. zu Hause geblieben
10. sie/ihn empfohlen
11. Sie/dich gefragt
12. sofort gekauft
13. Ihnen (dir) geholfen
14. nach Europa gefahren
15. Lehrer(in) geworden

Wiederholung

Complete the review on a separate piece of paper. Answers are located in the back of the book.

A. Put into the Comparative

BEISPIEL: Ich schlafe am Sonntag lang.
Und Ingrid schläft noch _____länger_____ .

1. Herbert spricht so schnell. Aber Richard spricht noch _____ .
2. Unser Auto ist groß. Müllers Auto ist noch _____ .
3. Gestern war es heiß. Aber heute ist es noch _____ .
4. Ein Fahrrad kostet viel. Aber ein Motorrad kostet noch _____ .
5. Sie haben wenig Geld. Und ich habe noch _____ .
6. Kuchen schmeckt gut. Aber Torte schmeckt noch _____ .

7. Ich esse Fisch gern. Aber Wienerschnitzel esse ich noch _____.

8. Mein Fernseher ist gut. Aber Ihrer ist noch _____.

B. Say the Superlative.

> **BEISPIEL:** Dieser Film dauert lang. Aber „Vom Winde verweht"
> *(Gone With the Wind)* _____ dauert am längsten. _____

1. Bei uns ist es kalt. Doch in Sibirien ist es _____.

2. Mein Job ist schwer. Aber deiner ist _____.

3. Ich esse Bratwurst gern. Doch Steak esse ich _____.

4. Im Hotel „Adler" isst man gut. Doch im „Grazerhof" isst man

   _____.

5. Nach Italien fahre ich gern. Doch nach Schweden fahre ich

   _____.

C. Contrary-to-Fact Condition

Change the sentences from indicative into *subjunctive*. Make it easy on yourself and use **würde** + *infinitive*.

> **BEISPIEL:** Ich bleibe gern länger hier.
> Ich würde gern länger hier bleiben.
>
> Wir sind nach Amerika geflogen.
> Wir wären nach Amerika geflogen.

1. Im Sommer wandern wir gern in den Bergen.
2. Ich frage sie nicht.
3. Ernst glaubt ihr nicht.
4. Wer bekommt das Geld?
5. Gestern bin ich Schi gelaufen.
6. Anke ist zu spät gekommen.
7. Du hast das nicht getan.

D. Wie sagt man auf englisch . . .

Translate these contrary-to-fact statements into good English. Try to be precise. Use the correct tense, too.

1. Wenn wir länger Urlaub gehabt hätten, wären wir noch eine Woche länger in der Schweiz geblieben.

2. Ich ginge heute ins Kino, wenn ich nicht arbeiten müsste.

3. Wäre ich Politiker, so würde ich das nicht sagen.

4. Wenn das Wetter besser gewesen wäre, hätten wir einen Ausflug gemacht.

5. Was hätten Sie gern gesehen, wenn Sie nach Deutschland gefahren wären?

Wortschatz

Nouns

die Abrechnung, -en	settlement (of accounts)	der Nichtraucher, –	nonsmoker
		der Politiker, –	politician
		der Rasen, –	lawn
die Bundesrepublik Deutschland (BRD)	The Federal Republic of Germany	die Rast, -en	rest
		der Rechtsanwalt, ¨e	lawyer
		der Schnee	snow
die Chefin, -nen	female boss	der See, -n	lake
die Gegend, -en	area	die Steuerabrech-nung, -en	tax return
der Gipfel, –	peak, summit		
(das) Italien	Italy	die Wanderung, -en	hike
die Luft	air	die Wäsche	laundry
der Maßstab, ¨e	scale		

Verbs

besteigen, ie, ie	to climb	mit·kommen,* kam mit, ist mitgekommen	to come along
drücken	to press, to pinch		
ein·laden (lädt ein) lud ein, eingeladen	to invite	schaffen	to make, to accom-plish, to create
erledigen	to finish, to settle		
geschehen* (ie), a, e	to happen	schi·laufen* (ä), ie, au	to ski
gewinnen, a, o	to win		
heraus·kommen,* kam heraus, ist herausge-kommen	to come out	schussen	to ski straight downhill
		stimmen	to be correct
mähen	to mow	waschen (ä), u, a	to wash
		sich wohl·fühlen	to feel well

Other Words

herrlich	wonderful, marvelous	**trocken**	dry
hinauf	up, upward	**unfreundlich**	unfriendly
höflich	polite	**unglaublich**	unbelievable
langsam	slow	**vereist**	icy
peinlich	embarrassing	**windig**	windy
toll	fantastic, great		

Idiomatic Expressions

Das spielt keine Rolle.	That doesn't make any difference.
das Weiße Haus	The White House (Washington, D.C.)
Es fällt mir nichts ein.	I can't think of anything.
sich Zeit lassen	to take one's time

Communication: Telephone, Post Office, Newspapers, Train Station, and Airport

---
CULTURE NOTES

The systems of communication and transportation—such as the postal service, telephone, railroads, and airlines—are not precisely the same in the German-speaking countries (Federal Republic of Germany, Austria, and Switzerland). But there are some features they share.

Most of these services are owned or controlled by the government of the country except private cell-phone companies. Neither the postal service nor the railroads nor the telephone companies make money; on the contrary, they need to be heavily subsidized by the government. Still, they perform vital services. Here is a brief listing of some of the typical features of these services.

Trains are still a major means of public transportation in all German-speaking countries: Trains provide excellent and frequent service to places near and far; are usually on time, clean, and comfortable; and are reasonably priced. There are just two classes (no need to travel first class to have a comfortable trip) and special price reductions for senior citizens and students. **Liegewagen,** with makeshift beds that serve as seats during the day (three people to a compartment), provide an economical alternative to fairly expensive **Schlafwagen** (sleepers) on overnight trips. Foreign travelers should consider the purchase of a Eurail Pass, which allows unlimited travel for certain periods of time, usually one to three months, throughout many parts of Europe. Train stations in larger cities often have a **Bahnhof-Postamt,** a special post office that is also open on weekends and holidays, sometimes 24 hours a day.

Postal service is dependable and fast. At a post office one can buy stamps, pay bills (with **Zahlkarten**), use a **Postsparbuch** (post office savings account) for depositing and withdrawing money at any post office within the country, and make local and long-distance calls. The **Hauptpost** (main post office) in a large city is often open 24 hours a day throughout the year. The postal service also runs buses to places that cannot be reached by train.

Services and procedures for *airlines and airports* follow the pattern of air transportation throughout the Western world. Differences are negligible. Security may be tighter than at airports in the United States. Frisking with metal detectors or by airport personnel is often standard procedure.

For *newspapers and the press,* see the Lesestück on page 194.

DIALOGE

Read the dialogues aloud in German and check the English translations.

	Auf der Post*	**At the Post Office**
KUNDE:	Wieviel Porto brauche ich für diesen Brief nach Irland?	How much postage do I need for this letter to Ireland?
BEAMTER:	*(zeigt auf den Brief)* Ist das der Brief, den Sie schicken wollen?	*(pointing to the letter)* Is that the letter which you want to send?
KUNDE:	Ja, und diese Postkarte auch.	Yes, and this postcard too.
BEAMTER:	*(wiegt den Brief)* Ein Euro zehn (€1,10). Und für die Postkarte brauchen Sie zwei vierzig Cent Marken.	*(weighs the letter)* One euro ten (€1,10). And for the postcard, you need two forty-cent stamps.
KUNDE:	*(gibt dem Postbeamten zehn Euro)* . . . Es tut mir leid. Können Sie wechseln?	*(gives the postal clerk a ten-euro bill)* . . . I am sorry. Do you have change for this?

---

*The post office is also called **das Postamt.**

BEAMTER:	Hätten Sie es nicht kleiner?	Don't you have anything smaller?
	Ich habe heute wenig Kleingeld.	I have very little change today.
KUNDE:	Ich seh' nochmal nach. Leider nicht.	I'll check again. Sorry, no.
BEAMTER:	Na, es wird schon gehen. Aber ärgern Sie sich nicht über die 10 Eurocheine, die ich Ihnen geben muss.	Well, it will be okay. But don't become annoyed about the ten-euro bill that I have to give you now.
KUNDE:	Nein, nein, das macht nichts.	No, no, that's okay.

	Am Bahnhof	**At the Train Station**
KUNDE:	Bitte einmal Schnellzug, zweite Klasse nach Düsseldorf.	One ticket, second-class express train to Düsseldorf, please.
BEAMTER:	Einfach oder hin und zurück?	One way or a round trip?
KUNDE:	Hin und zurück, bitte. Ich habe zwei Koffer, die ich nicht ins Abteil nehmen will.	A round trip, please. I have two suitcases that I don't want to take into the compartment.
BEAMTER:	Geben Sie sie als Reisegepäck auf.	Check them through.
KUNDE:	Und wie kann ich das tun?	And how can I do that?
BEAMTER:	Gehen Sie zum Ausgang zurück, und dann links. Dort ist der Schalter fürs Reisegepäck.	Go back to the exit, and then left. There is the luggage window.
KUNDE:	Vielen Dank.	Many thanks.

	Am Flughafen	**At the Airport**
KUNDIN:	Entschuldigen Sie, bitte. Von wo fliegt Lufthansaflug 426 nach Madrid ab?	Excuse me, please. From where does Lufthansa Flight 426 to Madrid depart?

BEAMTIN:	Halle B. Gate 5.	Concourse B, gate 5.
KUNDIN:	Könnten Sie mir sagen, wie ich dorthin komme?	Could you tell me how to get there?
BEAMTIN:	Nehmen Sie die Rolltreppe dort drüben und folgen Sie dem Zeichen B.	Take the escalator over there and follow sign B.
KUNDIN:	Vielen Dank.	Many thanks.
BEAMTIN:	Gern geschehen.	My pleasure.

	Am Telefon	**On the Telephone**
J. TYLER:	*(wählt eine Nummer)* . . . Schon wieder besetzt. *(nach einer Minute wählt er wieder)*	*(dials a number)* . . . Busy again. *(after a minute he dials again)*
	Guten Tag. Hier spricht John Tyler. Könnte ich bitte mit Frau Leitner sprechen?	Hello, John Tyler speaking. Could I speak with Mrs. Leitner please.
SEKRETÄRIN:	**Mit wem wollen Sie sprechen?**	With whom do you want to speak?
J. TYLER:	**Mit Frau Leitner.**	With Mrs. Leitner.
SEKRETÄRIN:	**Einen Augenblick. Ich verbinde. Es tut mir leid. Frau Leitner spricht gerade. Möchten Sie warten, oder wollen Sie später wieder anrufen?**	Just a moment, I'll connect you. I am sorry, Mrs. Leitner is on the phone right now. Would you like to wait, or do you want to call back later?
J. TYLER:	**Ich rufe in fünfzehn Minuten zurück.**	I'll call back in fifteen minutes.
SEKRET.	**Gut. Wie war der Name, bitte?**	Fine. What was your name, please?
J. TYLER:	**John Tyler.**	John Tyler.
SEKRETÄRIN:	**Danke. Ich sage Frau Leitner, dass Sie angerufen haben.**	Thank you. I will tell Mrs. Leitner that you called.

KOMMUNIKATION

Aktivität A

Was stimmt: *a, b, c,* oder *d*? Mehr als eine Antwort kann richtig sein.

1. Porto braucht man für
    a. eine Autoreise.
    b. ein Telefongespräch.
    c. einen Brief.
    d. eine Postkarte.

2. Wenn man jemanden anruft, sagt man
    a. Hier spricht . . .
    b. Ich habe kein Porto.
    c. Können Sie wechseln?
    d. Kann ich mit . . . sprechen?

3. Am Schalter eines Bahnhofs frage ich
    a. Können Sie mich verbinden?
    b. Wieviel Porto brauche ich?
    c. Gibt es einen Schnellzug nach . . . ?
    d. Wieviel kostet die Fahrt hin und zurück?

4. Am Flughafen
    a. landen Flugzeuge.
    b. gibt es oft Rolltreppen.
    c. kaufe ich Reisegepäck.
    d. fliegen täglich Flüge ab.

GRAMMATIK

1. Relative Pronouns

What are relative pronouns and how are they used? Look at these examples and their English equivalents. The most frequent relative pronouns in English are *that, which, who, whom,* and *whose.*

Nominative: **Der Schaffner, der nach der Fahrkarte fragte, war ein junger Mann.**
The conductor who asked for the ticket was a young man.

Die Frau, die mit uns sprach, war Kanadierin.
The woman who talked to us was a Canadian.

Das Haus, das sehr groß ist, kostet €1.000 pro Monat.
The house, which is very large, costs 1,000 euros per month.

Die Freunde, die heute kommen, sind Deutsche.
The friends who are coming today are Germans.

Accusative: **Der Winter, den wir in der Schweiz verbrachten, war sehr kalt.**
The winter, which we spent in Switzerland, was very cold.

Die Information, die ich am Bahnhof bekam, war falsch.
The information that I received at the railroad station was wrong.

Das Gulasch, das meine Mutter kocht, schmeckt am besten.
The goulash that my mother cooks tastes best.

Die Briefmarken, die ich gekauft habe, sind Sondermarken.
The stamps that I bought are commemorative stamps.

Dative: **Der Geschäftsmann, mit dem wir arbeiten, ist noch sehr jung.**
The businessman with whom we are working is very young.

Die Friseuse, zu der ich immer gehe, ist leider auf Urlaub.
The hairdresser to whom I always go is unfortunately on vacation.

Das Flugzeug, mit dem ich flog, war eine Boeing 747.
The plane I took (with which I flew) was a Boeing 747.

Die Touristen, denen wir die Stadt zeigten, waren Österreicher.
The tourists whom we showed the city were Austrians.

Genitive: **Der Deutsche, dessen BMW eine Panne hatte, schimpfte sehr.**
The German whose BMW broke down complained a lot.

Die Schweizerin, deren Buch ich gelesen habe, ist sehr bekannt.
The Swiss woman whose book I read is very well known.

> **Das Auto, dessen Nummernschild ich nicht lesen konnte, fuhr sehr schnell.**
> The car, whose license plate I could not read, drove very fast.
>
> **Die Reisenden, deren Gepäck noch im Zug ist, fahren schon zum Hotel.**
> The travelers, whose luggage is still on the train, are already going to the hotel.

The chart below shows you the close relationship between the definite articles **der, die,** and **das** and the use of their forms as relative pronouns.

	Masculine	Feminine	Neuter	Plural
Nominative	der	die	das	die
Accusative	den	die	das	die
Dative	dem	der	dem	**denen**
Genitive	**dessen**	**deren**	**dessen**	**deren**

Keep in mind the following principles guiding the use of relative pronouns:

a. Relative pronouns are similar in form to the definite articles **der, die,** and **das.**
b. They have the same gender and number as the noun to which they refer.
c. The *case* of a relative pronoun is determined by its *function* in its clause (nominative, dative, accusative, or genitive).
d. Relative pronouns introduce a *dependent clause* and therefore cause *V-L* word order.
e. The clauses they introduce are always set off by commas.
f. They cannot be omitted, as they often are in English.

Übung A: Meine Reise nach Amerika

Complete with the appropriate relative pronoun.

> **BEISPIEL:** Illinois ist der Staat, _____den_____ ich besuchte.

1. Letztes Jahr machte ich eine Reise, _____ sehr teuer war.

2. Meine Eltern, _____ für die Reise bezahlten, wollten, dass ich nach Amerika flog.

3. Die Maschine, mit _____ ich flog, war eine Boeing 747.

4. Das Essen, _____ man servierte, schmeckte nicht gut.

5. Aber das Flugpersonal, _____ sehr freundlich war, sprach gut Deutsch und Englisch.

6. Die Leute, mit _____ ich mich unterhielt, waren schon zweimal in Amerika gewesen.

7. Die westlichen Staaten, _____ ihnen besonders gefallen hatten, konnte ich leider nicht besuchen.

8. Ich verbrachte den Sommer in Chicago bei Verwandten, bei _____ ich blieb.

9. Meine Tante, _____ Auto ich fahren durfte, ist Amerikanerin.

10. Ich lernte viele Menschen kennen, _____ sich alle sehr für Deutschland interessierten.

Remember: The case is determined by the preposition, but the gender and the number are determined by the noun to which it refers.

When referring to a place, **wo** is often used instead of a preposition and relative pronoun.

Dort ist das Gasthaus, *wo* (in dem) wir gegessen haben.
There is the inn where we ate.

Herr Mayer zeigte uns die Stadt, *wo* (in der) er aufgewachsen war.
Mr. Mayer showed us the city where he grew up.

A **wo** *compound* may also be used to replace a preposition and the indefinite pronoun **was**. The **wo** *compound* then serves as a relative pronoun.

Ich weiß nicht, *wofür* (für was) er sich interessiert.
I don't know in what he is interested.

Übung B

Complete with **wo** or a **wo** *compound* used as a relative pronoun.

BEISPIEL: Dort ist das Büro, _____wo_____ ich arbeite.   where
Ich weiß, _____wofür_____ ich arbeite.   for what

1. Ich zeige Ihnen das Haus, _____ ich gewohnt habe.   where

2. Wir wissen nicht, _____ er kommt.   from where

3. Sie hat uns nicht gesagt, _____ sie das bezahlen kann.   with what

4. Ich frage mich, _____ ich so schwer arbeite.   what for

5. Weißt du, _____ meine Schlüssel sind?   where

The indefinite pronouns **wer** and **was** are equivalent to *who, whoever, anyone, whatever,* or *what*. These two interrogatives are used as relative pronouns when they refer to nonspecific persons or things—for example, **alles** (everything), **etwas** (something), **nichts** (nothing), **vieles** (much). They can also refer to an entire clause or concept.

The *indefinite* pronoun wer		
Nominative	wer	who
Accusative	wen	whom
Dative	wem	(to) whom
Genitive	wessen	whose

Wer einen Brief schickt, muss Briefmarken kaufen.
Whoever mails a letter must buy stamps.

Chris weiß nicht, mit *wem* er telefoniert hat.
Chris doesn't know with whom he spoke on the phone.

Das ist *alles, was* sie uns gesagt haben.
That is all they told us.

Relative Pronouns in Action

Relative pronouns are not "grammatical baggage." They are used in literature as well as in daily life. Let's look at some examples from the world of communication and travel. Find the proper English translation for each of them.

Am Bahnhof

1. Am Bahnsteig 7 steht der Schnellzug, der nach Hannover fährt.

2. Am Schalter 2 wartet die Gruppe, die nach Hamburg reist.

3. Die Wechselstube, die sich in der Abfahrtshalle befindet, ist von 8 zu 18 Uhr geöffnet.

4. Die Amerikaner, denen man den Fahrplan erklärt, fahren nach Köln.

5. Der Fahrplan, den man mir gezeigt hat, gilt nicht mehr.

6. Das Restaurant, in dem wir gegessen haben, befindet sich im zweiten Stock.

7. Der Reisende, dessen Uhr stehengeblieben ist, kommt zu spät.

8. Das Reisegepäck, das zu schwer ist, schicken wir mit der Bahn.

Die Presse

1. Der Artikel, der mich interessierte, stand in der *Süddeutschen Zeitung*.

2. Der Artikel, den ich gern gelesen hätte, war in der gestrigen Zeitung.

3. Der Journalist, dessen Stil mir gut gefällt, heißt Peter Wallner.

4. Die Anzeigen, deren Inhalt ich manchmal nicht verstehe, findet man auf Seite 30.

5. Die Journalisten, mit denen wir diskutierten, glaubten alles zu wissen.

Auf der Post

1. Hier sind die Marken, mit denen Sie Ihre Briefe frankieren müssen.

2. Sie müssen die Zahlkarte, die Sie mir gegeben haben, ausfüllen.

3. Das ist ein Postsparbuch, mit dem man bei jeder Post Geld abheben kann.

4. Es gibt viele Postämter, wo man faxen kann.

5. Für jeden Anruf, den man auf der Post macht, muss man beim Schalter bezahlen. (Unless you use a postal phone credit card!)

Am Telefon

1. Die Dame, deren Namen ich nicht verstehen konnte, sprach zu leise.

2. Der Herr, der vor mir in die Telefonzelle ging, sprach sehr lange.

3. Die Telefonnummer, die man mir gegeben hat, stimmt nicht.

4. Das Telegramm, das ich erhielt, war von meinen Eltern.

5. Mein Postsparbuch, dessen Nummer ich vergessen habe, liegt bei mir zu Hause.

Lesestück: Etwas über die Presse in den deutschsprachigen Ländern

Es gibt keine Demokratie, die ohne Pressefreiheit eine Demokratie bleiben kann. Die ältere Generation in Deutschland, der man in der Nazizeit diese Freiheit nahm, weiß das.

In der Schweiz, wo es seit Jahrhunderten eine erfolgreiche Demokratie gibt, erschien 1597 in Goldach (Kanton St. Gallen) die erste Zeitung Europas. Das Recht auf unabhängige Information ist für ein Land, in dem man frei leben will, sehr wichtig. Jeder soll schreiben dürfen, was er will; und jeder soll lesen können, was er mag. Es ist kein Zufall, dass man in der kleinen Schweiz (7 Millionen Einwohner) über 400 Zeitungen finden kann.

In der Bundesrepublik Deutschland, in der heute über 80 Millionen Menschen leben, gibt es ungefähr 1.250 Zeitungen. Sie repräsentieren verschiedene politische Meinungen, so zum Beispiel die *Süddeutsche Zeitung* (liberal), die *Frankfurter Allgemeine Zeitung* (konservativ-liberal) oder *Die Welt* (konservativ). Dazu kommen noch politische Wochenblätter wie *Die Zeit* (liberal) oder der *Rheinische Merkur* (konservativ). Eine Sonderstellung hat in der deutschen Presse *Der Spiegel,* ein Nachrichtenmagazin, das dem amerikanischen *Time* und *Newsweek* ähnlich ist. *Der Spiegel* sieht seine Rolle als „politischer Wachhund." Politiker, mit denen *Der Spiegel* auf dem Kriegsfuß steht, fürchten die scharfe und oft arrogante Kritik dieser Zeitschrift.

Sieben von zehn Zeitungen, die die Deutschen täglich lesen, kommen als Abonnement ins Haus. In der Bundesrepublik gehört die Presse zur Privatwirtschaft.

Auch in Österreich garantiert die Verfassung die Pressefreiheit. Die *Neue Kronenzeitung, Der Kurier* und *Die Presse* zählen zu jenen Zeitungen Österreichs, die man überall im Lande kaufen kann. Von den regionalen Zeitungen sind besonders die *Salzburger Nachrichten* für ihre unabhängige Berichterstattung bekannt.

Interessant ist auch die Tatsache, dass es im heutigen Deutschland weniger Zeitungen als vor dem Zweiten Weltkrieg gibt. So erschienen im Jahre 1932 in Deutschland 2.889 Zeitungen, also mehr als doppelt so viele wie heute. Wer sind bei diesem „Zeitungssterben" die Verlierer gewesen? Es waren lokale Zeitungen, die mit den großen Zeitungen nicht mehr konkurrieren konnten, und Parteizeitungen, denen heute das politische „Hinterland" fehlt.

„Die Großen fressen die Kleinen auf." Dieser Trend im deutschen Pressewesen macht vielen Deutschen Sorgen. Es ist ein Trend, der ein Problem für die Pressefreiheit werden könnte. In einer echten Demokratie möchte man, ja muss man viele Stimmen hören.

Übung C: Leseverständnis (Reading Comprehension)

Answer the following questions by marking the correct answer(s). More than one answer may be possible.

1. Warum ist die Pressefreiheit wichtig?

   a. Viele Leute können Zeitungen lesen.
   b. Man braucht kein Fernsehen.
   c. Die Zeitungen bleiben billig.
   d. Sie ist so wichtig für die Demokratie.

2. Wann gab es die meisten Zeitungen in Deutschland?

   a. Während des Zweiten Weltkrieges.
   b. Nach dem Zweiten Weltkrieg.
   c. Vor dem Zweiten Weltkrieg.
   d. Heute.

3. Warum ist es kein Zufall, dass es in der Schweiz über 400 Zeitungen gibt?

   a. Die Schweiz ist groß.
   b. Die Schweiz hat eine alte Demokratie.
   c. Die Schweiz ist neutral.
   d. Der Staat kontrolliert die Presse.

4. Was ist *Der Spiegel*?

   a. Ein Nachrichtenmagazin.
   b. Eine berühmte Zeitung in der Schweiz.
   c. Das Äquivalent zu *Time* und *Newsweek*.
   d. Eine sehr alte Zeitung.

5. Was bedeutet „Zeitungssterben?"

   a. Es gibt mehr Zeitungen.
   b. Es gibt weniger Zeitungen.
   c. Die Zeitungen kosten zu viel.
   d. Man hört weniger Stimmen, weil es weniger Zeitungen gibt.

2. German Word Order in Main Clauses

The position of verbs, including auxiliaries and modals, plays a special role in German word order. Other words can be placed in different positions depending on what is emphasized, but verbs cannot. The summary below may help with the use of correct word order in the following exercises.

In a main clause, the verb follows the subject and is the second grammatical unit. However, if the subject does *not* begin the sentence (i.e., it begins with a prepositional phrase or other element), the order of subject and verb is reversed. Note the following examples:

Wir **fliegen** im Juli nach Deutschland.

Im Juli **fliegen** wir nach Deutschland.

Nach Deutschland **fliegen** wir im Juli.

A. Main Clause with Modals

The modal will be the second unit of a main clause, and the infinitive falls at the end of the clause or sentence.

Karin **will** bald ihre Freundin **besuchen.**

Bald **will** Karin ihre Freundin **besuchen.**

Ihre Freundin **will** Karin bald **besuchen.**

B. Main Clause with werden

Werden is the second unit of a main clause, and the infinitive falls at the end of the clause or sentence.

Du **wirst** viele Touristen in Wien **sehen**

In Wien **wirst** du viele Touristen **sehen.**

Viele Touristen **wirst** du in Wien **sehen.**

C. Main Clause with Separable-Prefix Verbs

The stem of the verb is the second unit; the prefix comes last (in present and simple past tenses). Note these examples are in the simple past:

Jens **fuhr** heute um 17:00 Uhr **ab.**

Heute **fuhr** Jens um 17.00 Uhr **ab.**

Um 17.00 Uhr **fuhr** Jens heute **ab.**

D. Main Clause with Compound Tenses

The auxiliary verb is the second unit; the past participle is last (in present and past perfect tenses). Examples are in present perfect tense.

Erika **hat** gestern mit mir **gesprochen.**

Gestern **hat** Erika mit mir **gesprochen.**

Mit mir **hat** Erika gestern **gesprochen.**

E. Main Clause in a Question

Without question words, the conjugated verb always begins the sentence:

Bleibst du diesen Sommer in den USA? *(present tense)*

Willst du diesen Sommer in den USA **bleiben?** *(present tense with modal)*

Bist du letzten Sommer in den USA **geblieben?** *(present perfect)*

With question words, the verb comes after the question word:

Warum **fragen** Sie ihn nicht? *(present tense)*

Wen **haben** Sie am Flughafen **abgeholt?** *(present perfect)*

F. Main Clause in Commands and Requests

In the imperative, the verb comes first:

Sprechen Sie langsam bitte!

Bitte **sprechen** Sie langsam!*

Übung D: Wie kann man das noch anders sagen/schreiben?

Write alternative sentences using various types of word order.

> **BEISPIEL:** Rolf hat gestern mit Christine telefoniert.
>
> Wann . . .
>
> **Wann hat Rolf gestern mit Christine telefoniert?**
>
> Gestern abend . . .
>
> **Gestern abend hat Rolf mit Christine telefoniert.**

1. Wir holen Frau Jung heute nachmittag vom Bahnhof ab.

   a. Heute nachmittag . . .
   b. Holen wir . . .
   c. Können wir . . .

2. Herr Müller stellt seinen Wagen immer auf meinen Parkplatz.

   a. Warum . . .
   b. Immer . . .
   c. Warum darf . . .

3. Erika geht abends oft mit ihrem Freund spazieren.

   a. Oft . . .
   b. Mit ihrem Freund . . .
   c. Wann . . .

---

*It is more common to begin a request with *bitte*. The verb follows.

4. Frau Klein will im Sommer nach Japan fliegen.

    a. Wann . . .
    b. Im Sommer . . .
    c. Wohin . . .

5. Wir möchten mit Ursula bald über dieses Problem sprechen.

    a. Bald . . .
    b. Mit Ursula . . .
    c. Über dieses Problem . . .

3. German Word Order in Dependent Clauses

A dependent clause is always set off by a comma.

    Der Junge weiß, **dass sein Vater nicht immer recht hat.**
    Dass sein Vater nicht immer recht hat, weiß der Junge.

A German sentence may begin with either a main clause or a dependent clause.

    Ich kann nicht kommen, weil ich keine Zeit habe.
    Weil ich keine Zeit habe, **kann ich nicht kommen.**

Verb-last (V-L) word order is always used in a dependent clause. Word order in the dependent clause does not change regardless of whether it precedes or follows the main clause.

    Man soll das Gepäck aufgeben, wenn man einen schweren Koffer hat.
    Wenn man einen schweren Koffer hat, **soll man das Gepäck aufgeben.**

If the dependent clause comes first, the word order is *verb-subject*.

    Weil Marion gut Deutsch spricht, **versteht sie das deutsche Fernsehen.**

In a dependent clause, a separable-prefix verb does not separate in the present and past tense.

    Wir wissen, **dass unsere Pläne vom Wetter abhängen.**
    Dass unsere Pläne vom Wetter abhängen, wissen wir.

SPRECHEN LEICHT GEMACHT

Aktivität A: Was für Leute haben Sie gern?

State your preference with any suitable match in the right column. Form a sentence starting with „Ich habe . . . gern" using the correct relative pronoun. Several choices may be appropriate, but keep in mind that they are scrambled as they appear here.

BEISPIEL: eine Lehrerin/von der ich viel lernen kann.
Ich habe eine Lehrerin gern, von der ich viel lernen kann.

1. einen Lehrer	a. der mir oft Urlaub gibt.
2. einen Freund	b. die für mich Zeit hat.
3. eine Chefin	c. der mich oft anruft.
4. einen Boss	d. deren Ego nicht zu groß ist.
5. eine Freundin	e. mit dem man über alles sprechen kann.
6. eine Lehrerin	f. dessen Ego nicht zu groß ist.
7. Leute	g. der mich versteht.
	h. der immer hilft.
	i. die nicht immer von sich sprechen.
	j. die mich wirklich gern hat.
	k. die mich respektiert.
	l. die mich versteht.
	m. der mich versteht.

Aktivität B: Kennst du das Land, wo . . .

Wo möchtest du leben? Start with „Ich möchte . . ." and match the country or city at the left with the appropriate statement on the right. Give each sentence using **wo-** as a relative pronoun.

BEISPIEL: In Wien/Es gibt viele schöne Konzerte.
Ich möchte in Wien leben, wo es viele schöne Konzerte gibt.

1. In Deutschland	a. Die Winter sind warm.
2. In einem Land	b. Es gibt wenig Smog.
3. In der Schweiz	c. Man spricht nur Englisch.
4. In Italien	d. Die Leute sind höflich.
5. In England	e. Es regnet wenig.
6. In Hawaii	f. Man trinkt guten Wein.
7. In Salzburg	g. Es gibt viele Museen.
8. In Florida	h. Man kann gut surfen.
9. In München	i. Es schneit viel.
10. In Frankreich	j. Es gibt das beste Bier.
	k. Es gibt hohe Berge.
	l. Man singt viel und liebt die Oper.
	m. Es gibt die berühmten Festspiele.
	n. Alles ist gut organisiert.

Wiederholung

Complete the review on a separate piece of paper. Answers are located in the back of the book.

A. You are first at a post office in Germany and then at a train station, and you want to do the following things: What would you say or ask to accomplish these tasks?

> **BEISPIEL:** Buy a stamp for a letter you're sending to America.
> Ich möchte eine Briefmarke für einen Brief nach USA.
> *oder* Bitte geben Sie mir eine Briefmarke für einen Brief nach USA.
> Wieviel kostet eine Briefmarke für einen Brief nach USA?

1. Send a postcard to Austria.
2. Buy a round trip ticket to Hamburg.
3. Check your heavy suitcases as "Reisegepäck."
4. Find a telephone booth.
5. Fill out a money order.

1. _____.
2. _____.
3. _____.

4. _____.
5. _____.

B. Rewrite each sentence using the cue as your new antecedent. Make all necessary changes.

> **BEISPIEL:** Dort ist der Mann, mit dem ich gesprochen habe. die Frau
> Dort ist **die Frau**, mit **der** ich gesprochen habe.

1. Bitte fragen Sie die Verkäuferin, die dort steht.   der Beamte
2. Hier ist der Artikel, den ich Ihnen zeigen wollte.   die Anzeige
3. Wo ist die Fahrkarte, die du gekauft hast?   der Fahrplan
4. Wie heißt das Kind, dessen Namen ich vergessen habe.   die Ärztin
5. Das ist der Koffer, der so schwer ist.   die Tasche

C. Schreiben Sie auf deutsch.

1. This is the article which I read.
2. The number is busy. Please call again in 15 minutes.
3. Is there a telephone booth from which I can call?
4. Who was the gentleman with whom I spoke?

Wortschatz

Nouns

die Abfahrtshalle, -n	departure hall	die Panne, -n	breakdown (car)
der Ausgang, ̈e	exit		
die Bahn, -en	*here:* railroad	das Postsparbuch, ̈er	postal savings book
der Bahnsteig, -e	platform (train station)		
		die Pressefreiheit	freedom of the press
der Baum, ̈e	tree		
der Beamte, -n	civil servant	die Privatwirtschaft	private industry
die Berichterstattung, -en	reporting	das Recht, -e	right
der Fahrplan, ̈e	timetable, schedule	der saure Regen	acid rain
		das Reisegepäck	baggage, luggage
das Flugpersonal	flight personnel		
		der Reisende, -n	traveler
die Freiheit, -en	freedom	die Rolltreppe, -n	escalator
die Friseuse, -n	hairdresser	der Schaffner, –	conductor, *m.*
die Hin- und Rück-fahrt, -en	round trip		
		die Schaffnerin, -nen	conductor, *f.*
der Hundertmark-schein, -e	hundred-mark bill	der Schalter, –	ticket window
der Inhalt, -e	content	der Sekretär, -e	secretary, *m.*
das Jahrhundert, -e	century	die Seite, -n	page
der Kanadier, –	Canadian, *m.*	die Sondermarke, -n	commemo-rative stamp
die Kanadierin, -nen	Canadian, *f.*		
der Kanton, -e	canton (of Switzer-land)	die Sonderstellung	special place, position
das Kleingeld	change (money)	der Stil, -e	style
		die Stimme, -n	voice
die Marke, -n	stamp	die Tante, -n	aunt
die Meinung, -en	opinion	die Telefonzelle, -n	telephone booth
der Mensch, -en	human being, person		
		die Verfassung, -en	constitution
das Nachrichten-magazin, -e	news-magazine	der Verlierer, –	loser
die Nazizeit	Nazi period (in Ger-many, 1933–1945)	der Wachhund, -e	watchdog
		die Wechselstube, -n	money exchange office
das Nummernschild, -er	license plate	das Wochenblatt, ̈er	weekly newsp᾽

die Zahlkarte, -n	money order	die Zeitschrift, -en	magazine
der Erlagschein, -e (in Austria)		das Zeitungssterben	demise of newspapers
das Zeichen, –	sign	der Zufall, ⸚e	coincidence

Verbs

ab·heben, o, o	to withdraw (money)	(sich) fürchten	to be afraid, to fear
sich ärgern	to be annoyed	gelten (i), a, o	to be valid
auf·wachsen* (ä), u, a	to grow up	lehren	to teach, to instruct
aus·füllen	to fill out (a form)	schimpfen	to complain, to scold
sich befinden, befand, befunden	to be located, to be situated	schneien	to snow
		stehen·bleiben,* ie, ie	to stop, to halt
bei·tragen, u, a	to contribute	sterben* (i), a, o	to die
erklären	to explain	verbinden, a, u	to connect
erscheinen,* ie, ie	to appear, to be published	verbringen, verbrachte, verbracht	to spend (time)
frankieren	to put on postage	wechseln	to change

Other Words

ähnlich	similar	grün	green
deutschsprachig	German-speaking	gültig	valid
		lokal	local
doppelt	double	nochmals	once more
dorthin	to that place, over there	scharf	sharp
		unabhängig	independent
echt	genuine	ungefähr	approximately
erfolgreich	successful		
gerade	just, at that moment	verschieden	different
		wichtig	important
gestrig	yesterday's		

Idiomatic Expressions

auf Kriegsfuß stehen	to be in conflict with, to be on the warpath
Das macht mir Sorgen.	That worries me.
Das macht nichts.	That doesn't matter.
Es steht in der Zeitung.	It's written in the newspaper.
Es wird gehen.	It will work out. I can manage.
Gern geschehen.	Gladly, don't mention it.
Hin- und zurück	*here:* a round-trip ticket

Cognates

das Abonnement, -s	garantieren
der Artikel, –	kontrollieren
die Demokratie, -n	korrespondieren
der Dialekt, -e	repräsentieren
die Halle, -n	
die Presse	

KAPITEL **10** Selbstbiographisches

In diesem letzten Kapitel möchten wir Ihnen zeigen, wie Sie auf deutsch über sich selbst sprechen können. Wir nennen das Kapitel „Selbstbiographisches," denn Sie sind der Mittelpunkt.

DIALOGE

Sie sind in Köln auf der Polizei, denn man hat Ihnen alle wichtigen Papiere gestohlen (Pass, Führerschein, Flugkarte, usw.). Der Polizist spricht kein Englisch. Aber das macht nichts, denn Sie können seine einfachen Fragen verstehen und auf deutsch beantworten. Zunächst müssen Sie ein Formular ausfüllen. Daher der Telegrammstil.

POLIZIST:	Nachname (Familienname)
SIE:	Cook
POLIZIST:	Vorname
SIE:	Richard
POLIZIST:	Wohnort
SIE:	zur Zeit Köln
POLIZIST:	Straße
SIE:	Rheinallee 27, bei Biebers
POLIZIST:	Geburtstag (Geburtsdatum)

SIE:	20. Juli 1979
POLIZIST:	Geburtsort
SIE:	Columbus, Ohio, USA
POLIZIST:	Staatsangehörigkeit
SIE:	Amerikaner
POLIZIST:	Beruf
SIE:	Drogist
POLIZIST:	Passnummer
SIE:	Weiß ich nicht, denn man hat mir meinen Pass gestohlen.
POLIZIST:	Größe
SIE:	1,68 m (ein Meter achtundsechzig)
POLIZIST:	Gewicht
SIE:	75 Kilo
POLIZIST:	Haarfarbe
SIE:	blond
POLIZIST:	Augenfarbe
SIE:	blau-grau
POLIZIST:	besondere Kennzeichen
SIE:	Narbe über dem rechten Auge
POLIZIST:	Wo können wir Sie erreichen?
SIE:	Ich bin bis Montag in Köln. Sie haben ja meine Adresse.

Wir sprechen natürlich nicht in Stichwörtern (Telegrammstil), sondern in Sätzen. Wiederholen wir also das Gespräch.

Wie heißen Sie?	Ich heiße Richard Cook.
Wo wohnen Sie?	Zur Zeit wohne ich in Köln auf der Rheinallee bei Biebers.
Wann und wo sind Sie geboren?	Ich bin am 20. Juli 1969 in Columbus, Ohio, USA, geboren.
Welche Staatsangehörigkeit haben Sie?	Ich bin Amerikaner.
Was sind Sie von Beruf?	Ich bin Drogist.
Wissen Sie Ihre Passnummer?	Nein, denn man hat mir meinen Pass gestohlen.
Wie groß sind Sie?	Ich bin 1,68 m groß.

Wieviel wiegen Sie?	Ich wiege 75 Kilo.
Was ist Ihre Haarfarbe?	Blond.
Und Ihre Augenfarbe ist?	Blau-grau.
Haben Sie besondere Kenn- zeichen	Ja, ich habe eine Narbe über dem rechten Auge.

Wir möchten noch viel mehr über Sie wissen. Jetzt sind Sie aber nicht mehr auf der Polizei, sondern auf einer Party, wo Sie mit einem Gast sprechen. Der Gast scheint sehr neugierig zu sein, denn Sie werden so richtig ausgefragt.

GAST: Also, Herr Cook, wie lange sind Sie schon in Köln?

SIE: Seit zwei Wochen.

GAST: Was bringt Sie denn in unsere Stadt?

SIE: Ich habe eine Konferenz besucht.

GAST: Was haben Sie denn in Ihrer Freizeit gemacht?

SIE: Mir wurden fast alle Sehenswürdigkeiten der Stadt gezeigt.

GAST: Haben Sie Ihre Frau mitgebracht?

SIE: Ich bin noch ledig. Und Sie?

GAST: Ich bin schon 20 Jahre verheiratet.

SIE: Haben Sie auch Kinder?

GAST: Ja, zwei Töchter und einen Sohn.
Die Älteste ist Volksschullehrerin, und die zweite ist Verkäuferin in einem Kinderwarengeschäft. Mein Sohn . . .

SIE: Entschuldigen Sie, ich muss noch schnell mit Frau Kurz sprechen.

Frau Kurz ist leider auch sehr neugierig, und so werden Sie weiter ausgefragt.

FRAU K.: Haben Sie schon unsere Oper besucht?

SIE: Ja, letzte Woche bin ich von einem Kollegen zum „Freischütz" eingeladen worden.

FRAU K.: Und wie hat Ihnen die Oper gefallen?

SIE: Ja, gut, aber mir ist Wagner lieber.

FRAU K.: Dann müssen Sie nach Bayreuth.

SIE: Das ist mir von anderen auch gesagt worden.

FRAU K.: Es ist aber schwer, Karten zu bekommen.

SIE: Man hat sie mir auf dem Reisebüro schon besorgt.

FRAU K.: Wie lange bleiben Sie in Köln?

SIE: Noch drei Tage. Entschuldigen Sie, ich sehe gerade Herrn Dietrich. Ich muss ihn etwas fragen.

FRAU K.: Natürlich.

KOMMUNIKATION

Interview Checklist

Jetzt müssen Sie keine Fragen mehr beantworten. Wir haben aber eine Interviewliste, die Sie vielleicht ausfüllen möchten. Wenn Sie eine Frage nicht beantworten können, sehen Sie sich die Listen über Berufe und Hobbys an.

Name:

Vorname:

Adresse: (Wohnort, Straße)

Telefonnummer:

Beruf:

Familienstand: (ledig, verheiratet, geschieden, Witwe, Witwer)

Hobbys:

Interessen:

Reisen, die Sie gemacht haben:

Klubs/Vereine:

Lieblings
Autor(in):   Stadt:
Komponist(in):   Sport:
Sänger(in):   Getränk:
Filmschauspieler(in):   Essen:
Film: (sehen sich die Liste in Kapitel 3 an)
Buch:

Und was sind Sie von Beruf?

architect	Architekt(in)	librarian	Bibliothekar(in)
artist	Künstler(in)	mechanic	Mechaniker(in)
baker	Bäcker(in)	minister	Pastor(in), Pfarrer(in)
bookkeeper	Buchhalter(in)		
businessman	Geschäftsmann	musician	Musiker(in)
businesswoman	Geschäftsfrau	nurse, *f.*	Krankenschwester
chemist	Chemiker(in)		
civil servant	Beamter (Beamtin)	nurse, *m.*	Krankenpfleger
		officer (military)	Offizier(in)
clerk	Angestellter, Angestellte	physician	Arzt, Ärztin
		pilot	Pilot(in)
computer programmer	Computer Programmierer(in)	plumber	Installateur(in)
		professor	Professor(in) für Musik, Chemie, Mathematik, usw.
dentist	Zahnarzt, Zahnärztin		
druggist	Drogist(in)		
electrician	Elektriker(in)	psychologist	Psychologe, Psychologin
engineer	Ingenieur(in)	sales clerk	Verkäufer(in)
judge	Richter(in)	secretary (skilled)	Sekretär(in) (Fach)
laborer	Arbeiter		
lawyer	Rechtsanwalt, Rechtsanwältin	teacher	Lehrer(in)

Was ist Ihr Hobby? *oder* Was machen Sie gern in Ihrer Freizeit?

Ich spiele Tennis, Golf, Karten, Basketball, Fußball, usw.

Ich spiele Klavier, Gitarre, Cello, Trompete, Flöte, Geige (Violine), usw.

Ich schwimme, lese, schreibe, koche, wandere, bastle (do crafts), surfe, laufe Schi, sehe fern, höre Radio, sammle (collect) Münzen, Briefmarken, arbeite im Garten, stricke, usw.

Wofür interessieren Sie sich?

Ich interessiere mich für Sport, Musik, Kunst, Politik, Literatur, Film, Tanz, Technik, Theater, Astrologie, Computer, alte Autos, usw.

Aktivität A

Find a suitable verb for these sentences. Choose from the list. More than one choice may be correct.

> **BEISPIEL:** Mein Freund ___geht___ gern ins Kino.

1. Mein Vater _____ gern Klavier.

2. Mein Bruder _____ gern Autos.

3. Meine Schwester _____ gern über Politik.

4. Mein Nachbar _____ gern im Garten.

5. Meine Nachbarin _____ gern Romane.

6. Mein Chef _____ gern Briefmarken.

7. Mein Sohn _____ gern CDs.

8. Meine Tante _____ gern.

9. Meine Tochter _____ gern lange am Telefon.

10. Mein Mann _____ gern in guten Restaurants.

sammeln/reparieren/spielen/lesen/sprechen/nähen/essen/diskutieren/
hören/basteln/arbeiten/stricken

Aktivität B

Answer these personal questions in complete German sentences or with just a phrase.

> **BEISPIEL:** Wie oft waren Sie schon in Europa?
> Ich war schon dreimal dort.
> Schon dreimal.

1. Woher kommen Sie?

2. Wo sind Sie geboren?

3. Sind Sie verheiratet?

4. Wie viele Kinder haben sie?

5. Was machen Sie meistens am Wochenende?

6. Wie oft gehen Sie ins Kino?

7. Was machen Sie in Ihren Ferien? (im Urlaub)

8. Welches Land möchten Sie besuchen? Warum?

9. Warum sind Sie mit Ihrem Beruf zufrieden? (unzufrieden)

10. Beschreiben Sie Ihren Chef/Ihre Chefin.
    Er (sie) ist . . .

11. Beschreiben Sie einen Freund/eine Freundin.

12. Was sagen Ihre Freunde über Sie?
    Sie sagen, dass ich . . . bin.

charmant/nett/intelligent/reich/freundlich/interessant/sportlich/
impulsiv/attraktiv/natürlich/pünktlich/eingebildet/liberal/konservativ/
vorsichtig/mutig/kräftig/schlank/scheu/populär/arm/jung/klug

Aktivität C: Was sind diese Menschen von Beruf?

Fill in the blanks with the appropriate occupation.

> **BEISPIEL:** Herr Frisch unterrichtet in der Schule. Er ist ___Lehrer.___

1. Peter verkauft Schuhe in einem Schuhgeschäft. Er ist _____.

2. Herr Klein reparierte gestern mein Auto. Er ist _____.

3. Mein Bruder predigt jeden Sonntag in der Kirche. Er ist _____.

4. Meine Schwester arbeitet im Krankenhaus, wo sie Patienten pflegt.
   Sie ist _____.

5. Ich verkaufe Aspirin, Hustensaft, usw. in einer Drogerie. Ich bin
   _____.

6. Herr Schmidt hat meinen elektrischen Ofen repariert. Er ist _____.

7. Frau Jung hilft uns, die richtigen Bücher zu finden. Sie arbeitet in
   einer Bibliothek und ist _____.

8. Karsten arbeitet für Delta. Er fliegt Flugzeuge. Er ist _____.

9. Karin hat Medizin studiert. Sie arbeitet jetzt im Johanniterkranken-
   haus. Sie ist _____.

10. Meine Tochter arbeitet im Büro. Sie schreibt am Computer, tele-
    foniert, öffnet Briefe für den Chef, macht Reservierungen, usw. Sie
    ist dort _____.

GRAMMATIK

1. The Future Tense

The future tense in German, as in English, is formed with an auxiliary plus an infinitive. In German the auxiliary is **werden.** The infinitive goes to the end of the main clause.

Ich *werde* nach Hause *fahren.*	I shall go home.
Wann *werden* Sie Ihr Buch *schreiben*?	When are you going to write your book?
Du *wirst* morgen krank *sein.*	You will be sick tomorrow.

Conjugation of *werden*			
	Singular		**Plural**
ich	werde	wir	werden
du	wirst	ihr	werdet
er, sie, es	wird	Sie, sie	werden

Übung A

Schreiben Sie auf deutsch. Use future tense.

1. I will receive mail soon.

   _____.

2. Will you write to me this week?

   _____.

3. When is she going to work?

   _____.

4. He is going to buy good tickets.

   _____.

5. The bus will come in 15 minutes.

   _____.

2. The Passive Voice

The passive voice is usually used to describe a condition in which the *subject* is acted upon. In other words, the subject is not doing the action, but someone or something is doing something to the subject. A form of the verb **werden** is needed to express the passive.

Because you have to know the verb forms of **werden** to express or to recognize the passive, we should review them quickly. If used as a main verb, **werden** means *to become*. (Do not confuse this with **bekommen** = *to receive*.) **Werden** plus *infinitive* denotes *future tense*.

Das Kind wird krank.	The child is getting sick.
Das Kind wurde krank.	The child was getting sick.
Das Kind ist krank geworden.	The child has become sick.
Das Kind war krank geworden.	The child had become sick.
Das Kind wird krank werden.	The child will become sick.

Übung B

Complete with the correct form of **werden**. Watch tense.

1. Jens _____ gestern krank.   simple past

2. Elke _____ Sekretärin.   present

3. Wir _____ nach Hause fliegen.   future

4. Wieviel _____ du verdienen?   future

5. Paul _____ berühmt _____.   present perfect

Übung C

Decide whether you should use **werden** or **bekommen**. Watch tense.

> **BEISPIEL:** Frau Braun ___bekommt___ jeden Tag die Zeitung.
> Chris ___wird___ Elektriker.

1. Mein Großvater _____ im Januar

   neunzig Jahre _____.   present perfect

2. _____ du auch einen Brief von

   Erika _____?   present perfect

3. Der bekannte Schauspieler _____

   achtzig Jahre alt.   past

4. Gestern _____ ich meinen Pass.   past

5. Wir _____ erst im Juli Urlaub.   present

Now let's see how **werden** is used in the *passive*.

The Passive

Das Buch *wird* geschrieben.	The book is being written.
Das Buch *wurde* geschrieben.	The book was being written.
Das Buch *ist* geschrieben *worden*.*	The book has been written.
Das Buch *war* geschrieben *worden*.	The book had been written.
Das Buch *wird* geschrieben *werden*.	The book will be written.
Unser Auto wird heute repariert.	Our car is being repaired today. (present)
Das Haus wurde von uns geputzt.	The house was being cleaned by us. (past)
Das Buch ist von allen Studenten gelesen worden.	The book has been read by all students. (present perfect)
Die Rechnung wird von den Gästen bezahlt werden.	The bill will be paid by the guests. (future)

Essentially, you need to know three things to form the passive from the active. Please compare:

Er hat den Brief geschrieben.	He has written the letter.
Der Brief ist von ihm geschrieben worden.	The letter has been written by him.

1. The accusative object of the active sentences becomes the nominative subject of the passive sentence: *Der Brief . . .*

2. The active verb form is replaced by a form of **werden**: *ist . . . geschrieben worden.*

3. The subject of the active sentence is replaced by **von** + *dative* (of subject in the active sentence): *von ihm . . .*

Therefore, the new passive sentence reads: *Der Brief ist von ihm geschrieben worden.*

Übung D

---

*In the perfect tense of the passive, the special form of **worden** (not **geworden**) is used.

Supply the correct form of **werden**. All the sentences are in the passive voice.

BEISPIEL: Diese Geschichte ___ist oft erzählt worden___.   present perfect

1. Der Student _____ von dem Professor
   gefragt.   present

2. Die Schauspielerin _____ interviewt.   past tense

3. Die Briefe _____ geschickt _____.   present
                                                          perfect

4. Du _____ von mir angerufen _____.   future

5. Die Kinder _____ zur Party eingeladen

   _____.   present
                                                          perfect

6. Ich _____ von Dr. Lange untersucht.   past tense

7. Die Zeitung _____ von uns allen gelesen

   _____.   present
                                                          perfect

8. Dieses Lied _____ oft gesungen.   present

Übung E

Translate these sentences into English. Note that not all sentences have an agent.

BEISPIEL: **Das Haus wird verkauft.**   The house is being sold.

1. Sein Buch wurde in zwei Sprachen übersetzt.

2. Das Paket ist gestern abgeschickt worden.

3. Der Gast wurde ausgefragt.

4. Frau Kleins Pass ist gestohlen worden.

5. Während des Krieges ist Hamburg durch Bomben zerstört worden.*

---

*When the agent is an impersonal force such as the natural elements or a concept, **durch** is used with an accusative object.

6. Amerika wurde 1492 von Columbus entdeckt.

7. Der Film wird hoffentlich gemacht werden.

8. Der Verbrecher ist in Los Angeles gesehen worden.

9. Die Wohnung wird einmal die Woche geputzt.

10. Wo wird der Volkswagen hergestellt?

3. *Man* as a Substitute for the Passive

Man—*one, a person, you, they*—is often used to avoid the passive, especially in spoken German. The **man** construction expresses essentially the same idea as the passive construction.

Ich werde angerufen.	I am being called.
Man ruft mich an.	They are calling me.
Jens ist ausgefragt worden.	Jens was being (has been) questioned.
Man hat Jens ausgefragt.	They questioned Jens.

Übung F

Restate in the active voice, using the **man** construction.

1. Es wurde viel getanzt.

2. Wir sind nie besucht worden.

3. Ich bin oft gefragt worden.

4. Die Frau wird interviewt.

5. Dort wurde viel gegessen und getrunken.

6. In dem Zimmer ist nicht geraucht worden.

7. Dem Lehrer wurde das Auto gestohlen.

Wie schreibt man eine Karte oder einen Brief?

In German correspondence, all *personal pronouns* are capitalized. Note the basic writing styles in the following examples:

Eine Geburtstagskarte an eine Freundin

. . . den 13. Oktober 2006

Liebe Karin,

zu Deinem 35. Geburtstag gratuliere ich Dir recht herzlich. Ich wünsche Dir fürs nächste Jahr vor allem gute Gesundheit und weiteren Erfolg in Deiner neuen Stellung.

Herzlichst

Deine Tina

A Birthday Card to a Friend

October 13, 2006

Dear Karin,

For your 35th birthday I am sending you my heartiest congratulations. For the next year I wish you above all good health and continued success in your new job.

Yours,

Tina

Eine Einladung an einen Kollegen zu einer Party

Lieber Herr Schmidt,

am 22. Juli wollen wir den Geburtstag von Herrn Kluge bei uns zu Hause feiern. Wir möchten Sie und Ihre Frau recht herzlich zu einer Party einladen. Wir erwarten Sie zwischen 20.00 und 20:30 Uhr.

Mit freundlichen Grüßen

Ihre Gabriele Jost

An Invitation to a Colleague to a Party

Dear Mr. Smith,

on July 22nd we want to celebrate Mr. Kluge's birthday at our house. We would like to cordially invite you and your wife to a party. We will be expecting you between 8:00 and 8:30 P.M.

Best regards,

(Your) Gabriele Jost

Ein Dankschreiben

Sie möchten sich für ein Geschenk von guten Freunden bedanken.

Liebe Ingrid und lieber David,

herzlichen Dank für die schöne CD, die Ihr mir zum Geburtstag geschenkt habt. Sie hat mir schon viel Freude gemacht. Es war besonders nett von Euch, dass Ihr Euch an meinen Lieblings-

A Thank-You Note

You would like to thank good friends for a present.

Dear Ingrid and (dear) David,

Thank you so much for the beautiful CD that you sent for my birthday. I have enjoyed it a lot already. It was especially nice that you remembered my favorite

komponisten Mozart erinnert habt.

Viele liebe Grüße

Eure Elke

composer, Mozart.

With love,

(Your) Elke

Beschwerdeschreiben/Reklamation

Manchmal muss man leider auch einen Beschwerdebrief schreiben.

An das

Versandhaus Kabler

Landstraße 32

45127 Essen

Sehr geehrte Damen und Herren!

Am 11. August bestellte ich bei Ihnen vier blaue Badehandtücher mit passenden Waschlappen. Das Paket, das Sie mir am 20. August schickten, enthielt aber vier gelbe Badehandtücher und vier blaue Waschlappen. Leider bezahlte ich die Nachnahme, bevor ich das Paket öffnete. Ich bitte Sie daher, mir die blauen Badehandtücher zu schicken. Sobald ich die neue Ware erhalten habe, werde ich die gelben Handtücher zurückschicken.

Hochachtungsvoll

Karin Maier

Letter of Complaint

Unfortunately, sometimes one has to write a letter of complaint.

The Kabler Company

Landstraße 32

45127 Essen

Ladies and Gentlemen
(To whom it may concern):

On August 11th I ordered from you (your company) four blue bath towels with matching washcloths. However, the package that you mailed to me on August 20th contained four yellow bath towels and four blue washcloths. Unfortunately, I paid the C.O.D. charge before I opened the package. Therefore, please send me the blue bath towels. After I have received the new merchandise, I will return the yellow towels immediately.

Sincerely,

Karin Maier

Die Antwort der Firma Kabler

Frau Karin Maier

Henri-Spaak-Str. 73

53347 Oedekoven

The Answer from the Kabler Company

Mrs. Karin Maier

Henri-Spaak-Str. 73

53347 Oedekoven

Sehr geehrte Frau Maier!	Dear Mrs. Maier,
Wir bedauern außerordentlich, dass Ihr Auftrag vom 11. August nicht richtig ausgeführt wurde. Mit gleicher Post wurden Ihnen die blauen Badehandtücher zugeschickt. Sobald Sie die falsche Ware zurückgeschickt haben, werden wir natürlich für Ihre Unkosten aufkommen. Es liegt uns viel daran, dass unsere Kunden zufrieden sind.	We are very sorry that your order of August 11th was filled incorrectly. With the same mail we have sent you the blue bath towels. As soon as you have returned the wrong merchandise, we will of course cover your costs. We are very interested in keeping our customers satisfied.
Hochachtungsvoll	Sincerely,
gez. Franz Kraft	(signed Franz Kraft)

Hints on Letter Writing

die Anrede	**Addressing a Person**
Lieber Vater,	Dear Father,
Lieber Karl,	Dear Karl,
Mein lieber Freund,	My dear friend,
Mein lieber Johann,	My dear Johann,
Lieber Herr Müller,	Dear Mr. Müller,
Sehr geehrter Herr Klein!	Dear Mr. Klein,
Liebe Mutter,	Dear Mother,
Liebe Heidi,	Dear Heidi,
Meine liebe Freundin,	My dear friend,
Meine liebe Sabine,	My dear Sabine,
Liebe Frau Carsten,	Dear Mrs. Carsten,
Sehr geehrte Frau Braun,	Dear Mrs. Braun,
Liebe Mutter und lieber Vater,	Dear Mother and Father,
Liebe Ellen und lieber Michael,	Dear Ellen and Michael,
Sehr geehrte Herren, (*oder* Herren!)	Gentlemen:
Sehr geehrte Frau Dr. Kurz, (*oder* Kurz!)	Dear Dr. Kurz:
Sehr geehrter Herr Professor Lange, (*oder* Lange!)	Dear Professor Lange:
Sehr geehrte Damen und Herren, (*oder* Herren!)	Dear Ladies and Gentlemen:

Note: When addressing a letter, consider whether you are addressing a family member, a good friend, someone whom you address by a last name, a businessperson, official letters, or those whose status requires a special form of address.

Briefschluss	**How to End a Letter**
Privatbriefe	Personal Letters

Herzliche Grüße	Cordially, *or* With love,
Dein Freund Martin	Your friend, Martin
Viele Grüße an Euch alle	Greetings to all of you,
Herzlichst, Deine	With all my best,
Es grüßt Sie herzlich	Cordially,
Ihr (Ihre)	Your,

Geschäftsbriefe	Business Letters

Mit freundlichen Grüßen	Sincerely, *or* Respectfully,
Freundliche Grüße	Sincerely,
Hochachtungsvoll	Respectfully,

One final note: When addressing the envelope, Europeans usually write the return address on the back and the address in the center of the front. Never forget the **Postleitzahl** (ZIP code) at the end of the address.

(return address) **Absender:**	Dr. Karl Jost Gustav-Heinemann-Ufer 72 50968 Köln
(address) **Adresse:**	Herrn Dr. Fritz König Bahnhofstraße 5 60327 Frankfurt a.M.

Übung G

1. Sie möchten Ihre gute Freundin Klara zum Abendessen einladen. Schreiben Sie eine kurze Einladung.

2. Ihr Chef hat Sie zum Wochenende eingeladen. Sie können leider nicht kommen. Schreiben Sie einen kurzen Entschuldigungsbrief.

3. Sie bedanken sich bei Ihren Eltern (Kindern) für ein Geschenk.

Wiederholung

A. Was passt zusammen?
Match the occupations on the left with the activities on the right.

_____ 1. Zahnarzt   a. reparierte meinen Toaster

_____ 2. Bäcker   b. verkauft Schuhe

_____ 3. Elektriker   c. arbeitet in einem Krankenhaus

_____ 4. Professor   d. arbeitet auf der Post

_____ 5. Verkäuferin   e. hilft mir, wenn ich Zahnschmerzen habe.

_____ 6. Krankenschwester   f. backt jeden Tag Brot

_____ 7. Drogist   g. schreibt ein Buch

_____ 8. Postbeamter   h. verkauft Aspirin, Hustensaft, usw.

B. Ein Brief an einen Freund
You are writing a letter to a German friend. Fill in the blanks of the letter with appropriate words from the list below.

Lieber Gerd,

Jetzt bin ich schon drei _____ in Bonn. Es gefällt mir wirklich gut.

Jeden Tag gehe ich am Rhein spazieren. Leider ist das _____ nicht so

schön. Es hat jeden Tag _____. Letzten Sonntag war ich bei Familie

König _____. Sie gaben eine große Party für mich. Die meisten Gäste

wollten wissen, wo ich _____, ob ich verheiratet bin, und was ich in

Bonn mache. Ich war auch schon in der Oper in Köln. Wie Du weißt, ist Köln

nicht _____ von Bonn. Natürlich vermisse ich meine lieben

_____ in Amerika. Aber bald sehe ich Dich und die anderen wieder.

Für heute also _____ Grüße

_____ Bob

eingeladen/lieber/herzliche/Wochen/geregnet/Dein/wohne/Wetter/weit/Freunde/
liebe/Dein/mache

Wortschatz

Nouns

der Auftrag, ∸e	order	das Gewicht, -e	weight
die Augenfarbe, -n	eye color	die Größe, -n	size, height
die Auskunft, ∸e	information	die Haarfarbe, -n	hair color
das Badehandtuch, ∸er	bath towel	der Hustensaft, ∸e	cough syrup
Bayreuth	city in Bavaria (site of Wagner festivals)	der Installateur, -e	plumber
		der Kaufmann, die Kaufleute	businessman
der Beruf, -e	occupation	das Kennzeichen, –	identification
der Beschwerdebrief, -e	letter of complaint	der Komponist, -en	composer
		das Krankenhaus, ∸er	hospital
der Bibliothekar, -e	librarian	der Krankenpfleger, –	nurse, *m.*
das Dankschreiben, –	thank-you note	die Krankenschwester, -n	nurse, *f.*
der Drogist, -en	druggist	die Liste, -n	list
der Entschuldigungsbrief, -e	letter of apology	die Manieren *(pl.)*	manners
		der Mittelpunkt, -e	center (*here:* of attention)
der Erfolg, -e	success		
der Familienname, -n	last (family) name	die Münze, -n	coin
		die Nachnahme, -n	cash on delivery (C.O.D.)
der Familienstand	marital status		
die Ferien *(pl.)*	vacation	der Nachname, -n	last name
der Filmschauspieler, –	movie actor	die Narbe, -n	scar
		das Paket, -e	parcel, package
die Flöte, -n	flute		
der Fluggast, ∸e	airline passenger	die Papiere *(pl.)*	documents
		die Polizei	police
die Flugkarte, -n	airline (flight) ticket	das Reisebüro, -s	travel agency
		der Richter, –	judge
der „Freischütz"	opera by Karl Maria von Weber	der Roman, -e	novel
		der Sänger, –	singer
		der Satz, ∸e	sentence
die Freizeit	leisure time, free time	die Sehenswürdigkeit, -en	site of interest
der Führerschein, -e	driver's license	das Selbstbiographische	autobiographical matter
die Gartenarbeit, -en	gardening		
der Geburtstag, -e	birthday	die Staatsangehörigkeit	citizenship
die Geige, -n	violin		
das Geschenk, -e	present	die Stellung, -en	position
die Gesundheit	health	das Stichwort, ∸er	key word, cue

die Technik	technology	erwarten	to expect
der Telegrammstil	telegram style (very brief)	feiern	to celebrate
		her·stellen	to manufacture
der Tierarzt, ⁻e	veterinarian		
die Trompete, -n	trumpet	mit·bringen, brachte mit, mitgebracht	to bring along
die Unkosten (pl.)	expenses		
der Verbrecher, –	criminal	nähen	to sew
der Verkäufer, –	sales clerk	pflegen	to take care of, to nurse
der Verein, -e	club, association		
das Versandhaus, ⁻er	mail-order house	predigen	to preach
		sammeln	to collect
		stehlen (ie), a, o	to steal
der Volksschullehrer, –	elementary school teacher	stricken	to knit
		übersetzen	to translate
		unterrichten	to teach
der Vorname, -n	first name	verdienen	to earn
die Witwe, -n	widow	vermissen	to miss
der Wohnort, -e	place of residence	zerstören	to destroy
		zurück·senden	to return, to send back
der Zahnarzt, ⁻e	dentist		

Verbs

ab·schicken	to send off, to mail	

Other Words

auf·kommen* (für), kam auf, ist aufgekommen	to assume the cost	arm	poor
		berühmt	famous
		besonders	especially, special
aus·fragen	to question, to quiz	dasselbe	the same
		eigentlich	actual(ly)
aus·führen	to carry out, to implement	einfach	simple
		eingebildet	arrogant
		falsch	false
basteln	to do crafts, to tinker	freundlich	friendly
		geschieden	divorced
sich bedanken (für)	to thank, to say thanks	hochachtungsvoll	respectful(ly)
		klug	smart, intelligent
bedauern	to regret	kräftig	strong
behandeln	to treat	ledig	single
entdecken	to discover	meistens	mostly, most of the time
erreichen	to reach, contact	natürlich	naturally

*auxiliary is **sein**

neugierig	curious, nosy
passend	suitable, matching
reich	rich
scheu	shy
schlank	slender
sondern	but, on the contrary
sportlich	athletic
verheiratet	married
vorsichtig	careful

Idiomatic Expressions

Es liegt uns viel daran.	We are very much concerned./It matters to us.
Freude machen	to give joy, to bring joy

Cognates

der Architekt, -en	der Pastor, -en	diskutieren
die Bombe, -n	der Psychologe, -n	operieren
der Chemiker, –	der Physiker, –	reparieren
der Ingenieur, -e	der Pilot, -en	surfen
die Konferenz, -en	der Toaster, –	attraktiv
der Klub, -s	impulsiv	

Answers for Activities, Exercises, and Reviews

This section of the book provides answers for most activities, exercises, and reviews in the 10 chapters. We suggest that you check each answer *after* you have done the exercises.

<tr><td>

**KAPITEL 1
(Chapter 1)**

</td><td>

KOMMUNIKATION (Communication)

Aktivität A (p. 14)
Sample Responses:
1. Wo wohnen Sie? Wo arbeiten/leben/spielen/bleiben . . . Sie?
2. Wie heißen Sie? Wie heißt er/sie? Wie ist das Wetter? Wie geht's?
3. Wer ist sie/er? Wer kommt heute? Wer spielt Tennis/Golf?
4. Was machen Sie? Was trinken Sie? Was fragt er/sie?
5. Wieviel kostet das? Wieviele Kinder haben Sie? Wieviele Kinder hat sie/er?
6. Wohin gehen wir? Wohin fährst du? Wohin reisen Sie?
7. Woher kommen Sie? Woher kommt sie/er? Woher kommen sie?
8. Wann kommen Sie? Wann gehst du nach Hause? Wann fährt er?

</td></tr>

Aktivität B (matching answers) (p. 14)

1. c. In Chicago.	6. a. Fünfzig Euro.
2. d. Karl Schmidt.	7. g. Am Montag.
3. j. Ich gehe ins Konzert. Ich spiele Tennis.	8. h. Zwei Monate.
4. i. Aus Bonn.	9. l. Nach Frankfurt.
5. b. Danke gut / f. Nicht gut.	10. m. Die nächste Straße rechts.

Aktivität C (p. 15)

1. Wie geht es Ihnen?/Wie geht's?	7. Wohin gehen Sie?/Wohin fahren Sie?
2. Wieviel kostet das?	8. Ich heiße . . .
3. Wie heißen Sie?	9. Ich komme aus . . .
4. Was machen Sie heute?/ Was machst du heute?	10. Ich wohne in . . .
5. Wo wohnen Sie?	11. Vielen Dank.
6. Was machen Sie heute abend? Was machst du heute abend?	12. Ich fahre nach Berlin.

GRAMMATIK (Grammar)

Übung A (p. 17)

1. er	3. sie	5. du	7. es	9. sie
2. wir	4. sie	6. Sie	8. ich	10. sie

Übung B (p. 18)

1. heißen	3. kommt	5. studiert	7. fragst
2. wohnt	4. kaufe	6. arbeitet	8. wandern

Übung C (p. 19)

1. Christian tanzt gern.
2. Wir lernen gern Deutsch.
3. Ich trinke gern Kaffee.
4. Sie arbeiten hier gern.
   Sie arbeiten gern hier.
5. Karin schwimmt gern.
6. Ich spiele gern Tennis.
7. Sie reisen gern.
8. Sie singen gern.
9. Er wandert gern.
10. Wir leben gern in Florida.

Übung D (p. 21)

1. Eltern
2. Geld
3. Taxi (*or:* Bus)
4. Polizist/in
5. Bruder
6. Schwester
7. Telefon
8. Milch
9. Messer und Gabel
10. Amerikaner

Übung E (p. 22)

1. es	3. er	5. er	7. sie	9. er
2. sie	4. es	6. es	8. sie	10. sie

Übung F (p. 23)

1. teuer	3. warm	5. wenig	7. lang	9. selten	11. heiß
2. schlecht	4. gesund	6. alt	8. schwer	10. fleißig	12. groß

Übung G (p. 24)

1. ist	3. bist	5. sind	7. sind	9. Sind
2. ist	4. ist	6. ist	8. sind	10. ist

Übung H (p. 24)

1. haben	3. habe	5. hat	7. Hat
2. hat	4. hat	6. Hast	8. Haben

Übung I (p. 25)

(Translation for *Übung G*)

1. Mr. Braun is an American.
2. Beer is inexpensive in Germany.
3. Are you sick today?
4. Monika is intelligent.
5. The computers are new.
6. The luggage is heavy.
7. The children are diligent.
8. We are from Switzerland.
9. Are you an American, Mr. Brown?
10. Karin is healthy again.

(Translation for *Übung H*)

1. We have a lot of time.
2. Robert has an expensive car.
3. I have an old house.
4. Karin has a new friend.
5. The child has a ball.
6. Do you have a computer?
7. Does he have money?
8. Do Mr. and Mrs. Schmidt have children?

Übung J (p. 25)

1. spricht	3. liest/liest	5. fährst/fährt
2. siehst	4. isst/isst	6. schläfst/schläft

WIEDERHOLUNG (Review)

A (p. 27)

1. Guten Tag! (*or:* Grüß Gott!)	3. Guten Abend!	5. Guten Tag!
2. Guten Morgen!	4. Guten Tag!	6. Gute Nacht!

B (p. 27)

1. Wann arbeitet Herr Schmidt?	3. Wie ist das Wetter?	5. Wo wohnt Frau Bieber?
2. Was kauft Martin?	4. Wieviel kostet es?	

C (p. 27)

1. Ich reise gern.
2. Wie heißen Sie? (*or:* Wie heißt du?)
3. Wieviel kostet das Radio?
4. Wir spielen gern Golf.
5. Sie haben viel Zeit.
6. Sie wohnt (lebt) in München.
7. Entschuldigen Sie, bitte.
8. Wohin gehen Sie jetzt?/Wohin gehst du jetzt?

D (p. 27)

1. Ja, ich bin Amerikaner.
2. Ich fahre nach . . .
3. Ich wohne in . . .
4. Ich reise/spiele/gehe/ . . .
5. Ich bleibe . . .

KAPITEL 2

Aktivität B (p. 36)

1. Meine Telefonnummer ist . . .
2. Meine Zimmernummer ist . . .
3. Meine Hausnummer ist . . .
4. Meine Schuhgröße ist . . .
5. Ich weiß nicht./4.542 Kilometer (2,823 Meilen)
6. Meine Sozialversicherungsnummer ist . . .

Aktivität C (p. 37)

1. dreiunddreißig plus vierzehn ist siebenundvierzig
2. siebenundachtzig minus dreizehn ist vierundsiebzig
3. siebenmal drei ist einundzwanzig
4. vierzig durch acht ist fünf
5. siebzehn plus sechs ist dreiundzwanzig
6. fünfmal sieben ist fünfunddreißig
7. zweiundvierzig minus acht ist vierunddreißig
8. fünfzig durch zehn ist fünf
9. zwölf plus neun ist einundzwanzig
10. fünfundzwanzig minus sechs ist neunzehn

Aktivität D (p. 37)

1. Ich bin . . . Meter
2. Man bekommt heute . . . Euro/Schweizer Franken
3. Ich habe . . . Bruder (Brüder) und . . . Schwester (Schwestern)
4. Ich bin . . .
5. Ich trinke täglich . . .
6. Mt. McKinley ist 6.194 Meter. (*or:* 20,300 feet)
7. Heute ist es . . .

GRAMMATIK

Übung A (p. 38)
1. Haben wir jetzt eine Wohnung?
2. Hat Robert ein Haus?
3. Ist es weit von Berlin nach Wien?
4. Bleiben wir zwei Wochen in Europa?
5. Hat Inge drei Brüder?
6. Hat Herr Braun viel Geld?

Übung B (p. 38)
1. Wo
2. Wann
3. Wohin
4. Wer
5. Wie
6. Warum
7. Wieviel
8. Woher
9. Was
10. Wie lange

Übung C. (p. 40)
1. Wieviel kostet es?
2. Haben sie Kinder?
3. Bleibt sie drei Tage oder vier Tage?
4. Kostet es 38 Euro oder 83 Euro?
5. Wie weit ist es von hier?
6. Hast du Geld?

Übung D (p. 40)
1. Es kostet 15 Mark.
2. Ich habe zwei Brüder und drei Schwestern.
3. Er kauft das Radio.
4. Es ist heute 12 Grad.
5. Ihr bekommt morgen das Geld.
6. Ich habe nicht genug Zeit.

Übung E (p. 42)
1. Ich nehme einen Zug.
2. Wir finden ein Restaurant.
3. Gregor sucht ein Buch.
4. Brauchen Sie eine Wohnung?
5. Kennt sie eine Journalistin?
6. Maria kauft eine Jacke.

Übung F (p. 42)
1. kein Auto
2. kein Geld
3. keinen Pulli
4. kein Bier
5. keinen Bus
6. keine Kinder
7. keinen Fisch

Übung G (p. 44)
1. mich 2. sie 3. uns 4. ihn 5. dich 6. Sie 7. sie 8. euch

Übung H (p. 45)
1. Es/es
2. Sie/sie
3. Er/ihn
4. Es/es
5. Es/es
6. Er/ihn
7. Sie/sie
8. Er/ihn

Übung I (p. 46)
1. einen Regenschirm
2. den Park
3. die Stadt
4. das Geschäft
5. den Tisch
6. das Haus
7. das metrische System
8. die Kinder

Übung J (p. 47)
1. nicht im Hotel
2. es nicht
3. nicht oft
4. morgen nicht
5. nicht schnell
6. heute abend nicht

Übung K (p. 47)
A. Fährt Gregor heute abend?
B. Nein, ich glaube nicht. Er hat kein Auto.
A. Herr Scholz, wann fliegen Sie nach Deutschland?
S. Morgen.
A. Haben Sie einen Pass?
S. Oh ja, ich reise viel.

A. Wie heißt der Mann?

B. Wir kennen ihn nicht.

A. Spricht er Deutsch?

B. Ja, er ist aus Österreich.

Übung L (p. 48)

1. Sie geht nicht schnell.
2. Sie sprechen nicht zu laut.
   (*or:* Du sprichst nicht zu laut.)
3. Er arbeitet nicht am Abend.
4. Wir zahlen die Rechnung nicht.
5. Sie essen nicht viel.

Übung M (p. 49)

1. Sind Sie heute abend allein?
   (*or:* Bist du heute abend allein?)
2. Sind wir heute pünktlich?
3. Ist er wieder krank?
4. Fährt der Zug jeden Tag?

Übung N (p. 50)

1. Herr Schulz kommt pünktlich ins Hotel.
2. Bettina ist heute nicht zu Hause.
3. Sie bleiben bis morgen hier.
4. Dieter fliegt morgen sofort nach Hause.
5. Der Bus hält immer hier.

SPRECHEN LEICHT GEMACHT

Aktivität A (p. 50)

1. Heute ist . . .
2. Nach Dienstag kommt Mittwoch.
3. Morgen ist . . .
4. Vor Samstag kommt Freitag.
5. Gestern war . . .

Aktivität B (p. 51)

1. e. 2. c. 3. b. 4. a. 5. d.

WIEDERHOLUNG

A (p. 51)

1. Ich trinke Milch.
2. Mein Freund ist krank.
3. Ich sehe dort eine Freundin.
4. Ich brauche 100 Euro.
5. Sabine kommt am Dienstag.
6. Ich fahre heute nach Hamburg.
7. Ich komme aus Texas.
8. Ich bleibe drei Tage.

B (p. 51)

1. kein 2. nicht 3. keinen 4. keine 5. nicht 6. nicht 7. nichts

C (p. 52)

1. Achtundsechzig Grad Fahrenheit ist zwanzig Grad Celsius.
2. Dreimal vier ist zwölf.
3. Ein Kilo hat 1.000 Gramm.
4. Was ist Ihre Zimmernummer?
5. Meine Telefonnummer ist . . .
6. Welcher Tag ist heute? (*or:* Der Wievielte ist heute?)

KAPITEL 3

KOMMUNIKATION

Aktivität A (p. 58)

1. e. 2. a. 3. c. 4. d. 5. e. 6. f. 7. b., g.

Aktivität B (p. 61)

1. gedämpft/gekocht
2. gebacken/gebraten/gegrillt
3. vom Rost/gegrillt/gebraten
4. gebacken/gekocht/gefüllt/gedämpft
5. gebraten/gebacken
6. gebacken/gefüllt/gekocht/gegrillt

Aktivität C (p. 61)

1. Karotten 2. Äpfel 3. Spargel 4. Rotkohl 5.Trauben

Aktivität D (p. 62)

1. c. 2. b. 3. b., c., e.

Aktivität E (p. 63)

1. b. 3. f. 5. e. 7. i. 9. h. 11. m. 13. k.
2. c. 4. j. 6. d. 8. g. 10. a. 12. l.

GRAMMATIK

Übung A (p. 64)

1. Bringen Sie ein Glas Wein!
2. Versuchen Sie diese Suppe!
3. Kochen Sie ohne Salz!
4. Warten Sie auf den nächsten Bus!
5. Kommen Sie heute abend!
6. Gehen Sie zur Ecke!
7. Wählen Sie das Steak!
8. Fragen Sie den Ober!
9. Nehmen Sie ein Taxi!
10. Fahren Sie nach Hause!

Übung B (p. 66)

1. können 3. kann 5. wollen 7. darf 9. dürfen
2. will 4. soll 6. musst 8. können 10. willst

Übung C (p. 67)

1. möchte heute Tennis spielen.
2. möchte einen Tee trinken.
3. möchte jetzt essen.
4. möchten Sie wohnen?
5. möchte nach Wien reisen.
6. möchten zahlen, bitte.
7. möchtest du trinken?
8. möchte einen Tisch bestellen.
9. möchtet ein Gasthaus finden.
10. möchten Sie fahren?

Übung D (p. 68)

1. Weihnachten ist am fünfundzwanzigsten Dezember.
2. Der Nationalfeiertag der USA ist am vierten Juli.
3. Silvester ist am einunddreißigsten Dezember.
4. Neujahr ist am ersten Januar.
5. Ich fliege am . . . nach Europa.
6. Ich fahre am . . . nach Deutschland.
7. Ich habe am . . . Geburtstag.
8. Ich fahre am . . . nach Hause.

Übung E (p. 69)

1. Hälfte 2. viertel 3. Achtel 4. siebenzehntel 5. Dreiviertel

Übung F (p. 70)

1. Fliegt sie am zwanzigsten nach Berlin?
2. Heiratet Gregor am siebzehnten Juni?
3. Welcher Tag ist heute? (*or:* Der Wievielte ist heute?)

4. Kommen Sie am vierzehnten?
5. Ist der dreiundzwanzigste ein Montag?

Übung G (p. 71)

1. Sie ist am einundzwanzigsten hier.
2. Der fünfte ist ein Samstag.
3. Er kommt am dreißigsten.
4. Wir fliegen am achtzehnten nach Österreich.
5. Ich kaufe am zehnten Mai ein Haus.

Übung H (p. 71)

1. wann der Zug kommt?
2. wohin die Straßenbahn fährt?
3. wo hier ein Telefon ist?
4. wie teuer das ist?
5. wen ich dort frage?
6. warum heute kein Bus fährt?
7. wann Frau Schmidt nach Hause geht?

Übung I (p. 72)

1. Suchen Sie eine Milchbar?
2. Bestellt er einen Salat?
3. Nimmt Helga ein Taxi?
4. Kommst du ins Hotel?
5. Seht ihr die Post?
6. Finde ich das Restaurant?
7. Wartet sie auf den Zug?
8. Bestellt er das Menü?
9. Geht Bernd zum Schnellimbiss?
10. Steht das Auto vor dem Hotel?

Übung J (p. 73)

1. weiß
2. wissen
3. weiß
4. wissen
5. Wissen
6. weiß
7. weiß
8. Weißt

Übung K (p. 73)

1. Wo ist der Bahnhof?
2. Weiß Gregor, wie teuer das Restaurant ist?
3. Weißt du, was der Polizist sagt?
4. Wissen sie, wo ich wohne?
5. Wieviel kostet die Zeitung?

Übung L (p. 75)

1. die Restaurants zu teuer sind.
2. er mit dem Taxi fährt.
3. das Essen dort billig ist.
4. es ein preiswertes Hotel gibt.
5. ich wenig Geld habe.
6. das Wetter kalt ist.

Übung M (p. 76)

1. Ich bin glücklich, weil ich jetzt in Deutschland bin.
2. Wir zahlen jetzt, damit wir nach Hause gehen können.
3. Der Kellner empfiehlt das Menü, obwohl es nicht gut ist.
4. Meine Frau bleibt in Europa, während ich hier arbeite.
5. Ich weiß nicht, ob ich zur Party kommen kann.
6. Die Kellnerin gibt uns einen Tisch am Fenster, weil sie uns kennt.
7. Herr König fährt oft mit dem Auto, obwohl das Benzin teuer ist.
8. Wissen Sie, dass es schon sehr spät ist?

Übung N (p. 77)

1. Wir wohnen im Hotel Dresden, bis wir ein Haus kaufen.
2. Ich möchte dich sehen, obwohl ich krank bin.
3. Sie gehen nicht nach Hause, bist du kommst.
4. Meine Eltern können reisen, wenn sie Zeit haben.
5. Elke möchte bis fünfzehnten Juni hier bleiben.

Übung O (p. 78)

1. der Käsekuchen
2. die Obsttorte
3. die Gulaschsuppe
4. das Fruchteis
5. das Gasthaus

Übung P (p. 78)

1. die Straßenbahn
2. das Gasthaus
3. die Bushaltestelle
4. der Käsekuchen
5. der Stadtplan
6. die Haustür
7. der Hotelportier

WIEDERHOLUNG

A (p. 80)

1. Gehen Sie/Fahren Sie geradeaus/nach links/nach rechts
2. Gehen Sie bis zur Ecke/bis zum Schild/über die Brücke
3. Nehmen Sie den Bus/die Straßenbahn/ein Taxi
4. Bringen Sie die Speisekarte/die Zeitung/das Telefonbuch

B (p. 80)

1. Ich möchte das Fleisch nicht durchgebraten/durchgebraten.
2. Ich möchte das Gemüse gedämpft.
3. Ich möchte den Nachtisch mit Schlag (mit Sahne) ohne Schlag (ohne Sahne).

C (p. 80)

1. Wir warten schon lange./Ich warte schon lange.
2. Die Suppe ist kalt.
3. Das Bier ist warm.
4. Das ist versalzen.
5. Das Tischtuch ist nicht sauber.
6. Das Fleisch ist zäh.

D (p. 80)

1. Bitte, ist der Platz besetzt/ist der Platz noch frei?/Gibt es noch Platz?
2. Bitte, gibt es noch etwas Warmes zu essen?/Bitte, gibt es noch ein Mittagessen/ein Abendessen?
3. Haben Sie noch ein Menü?

E (p. 81)

1. Die Rechnung, bitte. (*or:* Bitte zahlen.)   3. Entschuldigen Sie, bitte. *or:* Verzeihung.
2. Wir waren zufrieden.

F (p. 81)

1. f.   2. f.   3. d.   4. d.   5. f.   6. c.   7. b.   8. a.
9. f.   10. b.   11. f.   12. c.   13. d.   14. g.   15. f.   16. c.

KAPITEL 4

KOMMUNIKATION

Aktivität A (p. 88)

1. c.   2. e.   3. h.   4. d.   5. g.   6. a.   7. f.   8. b.   9. j.   10. i.

Aktivität B (p. 88)

1. einen Koffer
2. dem Doppelzimmer
3. in die Dusche
4. ein Gepäck

GRAMMATIK (p. 89)

Übung A (p. 90)

1. den Freunden
2. dem Arzt
3. dem Kind
4. dem Professor
5. dem Mädchen
6. der Managerin

Übung B (p. 91)

1. dem Herrn	4. dem Freund	6. dem Touristen
2. den Amerikanern	5. den Freunden	7. den Touristen
3. den Studenten		

Übung C (p. 91)

1. Geben Sie es den Touristen.
2. Wir zeigen es der Mutter.
3. Ich sage es dem Lehrer.
4. Karl schreibt dem Geschäftsmann.
5. Ich sage es den Leuten.

Übung D (p. 92)

1. dem Bus	3. der Kollegin	5. dem Konzert
2. dem Geschäft	4. einem Monat	

Übung E (p. 93)

1. ihm 2. uns 3. ihr 4. mir 5. ihnen 6. dir

Übung F (p. 94)

1. übers Wetter	3. vorm Geschäft	5. im Koffer
2. ans Fenster	4. ins Büro	6. unterm Tisch

Übung G (p. 94)

1. Wir wohnen im Hotel.
2. Bringen Sie den Brief ins Büro?
3. Ich arbeite jetzt im Geschäft.
4. Frau Müller reist in die Schweiz.
5. Karin fährt vor das Gasthaus.

Übung H (p. 95)

1. ihr 2. ihm 3. ihnen 4. ihnen 5. ihm 6. ihr 7. ihm 8. ihr

Übung I (p. 95)

1. Bitte helfen Sie der Frau.
2. Glaubt er dem Amerikaner nicht?
3. Das passt den Österreichern nicht.
4. Wir danken den Deutschen.
5. Diese Wohnung gefällt der Studentin.
6. Das Haus gehört der Firma.
7. Schmeckt es den Gästen?
8. Leider kann ich dem Kind nicht helfen.

Übung J (p. 97)

1. Wann zieht Lisa in die neue Wohnung ein?
2. Bitte nehmen Sie das Buch mit.
3. Herr Emmerich, rufen Sie morgen an!
4. Bitte machen Sie das Fenster zu.
5. Wann fliegen Sie nach Amerika zurück?
6. Der Zug fährt um 16 Uhr 40 ab.
7. Herr Richter kommt am Freitag an.
8. Wann fängt das Konzert an?

Übung K (p. 98)

1. . . . Tina am Mittwoch zurückfliegt.
2. . . . Ernst im Sommer umzieht.
3. . . . das Spiel um 19 Uhr anfängt.
4. . . . Ingrid nach Österreich mitkommt.
5. . . . er am Sonntag abfährt.
6. . . . dort immer aussteigt.

Übung L (p. 100)

1. a. ihr den Koffer	b. ihn Elke	c. ihn ihr
2. a. ihnen einen Fernseher	b. ihn den Amerikanern	c. ihn ihnen
3. a. ihnen das Geschäft	b. es den Freunden	c. es ihnen

Übung M (sample answers) (p. 101)
1. Wir zeigen den Deutschen ein Auto.
2. Ich bringe ihnen einen Koffer.
3. Er kauft es ihr.

Kurzer Geschäftsbrief (translation) (p. 101)
Dear Mr. Müller,

My colleague John Tyler and I will arrive in Düsseldorf on June 23rd at 3:30 P.M. with Lufthansa flight 79 from Hamburg. Are you picking us up or should we go directly to the hotel? We would be happy if you could pick us up, but it is not necessary.

Please let us know (write to us) before we leave here.

Cordially,

yours . . .

Übung N (p. 102)
1. die Stadt
2. dem Hotel
3. das Haus
4. einem Österreicher
5. dem Tisch
6. einen Berg
7. einem Gasthof
8. dem Gasthaus
9. dem Sofa
10. die Ecke

SPRECHEN LEICHT GEMACHT

Aktivität A (p. 103)
1. ihnen Kuchen
2. ihr das Einzelzimmer
3. ihr ein Trinkgeld
4. ihm ein Buch
5. ihm eine Limonade
6. ihm das Gepäck

Aktivität B (p. 104)
Ich wohne in der Schweiz/in dem (im) Hotel/in der Jugendherberge/ in dem (im) Gasthof/in dem (im) Studentenheim/in der Ferienwohnung/in dem (im) Haus/in der Wohnung

Aktivität C (p. 104)
Ich fahre in das (ins) Büro/in die Schweiz/in das (ins) Theater/in das (ins) Geschäft/in die Berge

Aktivität D (p. 104)
(Sample answers).
Guten Abend. Haben Sie noch ein Zimmer frei?/ . . . ein Doppelzimmer?
Wieviel kostet ein Einzelzimmer mit Dusche?/ . . . ein Doppelzimmer?
Ich nehme das Einzelzimmer mit Dusche./ . . . das Doppelzimmer mit
    Dusche./ . . . das Doppelzimmer mit Bad.
Wo ist das Frühstückszimmer?/ . . . die Toilette?/ein Telefon?
Soll ich jetzt zahlen oder kann ich später zahlen?

Aktivität E (p. 104)
Ich gehe gern in die Oper/in das (ins) Geschäft/in das (ins) Büro/in das (ins) Hotel/in das (ins) Restaurant/auf die Universität/auf das (aufs) Zimmer/in das (ins) Konzert

WIEDERHOLUNG

A (p. 105)
1. Gibt es noch ein Zimmer?
2. Ist es ein Einzelzimmer oder ein Doppelzimmer?
3. Kann ich die Wohnung sehen?
4. Wann kann ich einziehen?
5. Wieviele Zimmer hat die Wohnung?

B (p. 105)
1. Ich ziehe diesen Sommer nach Zürich um.
2. Sie bleiben gern in New York.
3. Ich fahre nach Deutschland.

C (p. 105)
1. ihnen   2. ihr   3. ihm   4. uns

D (p. 105)

1. Wir holen Franz am Wochenende ab.	We pick up Franz on the weekend.
2. Ich rufe am Sonntag an.	I'll call on Sunday.
3. Ich lerne ihn auf der Party kennen.	I am meeting him at the party.
4. Er nimmt den Koffer nicht mit.	He is not taking along the suitcase.
5. Wo steigen wir aus?	Where are we getting off?
6. Wann ziehe ich dort ein?	When am I moving in there?
7. Elfe kommt am Freitag an.	Elfe is arriving on Friday.
8. Das Konzert fängt um 19 Uhr an.	The concert begins at 7 P.M.

E (p. 106)
1. Das Fahrrad gehört ihr.
2. Wann kommen Sie in Frankfurt an?
3. Das Haus gefällt uns nicht.
4. Sie kommt am Mittwoch zurück.
5. Der Gast möchte ein Zimmer mit Dusche.
6. Ich muss um sieben Uhr aufstehen.

KAPITEL 5

Kommunikation
Aktivität A (p. 112)
1. viertel nach sechs (*or:* viertel sieben)
2. halbe Stunde
3. neun Uhr fünfunddreißig
4. viertel vor zwölf (*or:* dreiviertel zwölf)
5. ein Uhr
6. viertel nach fünf (*or:* viertel sechs)
7. halb elf

Aktivität B (p. 112)
1. Um sechzehn Uhr fünfundvierzig (*or:* dreiviertelfünf)
2. Elf Uhr fünfzehn (*or:* viertel nach elf)
3. Um zwanzig Uhr
4. Bis viertel vor sechs (*or:* dreiviertel sechs)
5. Zweiundvierzig Stunden
6. Um halb fünf (*or:* vier Uhr dreißig)

GRAMMATIK
Übung A (p. 114)
1. gewohnt   2. gelernt   3. gemacht   4. gearbeitet   5. gekauft

Übung B (p. 115)
1. geschrieben   2. gefahren   3. gegangen   4. gefunden   5. gegessen

Übung C (p. 115)
1. angerufen
2. abgeflogen
3. angefangen
4. aufgehört
5. vorbeigekommen
6. zurückgekommen

Übung D (p. 117)

1. reserviert	3. gegessen	5. besucht
2. studiert	4. vergessen	6. angerufen

Übung E (p. 119)

1. gefahren/gegangen/gereist
2. gelesen/gekauft
3. abgefahren/angekommen
4. gesehen/gehört/gekauft
5. gereist/gefahren
6. gefallen
7. getroffen/gesehen/gefunden
8. gewesen/geblieben
9. gefahren/gegangen
10. getroffen/gefunden/gesehen

Übung F (p. 121)

1. Wo ist Karins Vater?
2. Ist das Karls Zimmer?
3. Wissen (Kennen) Sie den Namen des Professors?
4. Ich habe die Adresse des Restaurants nicht.
5. Die Eltern der Kinder sind abgefahren.
6. Möchten Sie Heidis Fotos sehen?
7. Wir können Johns Auto nicht kaufen.

SPRECHEN LEICHT GEMACHT

Aktivität B (p. 122)

1. in die Schweiz/nach Österreich/nach Frankreich gefahren
2. einem Freund/meinen Eltern gereist
3. mit dem Zug/dem Autobus/dem Camper gefahren
4. ein paar Tage/Wochen/Monate Urlaub gemacht
5. die Schweiz/Frankreich/Italien besucht
6. nicht viel gepackt/mitgenommen
7. Kreditkarte/Scheck/Bargeld/Euro/Franken bezahlt
8. Euro/Schweizer Franken mitgenommen
9. drei Tage/eine Woche dort gewesen
10. gefallen
11. verstanden/gesprochen
12. reserviert

WIEDERHOLUNG

A sample answers (p. 124)

7:00 ich stehe auf/ich frühstücke
7:45 ich fahre zur Arbeit/ich komme im Büro an
8:15 ich komme im Büro an/ich gehe zur Arbeit
9:30 ich spreche mit Kunden/ich lese die Post
10:30 ich trinke einen Kaffee/ich spreche mit Kunden
12:30 ich gehe Mittagessen/ich gehe in den Park
13:45 ich gehe ins Büro zurück/ich lese die Zeitung
15:00 ich spreche mit dem Chef/ich telefoniere
16:30 ich arbeite im Büro/ich diskutiere mit Kollegen
17:15 ich gehe nach Hause/ich fahre nach Hause/ich rufe meine Frau/meinen Mann an
17:45 ich kaufe etwas ein
18:00 ich komme zu Hause an/ich lese die Zeitung

19:00 ich habe Abendessen/ich höre mir die Nachrichten an
20:00 ich besuche einen Nachbarn/ich spiele mit den Kindern
21:00 ich sehe fern/ich lese ein Buch/ich spiele Klavier
22:30 ich gehe ins Bett/ich lese noch im Bett

B (p. 124)

ich bin aufgestanden/ich habe gefrühstückt
ich bin zur Arbeit gefahren/ich bin im Büro angekommen
ich bin im Büro angekommen/ich bin zur Arbeit gegangen
ich habe mit Kunden gesprochen/ich habe die Post gelesen
ich bin Mittagessen gegangen/ich bin in den Park gegangen
ich bin ins Büro zurückgegangen/ich habe die Zeitung gelesen
ich habe mit dem Chef gesprochen/ich habe telefoniert
ich habe im Büro gearbeitet/ich habe mit Kollegen diskutiert
ich bin nach Hause gegangen/ich bin nach Hause gefahren
ich habe meine Frau angerufen/ich habe meinen Mann angerufen
ich habe etwas eingekauft
ich bin zu Hause angekommen/ich habe die Zeitung gelesen
ich habe Abendessen gehabt/ich habe mir die Nachrichten angehört
ich habe einen Nachbarn besucht/ich habe mit den Kindern gespielt
ich habe ferngesehen/ich habe ein Buch gelesen/ich habe Klavier gespielt
ich bin ins Bett gegangen/ich habe noch ein Buch gelesen

C (p. 124)

   Am 8. Mai bin ich um 18:15 in Berlin angekommen. Vom Flughafen habe ich ein Taxi genommen und bin sofort zum Hotel gefahren. Ich habe den Portier gefragt, ob er ein Zimmer für mich reserviert hat. Ja, ich habe Glück gehabt. Ich habe ein Zimmer für drei Tage bekommen. Ich bin drei Tage in Berlin gewesen. Ich habe einige deutsche Firmen besucht und ich bin auch öfters bei deutschen Kollegen gewesen. Herr Müller von der Firma Siemens hat mir auch eine neue Fabrik gezeigt. Am Wochenende haben wir einen Ausflug in den Grunewald gemacht. An einem Abend bin ich ins Konzert gegangen. Es hat mir gut gefallen. Die Berliner Philharmoniker haben Beethoven und Mozart gespielt.

KAPITEL 6

KOMMUNIKATION

Aktivität A (correct answers) (p. 131)

1. zum Arzt/ins Krankenhaus
2. nichts machen/viel trinken/Aspirin nehmen
3. Ist Ihnen schwindelig?/Wo tut's weh?
   Wie fühlen Sie sich?/Haben Sie Fieber?
4. hohen Blutdruck haben/Ohrenschmerzen haben.

Aktivität B (p. 133)

1. a., d.   2. b.   3. b., c., d.   4. c., d.   5. a., c., d.   6. c.   7. b., c.

GRAMMATIK

Übung A (p. 134)

1. Ich fühlte mich nicht wohl.
2. Wir holten den Arzt.
3. Ich antwortete auf seine Fragen.
4. Er sagte nicht viel.
5. Ich kaufte mir Tabletten.
6. Bald war ich wieder gesund.

Übung B (p. 135)

1. Sarah war krank.	Sarah was sick.
2. Sie rief die Ärztin an.	She called the doctor.
3. Sie kam und verschrieb Tabletten.	She came and wrote a prescription (for tablets).
4. Sarah trank viel Tee und Saft.	Sarah drank a lot of tea and juice.
5. Sie aß nur Suppe.	She ate only soup.
6. Bald ging es ihr besser.	Soon she felt better.

Übung C (p. 136)

1. wolltet	3. konnten	5. musste
2. musste	4. durfte	6. konnten

Übung D (p. 136)
Dialog 1

1. Er hatte Halsschmerzen	3. Er hieß Dr. Jung.
2. Er wollte noch warten.	4. Klaus fuhr ihn zum Arzt.

Dialog 2
1. Ihr Blinddarm musste raus.
2. Der Arzt empfahl das Universitätskrankenhaus.
3. Die Mutter von Frau K. war auch im Universitätskrankenhaus.

Dialog 3
1. Elke war schwindelig.
2. Karin besuchte sie.
3. Sie nahm vor einer Stunde Aspirin.
4. Sie hatte zwei Liter getrunken.
5. Sie sagte: „Hoffentlich fühlst du dich bald besser."

Dialog 4
1. Er hatte schreckliche Ohrenschmerzen.
2. Nein, seine Mandeln waren auch geschwollen.
3. Der Arzt verschrieb ihr Penicillintabletten.

Übung E (p. 139)

1. sich	3. sich	5. mir	7. sich	9. mir
2. sich	4. sich	6. uns	8. mich	10. sich

Übung F (p. 140)
1. Kinder, wir müssen uns beeilen.
2. Ich muss mich zuerst (noch) duschen.
3. Vater rasiert sich noch.
4. Wer zieht das Baby an?
5. Ich weiß nicht.
6. Paul, warum hast du dir deine Haare nicht gekämmt?
7. Ich habe mein Haare gekämmt.
8. Mutti, Paul und Peter haben ihre Zähne nicht geputzt.
9. Ich bleibe zu Hause.   Ich fühle mich nicht wohl.
10. Wir gehen alle ins Restaurant.
11. Freust du dich nicht auf das Essen bei . . . ?
12. Nein, ich bin wirklich krank.
13. Dann bleiben wir alle zu Hause.

Übung G (p. 142)

1. Als	3. wann	5. Wenn	7. Als	9. wann
2. wann	4. Wenn	6. wenn	8. Wann	10. als

SPRECHEN LEICHT GEMACHT

Aktivität A (p. 142)

1. stand ich auf.
2. frühstückte ich.
3. las ich ein Buch.
4. ging ich einkaufen.
5. besuchte ich einen Freund.
6. aßen wir wieder.
7. ging ich nach Hause.
8. arbeitete ich im Garten.
9. sah ich einen Film.
10. ging ich ins Bett.

Aktivität B (sample responses) (p. 142)

1. Ich blieb im Bett./Ich trank viel Tee, Wasser, Saft./Ich nahm Aspirin.
2. Ich hatte Halsschmerzen/Ohrenschmerzen/Kopfschmerzen.
3. Bei einer Blinddarmentzündung/Lungenentzündung/muss man ins Krankenhaus/ Wenn man sich ein Bein bricht./Wenn man Krebs hat.
4. Wenn man Fieber/Grippe/einen Husten hat.
5. Ich blieb zu Hause./Ich legte mich ins Bett. Ich nahm Aspirin und trank viel Tee/Wasser/Saft.
6. Ja, ich habe einen Hausarzt./Nein, ich habe keinen Hausarzt.
7. Viele Menschen haben Lungenkrebs, weil sie rauchen.
8. Ich gehe oft/nie/manchmal/selten in die Apotheke.
9. Ja, ich schlafe genug./Nein, ich schlafe nicht genug.
10. Man soll gesund essen./ Man soll fit bleiben./Man soll nicht rauchen und nicht zuviel Alkohol trinken./Man soll Sport treiben.

WIEDERHOLUNG

A (p. 143)

Norbert blieb heute zu Hause. Er hatte Hals- und Kopfschmerzen und fühlte sich nicht wohl. Auch sah er sehr blass aus. Am Nachmittag ging er zum Arzt, denn sein Fieber war sehr hoch. Er war wohl wirklich krank. Er musste sich untersuchen lassen. Der Arzt glaubte, dass er eine schwere Erkältung oder vielleicht sogar eine Grippe hatte. Er gab ihm Penicillintabletten. Bald ging es ihm besser.

B (p. 143)

1. Wann war Kim nicht im Büro?
2. Wer hat sich ein neues Auto gekauft?
3. Wie hat sich Kurt gestern gefühlt?
4. Wer schläft nicht genug?
5. Wohin fuhr Herr Schwarz?

KAPITEL 7

KOMMUNIKATION

Aktivität A (p. 148)

1. gut durchgebraten
2. Bibliotheken
3. sehe ich nichts/verpasse ich alle Programme/ höre ich das Radio
4. muss nichts bezahlen

GRAMMATIK

Übung A (p. 151)

1. deinen	3. unsere	5. meinen	7. Ihr
2. seine	4. ihr	6. eure	8. ihre

Übung B (p. 151)
1. unsere Autoschlüssel
2. meinen Regenschirm
3. seinen Koffer
4. ihr Auto
5. ihre Theaterkarte
6. Ihr Buch
7. deine CDs

Übung C (p. 152)
1. jenen   2. dieses   3. welche   4. solche   5. manchen   6. jedes

Übung D (p. 153)
1. krank
2. fleißig
3. spät
4. alt
5. jung
6. schlecht
7. kalt
8. kurz
9. laut
10. leicht

Übung E (p. 155)
1. kurzer
2. warmen
3. heiße
4. lange/teure
5. langweiligen
6. kühlen
7. kurze
8. schöne/weiße
9. kalte
10. kalten/lang

Übung F (p. 156)
1. Sie haben nicht viele Werbungen.
2. Ich interessiere mich nicht fürs ausländische Fernsehen. (*or:* Ich habe kein Interesse am ausländischen Fernsehen.)
3. Elke hört sich nur klassische Musik an.
4. Paul gefällt amerikanischer Jazz. or: Paul hat amerikanischen Jazz gern.
5. Möchten Sie/Möchtest du dieses verrückte Programm sehen?
6. Ja, weil es interessant ist.
7. Dieser langweilige Film hat mir nicht gefallen. (*or:* Dieser langweilige Film gefiel mir nicht.)
8. Mein Vater gab (schenkte) meinem kleinen Bruder einen neuen Fernseher.

Übung G (p. 157)
1. Mein Ältester
2. Der Große
3. den Neuen
4. meine Jüngste
5. der Kranken
6. Arme
7. der Beste

Übung H (p. 159)
1. roten Ball
2. großen Rosenbusch
3. guter Marmelade
4. junger Mann
5. langes blondes Haar
6. kühl
7. neu
8. gute Schwimmer

SPRECHEN LEICHT GEMACHT
Aktivität A (p. 159)
1. f.   2. h.   3. h.   4. a.   5. c., d.   6. b., h.   7. g.

Aktivität B (sample answers) (p. 160)
1. in einem österreichischen Restaurant/in einem eleganten Hotel
2. schwindelig/krank
3. eine nette Frau/eine gute Freundin
4. in einer kleinen Stadt/an einer lauten Straße
5. bei einer kleinen Firma/in einem modernen Büro
6. blondes Haar/braune Augen
7. billiges/schönes Auto
8. in die schöne Schweiz/in die hohen Berge gefahren.

WIEDERHOLUNG

A (p. 161)

1. Ich höre jeden Abend die Nachrichten.
2. Wir kaufen heute ein neues Auto.
3. Der Arzt kann dem Kranken nicht helfen.
4. Trinken Sie gern schwarzen Kaffee?
5. Weil das Wetter heiß ist, gehen wir heute schwimmen. (*or:* Wir gehen heute schwimmen, weil das Wetter heiß ist.)

B (p. 161)

1. u.	5. a.	9. k.	13. s.	17. q.
2. i.	6. b.	10. l.	14. o.	18. p.
3. c.	7. g.	11. h.	15. r.	19. m.
4. j.	8. f.	12. e.	16. t.	20. n.

KAPITEL 8

KOMMUNIKATION

Aktivität A (p. 165)

1. ist verreist.
2. kommt bald heraus.
3. ist heute peinlich.
4. machen wir das Wetter.
5. reinen Pulverschnee.

Aktivität B (p. 166)

1. b.   2. c.   3. b.

GRAMMATIK

Übung A (p. 167)

1. so alt wie Brigitte.
2. so schnell wie Peter.
3. so heiß wie heute.
4. so wenig Zeit wie du.
5. so gut wie Mary.
6. so viel wie Robert.

Übung B (p. 168)

1. noch größer.
2. noch weiter.
3. dauert noch länger.
4. noch billiger.
5. noch älter.
6. noch höher.
7. noch wärmer.

Übung C (p. 169)

1. jüngste   2. schnellste   3. größte   4. schönste   5. älteste

Übung D (p. 170)

1. mehr/meisten   2. besser/besten   3. höher/höchsten   4. lieber/liebsten

Übung E (p. 172)

1. Wenn Christopher nicht krank wäre, würde er täglich vier Kilometer laufen.
2. Was würden Sie machen, wenn Sie Kopfschmerzen hätten?
3. Wenn wir Urlaub hätten, würden wir ins Ausland reisen.
4. Würden Sie Deutsch lernen?
5. Ich würde gern wandern, wenn es warm wäre.
6. Wir würden mit Ihnen fahren, wenn es Ihnen recht wäre.

Übung I (p. 177)

1. hätten/hätten
2. hätte/hätte
3. wären/wäre
4. hätten/hätten
5. wäre/hätte

SPRECHEN LEICHT GEMACHT
Aktivität B (p. 179)
1. Ach, wenn ich nur einen Job hätte!
2. . . . wenn das Wetter nur nicht so schlecht wäre!
3. . . . wenn meine Eltern nur Geld hätten!
4. . . . wenn du mir nur helfen würdest!
5. . . . wenn mein Freund nur Briefe schriebe! (*or:* . . . wenn mein Freund nur Briefe schreiben würde!*)
6. . . . wenn sie nur mit uns wanderten! (*or:* . . . wenn sie nur mit uns wandern würden!)
7. . . . wenn unsere Freunde nur länger bei uns blieben! (*or:* . . . wenn unsere Freunde nur länger bei uns bleiben würden!)
8. . . . wenn Elfe im Sommer nur Urlaub hätte!
9. . . . wenn ich nur Kaffee trinken dürfte!
10. . . . wenn wir es nur wüssten. (*or:* . . . wenn wir es nur wissen würden.)

WIEDERHOLUNG

A (p. 180)
1. schneller. 3. heißer. 5. weniger. 7. lieber.
2. größer. 4. mehr. 6. besser. 8. besser.

B (p. 181)
1. am kältesten. 3. am liebsten. 5. am liebsten.
2. der Schwerste (am schwersten). 4. am besten.

C (p. 181)
1. Im Sommer würden wir gern in den Bergen wandern.
2. Ich würde sie nicht fragen.
3. Ernst würde ihr nicht glauben.
4. Wer würde das Geld bekommen?
5. Gestern wäre ich gern Schi gelaufen.
6. Anke wäre zu spät gekommen.
7. Du hättest das nicht getan.

D (p. 181)
1. If we had had a longer vacation, we would have stayed one more week in Switzerland.
2. I would go to the movies today if I didn't have to work.
3. If I were a politician, I wouldn't say that.
4. If the weather had been better, we would have gone on an outing.
5. What would you have liked to see if you had traveled to Germany?

KAPITEL 9

KOMMUNIKATION
Aktivität A (p. 188)
1. c., d. 2. a., d. 3. c., d. 4. a., d.

*Strict grammarians argue for the use of the subjunctive form (*here:* **schriebe** in a **wenn** clause). However, in colloquial German this rule is often ignored in favor of the *infinitive* + **würde** form.

GRAMMATIK

Übung A (p. 190)

1. die	3. der	5. das	7. die	9. deren
2. die	4. das	6. denen	8. denen	10. die

Übung B (p. 191)

1. wo 2. woher 3. womit 4. wofür 5. wo

Am Bahnhof (translation) (p. 192)

1. On track 7 is (stands) the express train that goes to Hannover.
2. The group that is traveling to Hamburg is waiting at window 2.
3. The exchange office, which is located in the departure hall, is open from 8 A.M. to 6 P.M.
4. The Americans to whom they explained the train schedule are going to Cologne.
5. The train schedule that they showed me is no longer valid.
6. The restaurant where we ate is located on the second (third) floor.
7. The traveler whose watch has stopped is (being) late.
8. The luggage, which is too heavy, we (will) send by rail.

Die Presse (translation) (p. 193)

1. The article that interested me was in the *Süddeutsche Zeitung*.
2. The article that I had wanted to read was in yesterday's paper.
3. The journalist whose style I like is Peter Wallner.
4. The classified ads, whose content I sometimes don't understand, are found (one finds) on page 30.
5. The journalists with whom we had a discussion believed they knew everything.

Auf der Post (p. 193)

1. Here are the stamps that you have to put on your letter.
2. You must fill out the money order that you have given me.
3. This is a post office savings book with which you can withdraw money at any post office.
4. There are many post offices from which one can send a fax.
5. For every call one makes from the post office, one has to pay at the window.

Am Telefon (translation) (p. 193)

1. The lady, whose name I couldn't understand, spoke too softly.
2. The gentleman who went into the telephone booth ahead of me talked very long.
3. The telephone number that was given to me was not correct.
4. The telegram that I received was from my parents.
5. My postal savings book, whose number I have forgotten, is at home.

Lesestück (translation) (p. 194)

Etwas über die Presse in deutschsprachigen Ländern (Something about the Press in German-Speaking Countries):

There is no democracy that can remain a democracy without freedom of the press. The older generation in Germany, from whom this freedom had been taken during the Nazi period, experienced that.

In Switzerland, where there has been a successful democracy for centuries, the first newspaper in Europe was published in 1597 in Goldach (Canton St. Gallen). The right to independent information is very important for a country in which one wants to live in freedom. Everybody should be able to write what he wants to write; and everybody should be able to read what he wants to read. It is no coincidence that one can find over 400 newspapers in little Switzerland (population 7 million).

In the Federal Republic of Germany, where more than 80 million people live today, there are about 1,250 newspapers. They represent different political opinions—for instance, the *Süddeutsche Zeitung* (liberal), the *Frankfurter Allgemeine Zeitung* (conservative-liberal), or *Die Welt* (conservative). Add to that (*literally:* to that, come) political weeklies like *Die Zeit* (liberal) or the *Rheinische Merkur* (conservative).

Der Spiegel, a weekly newsmagazine that is similar to the American *Time* and *Newsweek,* has a special position in the German press. *Der Spiegel* sees its role as a political watchdog. Politicians who are on the warpath with *Der Spiegel* are afraid of the biting (sharp) and often arrogant criticism from this magazine.

Seven of ten newspapers that Germans read every day come into the house as a subscription paper. In the Federal Republic the press belongs to the private sector. In Austria, too, the constitution guarantees the freedom of the press. *Die Neue Kronenzeitung,* the *Kurier* and *Die Presse* belong (count) to those newspapers in Austria that one can buy everywhere in the country. Of the regional papers, the *Salzburger Nachrichten* is especially well known for independent reporting of the news.

It is an interesting fact that in today's Germany there are fewer newspapers than there were before World War II. In 1932, 2889 newspapers were published (*literally:* appeared) in Germany—more than double the number of today. Who were the losers in this demise of newspapers? They were local newspapers that could no longer compete with the big newspapers, and the party newspapers, which are lacking the political hinterland today.

"The big ones are devouring the little ones"; this trend in the German press worries many Germans. It is a trend that could become a problem for the freedom of the press. In a genuine democracy one would like to hear—yes, one *must* hear—many voices.

Übung C (p. 195)
1. d. 2. c. 3. b. 4. a., c. 5. b., d.

Übung D (p. 197)
1. a. Heute nachmittag holen wir Frau Jung vom Bahnhof ab.
   b. Holen wir heute nachmittag Frau Jung vom Bahnhof ab?
      Holen wir Frau Jung heute nachmittag vom Bahnhof ab?
   c. Können wir heute nachmittag Frau Jung vom Bahnhof abholen?
      Können wir Frau Jung heute nachmittag vom Bahnhof abholen?
2. a. Warum stellt Herr Müller seinen Wagen immer auf meinen Parkplatz?
   b. Immer stellt Herr Müller seinen Wagen auf meinen Parkplatz.
   c. Warum darf Herr Müller seinen Wagen immer auf meinen Parkplatz stellen?
3. a. Oft geht Erika abends mit ihrem Freund spazieren.
   b. Mit ihrem Freund geht Erika abends oft spazieren.
   c. Wann geht Erika oft mit ihrem Freund spazieren?
4. a. Wann will Frau Klein nach Japan fliegen?
   b. Im Sommer will Frau Klein nach Japan fliegen.
   c. Wohin will Frau Klein im Sommer fliegen?
5. a. Bald möchten wir mit Ursula über dieses Problem sprechen.
   b. Mit Ursula möchten wir bald über dieses Problem sprechen.
   c. Über dieses Problem möchten wir bald mit Ursula sprechen.

SPRECHEN LEICHT GEMACHT (p. 198)

Aktivität A (sample responses) (p. 198)

1. einen Lehrer, der mich versteht/der immer hilft.
2. einen Freund, der mich oft anruft/mit dem man über alles sprechen kann/der immer hilft/dessen Ego nicht zu groß ist.
3. eine Chefin, deren Ego nicht zu groß ist/die mich respektiert/die mich versteht.
4. einen Boss, der mir oft Urlaub gibt/dessen Ego nicht zu groß ist/der immer hilft/der mich versteht.
5. eine Freundin, die für mich Zeit hat/deren Ego nicht zu groß ist/die mich wirklich gern hat/die mich respektiert/die mich versteht.
6. eine Lehrerin, die für mich Zeit hat/die mich respektiert/die mich versteht.
7. Leute, die nicht immer von sich sprechen/deren Ego nicht zu groß ist.

Aktivität B (sample completions) (p. 199)

1. in Deutschland leben, wo alles gut organisiert ist.
2. in einem Land, wo es wenig Smog gibt.
3. in der Schweiz, wo es hohe Berge gibt.
4. in Italien, wo man viel singt und die Oper liebt.
5. in England, wo die Leute höflich sind.
6. in Hawai, wo man gut surfen kann.
7. in Salzburg, wo es die berühmten Festspiele gibt.
8. in Florida, wo die Winter warm sind.
9. in München, wo es das beste Bier gibt.
10. in Frankreich, wo man guten Wein trinkt.

WIEDERHOLUNG

A (p. 200)

1. Ich möchte eine Postkarte nach Österreich schicken.
2. Einmal hin und zurück nach Hamburg, bitte.
3. Ich möchte meine schweren Koffer als Reisegepäck schicken (aufgeben).
5. Wo ist eine Telefonzelle, bitte? Bitte, wo kann ich eine Telefonzelle finden?
6. Ich möchte eine Zahlkarte ausfüllen.

B (p. 200)

1. Bitte fragen Sie den Beamten, der dort steht.
2. Hier ist die Anzeige, die ich Ihnen zeigen wollte.
3. Wo ist der Fahrplan, den du gekauft hast?
4. Wie heißt die Ärztin, deren Namen ich vergessen habe?
5. Das ist die Tasche, die so schwer ist.

C (p. 200)

1. Das ist der Artikel, den ich las (gelesen habe).
2. Die Nummer ist besetzt. Bitte rufen Sie wieder (nochmals) in 15 Minuten an.
3. Gibt es hier eine Telefonzelle, von der ich anrufen kann?
4. Wer war der Mann (der Herr), mit dem ich sprach (gesprochen habe)?

KAPITEL 10

Dialog (translation) (p. 204)

You are at the police station in Cologne because someone stole all your important documents (passport, driver's license, airplane tickets, etc.). The policeman doesn't speak any English. But that doesn't matter, because you can understand his simple questions and you can answer in German. First you have to fill out a form—therefore, in "telegram style" (no sentences, just single words).

Of course, we don't talk just in cues (telegram style) but in sentences. Let's therefore repeat the conversation.

What's your name?	My name is Richard Cook.
Where do you live?	Presently I live in Cologne on the Rheinallee 27 with the Biebers.
What's your telephone number?	My number is 63-54-72.
When and where were you born?	I was born on July 20, 1969, in Columbus, Ohio, USA.
What is your citizenship?	I am an American.
What's your profession?	I am a druggist.
Do you know your passport number?	No, because they stole my passport.
What's your height?	I am 1 meter and 68 centimeter (5'7").
How much do you weigh?	I weigh 75 kilos (165 pounds).
What's the color of your hair?	Blond.
And what is the color of your eyes?	Blue-gray.
Do you have any distinguishing marks?	Yes, I have a scar over my right eye.

We want to know much more about you, but now you are no longer at the police station but at a party where you are talking with a guest. The guest seems to be very curious, because he is really quizzing you.

"Now then, Mr. Cook, how long have you already been in Cologne?"—"For two weeks."—"And what brings you to our city?"—"I attended a conference."—"What have you done with your free time?"—"They showed me most of the special sights of the city."—"Did you bring your wife along?"—"I am still single.   And you?"—"Oh, I have been married for 20 years."—"Do you have any children?"—"Yes, two daughters and a son."—"The oldest is an elementary school teacher, and the second one is a saleswoman in a children's store.   My son . . ."—"Excuse me, I have to talk briefly with Mrs. Kurz."

Unfortunately, Mrs. Kurz is also very curious, and so you are being quizzed some more.

"Have you already attended our opera?"—"Yes, last week I was invited by a colleague to (a performance of) the 'Freischütz.'"—"Did you like the opera?"—"Yes, but actually I am a fan of Wagnerian music."—"Then you have to go to Bayreuth."—"Others have told me that, too."—"But it is difficult to get tickets."—"They already got those for me at the travel agency."

"How long are you going to stay in Cologne?"—"Three more days. Excuse me, please, I just see Mr. Dietrich. I have to ask him something."—"Of course."

Interview Checklist (translation) (p. 207)

Now you don't have to answer any more questions. But we have an interview list that you may want to fill out. If you can't answer a question, check the list about professions and hobbies.

name/first name/address/(place of residence and street)/telephone number/ profession/marital status (single/married/divorced/widow/widower)/hobbies/ interests/trips undertaken/clubs/associations /favorite author/composer/singer/ movie star/film /book/city/sport/beverage/meal

What is your hobby? (*or:* What do you like to do in your free time?)
   I play tennis/golf/cards/basketball/soccer, etc.
   I play the piano/the guitar/cello/trumpet/flute/violin, etc. I swim/read/write/cook/
   hike/do crafts/surf/ski/watch TV/listen to the radio/collect stamps, coins/work in
   the yard/etc.

Aktivität A (p. 209)

1. spielt	3. diskutiert/spricht	5. liest	7. hört	9. spricht
2. repariert	4. arbeitet	6. sammelt	8. strickt/näht	10. isst

Aktivität B (sample responses) (p. 209)

1. Ich komme aus Amerika/Kanada/Kalifornien/Miami.
2. Ich bin in Ohio/New York/in der Schweiz/Springfield geboren.
3. Nein, ich bin ledig/Ich bin verwitwet/Ja, ich bin verheiratet.
4. Ich habe zwei Kinder/ein Kind/keine Kinder.
5. Ich arbeite im Garten/repariere mein Auto/spiele Basketball.
6. Ich gehe einmal im Monat/dreimal im Jahr/nie ins Kino.
7. Ich fahre nach Österreich/bleibe zu Hause/wandere in den Bergen/schreibe ein
   Buch/besuche Freunde.
8. Ich möchte Italien/Deutschland/die Schweiz besuchen.
9. Ich liebe meinen Beruf/verdiene gut/interessiere mich für meinen Beruf/finde ihn
   langweilig/ verdiene nicht genug/habe zu wenig Zeit für meine Familie.
10. vorsichtig/populär/nett/kompetent/jung/alt /konservativ
11. nett/attraktiv/scheu/reich/arm/pünktlich /freundlich/arm
12. sportlich/vorsichtig/schlank/klug/liberal/impulsiv

Aktivität C (p. 210)

1. Verkäufer	5. Drogist/Drogistin	8. Pilot
2. Mechaniker	6. Elektriker	9. Ärztin
3. Pfarrer (Pastor)	7. Bibliothekarin	10. Sekretärin
4. Krankenschwester		

GRAMMATIK

Übung A (p. 211)

1. Bald bekomme ich Post. (*or:* Bald werde ich Post bekommen.)
2. Schreibst du mir diese Woche? (*or:* Wirst du mir diese Woche schreiben?)
3. Wann wird sie arbeiten?
4. Er wird gute Karten kaufen.
5. Der Bus kommt in 15 Minuten. (*or:* Der Bus wird in 15 Minuten kommen.)

Übung B (p. 212)

1. wurde   2. wird   3. werden   4. wirst   5. ist . . . geworden

Übung C (p. 212)

1. ist . . . geworden	3. wurde	5. bekommen
2. Hast . . . bekommen	4. bekam	

Übung D (p. 213)

1. wird	3. sind . . . worden	5. sind . . . worden	7. ist . . . worden
2. wurde	4. wirst . . . werden	6. wurde	8. wird

Übung E (p. 214)

1. His book was translated into two languages.
2. The package has been (was) mailed yesterday.
3. The guest was being quizzed.
4. Mrs. Klein's passport has been (was) stolen.
5. Hamburg has been (was) destroyed by bombs during the war.
6. America was discovered by Columbus in 1492.
7. I hope (one hopes) that the film will be made.
8. The criminal has been seen (was seen) in Los Angeles.
9. The apartment is being cleaned once a week.
10. Where is the Volkswagen being manufactured?

Übung F (p. 215)

1. Man tanzt viel.
2. Man hat uns nie besucht.
3. Man hat mich oft gefragt.
4. Man interviewt die Frau.
5. Dort aß und trank man viel.
6. Man hat in dem Zimmer nicht geraucht.
7. Man stahl dem Lehrer das Auto.

Übung G (sample letters) (p. 219)

1. Liebe Klara,

wir möchten Dich gern für nächsten Freitag (17.3.) um halb sieben zum Abendessen einladen. Hoffentlich kannst Du kommen. Bitte rufe mich vor Mittwoch an.

Auf ein baldiges Wiedersehen.

Deine Brigitte

2. Sehr geehrter Herr Dr. Müller,

besten Dank für Ihre freundliche Einladung. Ich würde sehr gern das Wochenende mit Ihrer Familie verbringen, aber wir erwarten am selben Wochenende Besuch von unseren Verwandten aus Österreich.

Ich hoffe, dass ich Ihre Familie ein anderes Mal besuchen darf.

Mit freundlichen Grüßen

Ihr

3. Liebe Mutti, lieber Vati, (*or:* Liebe Kinder,)

das war eine nette Überraschung, als gestern Euer großes Paket ankam. Vielen Dank für Euer Weihnachtsgeschenk, das wir gut gebrauchen können. Die zwei großen Tischdecken mit den 12 Servietten passen gut zu unseren Möbeln im Esszimmer. Und der Toaster, den Ihr geschickt habt, kam auch zur richtigen Zeit, denn unser alter ist seit zwei Wochen kaputt. Wie habt Ihr das gewusst?

Vielen Dank und alles Liebe. Fröhliche Weihnachten!

WIEDERHOLUNG

A (p. 220)

1. e. 2. f. 3. a. 4. g. 5. b. 6. c. 7. h. 8. d.

B (p. 220)

Wochen/Wetter/geregnet/eingeladen/wohne/weit/Freunde/herzliche/Dein

Reference Grammar

DECLENSION OF PERSONAL PRONOUN

	Singular		Plural
ich	*I*	**wir**	*we*
du	*you* (familiar)	**ihr**	*you* (familiar)
er, sie, es	*he, she, it*	**sie**	*they*
Sie	*you* (formal)	**Sie**	*you* (formal)

	Singular				Plural			
Nominative	ich	du	er	sie	es	wir	ihr	sie	Sie
Accusative	mich	dich	ihn	sie	es	uns	euch	sie	Sie
Dative	mir	dir	ihm	ihr	ihm	uns	euch	ihnen	Ihnen

CONJUGATION OF *SEIN* AND *HABEN*

	Singular			Plural		
sein	ich **bin**	*I am*		wir **sind**	*we are*
	du **bist**	*you are*		ihr **seid**	*you are*
	er, sie, es **ist**	*he, she, it is*		Sie, sie **sind**	*you, they are*
haben	ich **habe**	*I have*		wir **haben**	*we have*
	du **hast**	*you have*		ihr **habt**	*you have*
	er, sie, es **hat**	*he, she, it has*		Sie, sie **haben**	*you, they have*

VERB ENDINGS IN PRESENT TENSE

		Singular	Plural
kaufen	*to buy*	ich kauf**e**	wir kauf**en**
		du kauf**st**	ihr kauf**t**
		er, sie, es kauf**t**	Sie, sie kauf**en**

DECLENSION OF DEFINITE AND INDEFINITE ARTICLES

	Masculine	Feminine	Neuter	Plural
Nominative	der	die	das	die
	ein	eine	ein	keine
Accusative	den	die	das	die
	einen	eine	ein	keine
Dative	dem	der	dem	den
	einem	einer	einem	keinen
Genitive	des	der	des	der
	eines	einer	eines	keiner

CONJUGATION OF MODAL AUXILIARIES

	dürfen	können	müssen	sollen	wollen	mögen	
ich	darf	kann	muss	soll	will	mag	möchte
du	darfst	kannst	musst	sollst	willst	magst	möchtest
er, sie, es	darf	kann	muss	soll	will	mag	möchte
wir	dürfen	können	müssen	sollen	wollen	mögen	möchten
ihr	dürft	könnt	müsst	sollt	wollt	mögt	möchtet
sie,Sie	dürfen	können	müssen	sollen	wollen	mögen	möchten

"STUDENTEN-TYPE" NOUNS

	Singular	Plural
Nominative	der Student	die Student**en**
Accusative	den Student**en**	die Student**en**
Dative	dem Student**en**	den Student**en**
Genitive	des Student**en**	der Student**en**

DECLENSION OF POSSESSIVE ADJECTIVE

	Singular		Plural	
	Masculine	*Neuter*	*Feminine*	*All genders*
Nominative	ein	ein	eine	keine
	mein	mein	meine	meine
	unser	unser	uns(e)re	uns(e)re
Accusative	einen	ein	eine	keine
	meinen	mein	meine	meine
	uns(e)ren	unser	uns(e)re	uns(e)re

Dative	einem	einem	einer	keinen
	meinem	meinem	meiner	meinen
	uns(e)rem	uns(e)rem	uns(e)rer	uns(e)ren
Genitive	eines	eines	einer	keiner
	meines	meines	meiner	meiner
	uns(e)res	uns(e)res	uns(e)rer	uns(e)rer

REFLEXIVE PRONOUNS

	Personal Pronoun		Reflexive Pronoun	
Nominative	**Accusative**	**Dative**	**Accusative**	**Dative**
ich	mich	mir	mich	mir
du	dich	dir	dich	dir
er	ihn	ihm		
sie	sie	ihr	sich	
es	es	ihm		
wir	uns		uns	
ihr	euch		euch	
sie	sie	ihnen	sich	
Sie	Sie	Ihnen		

ENDINGS OF DEFINITE ARTICLE

	Masculine	Neuter	Feminine and Plural
Nominative	-er	-es	-e
Accusative	-en		
Dative	-em		-en
			-er
Genitive	-es		

ADJECTIVE ENDINGS AFTER *DER*-WORDS OR *EIN*-WORDS

	Masculine	Feminine	Neuter	Plural
Nominative	(der)-**e**		(das)-**e**	
		-e		-en
	(ein)-**er**		(ein-**es**	
Accusative	-en	-e	(das)-**e**	-en
			(ein)-**es**	
Dative	-en	-en	-en	-en
Genitive	-en	-en	-en	-en

PRINCIPAL PARTS OF STRONG AND IRREGULAR VERGS

Infinitive	Present*	Past	Past Participle	Basic Meaning
abfahren	fährt ab	fuhr ab	ist abgefahren	to leave
abnehmen	nimmt ab	nahm ab	abgenommen	to decrease
anfangen	fängt an	fing an	angefangen	to begin
anhalten	hält an	hielt an	angehalten	to stop
ankommen		kam an	ist angekommen	to arrive
(sich) anziehen		zog an	angezogen	to attract; to dress
aufgeben	gibt auf	gab auf	aufgegeben	to assign, mail
aufstehen		stand auf	ist aufgestanden	to get up
aussteigen		stieg aus	ist ausgestiegen	to get off
befehlen	befiehlt	befahl	befohlen	to command
beginnen		begann	begonnen	to begin
behalten	behält	behielt	behalten	to keep
bekommen		bekam	bekommen	to receive
bekommen		bekam	bekommen	to receive
bitten		bat	gebeten	to request

PRINCIPAL PARTS OF STRONG AND IRREGULAR VERBS *(continued)*

Infinitive	Present	Past	Past Participle	Basic Meaning
bleiben		blieb	ist geblieben	to stay
bringen		brachte	gebracht	to bring
denken		dachte	gedacht	to think
dürfen	darf	durfte	gedurft	to allow
einladen	lädt ein	lud ein	eingeladen	to invite
empfehlen	empfiehlt	empfahl	empfohlen	to recommend
(sich) entscheiden		entschied	entschieden	to decide
erhalten	erhält	erhielt	erhalten	to receive
ersteigen		erstieg	erstiegen	to climb
essen	isst	aß	gegessen	to eat
fallen	fällt	fiel	ist gefallen	to fall
finden		fand	gefunden	to find
fliegen		flog	ist geflogen	to fly
frieren		fror	gefroren	to be cold
geben	gibt	gab	gegeben	to give
gefallen	gefällt	gefiel	gefallen	to please
gehen		ging	ist gegangen	to go
gelingen		gelang	ist gelungen	to succeed
genießen		genoss	genossen	to enjoy
geschehen	geschieht	geschah	ist geschehen	to happen
gewinnen		gewann	gewonnen	to win
haben	hat	hatte	gehabt	to have
halten	hält	hielt	gehalten	to hold
heißen		hieß	geheißen	to be called
helfen	hilft	half	geholfen	to help
kennen		kannte	gekannt	to know
klingen		klang	geklungen	to sound
kommen		kam	ist gekommen	to come
können	kann	konnte	gekonnt	to be able to
lassen	lässt	ließ	gelassen	to let, leave
laufen	läuft	lief	ist gelaufen	to go, run
leiden		litt	gelitten	to suffer
leihen		lieh	geliehen	to borrow
lesen	liest	las	gelesen	to read
liegen		lag	gelegen	to lie, to be located
lügen		log	gelogen	to tell a lie
messen	misst	maß	gemessen	to measure
mögen	mag	mochte	gemocht	to like to
müssen	muss	musste	gemusst	to have to
nehmen	nimmt	nahm	genommen	to take
nennen		nannte	genannt	to call, name
raten	rät	riet	geraten	to advise

*Only verbs with a vowel change in the third-person singular are listed.

PRINCIPAL PARTS OF STRONG AND IRREGULAR VERBS *(continued)*

Infinitive	Present*	Past	Past Participle	Basic Meaning
rennen		rannte	ist gerannt	to run
rufen		rief	gerufen	to call
scheinen		schien	hat *or* ist geschienen	to appear, shine
schlafen	schläft	schlief	geschlafen	to sleep
schreiben		schrieb	geschrieben	to write
schwimmen		schwamm	geschwommen	to swim
sehen	sieht	sah	gesehen	to see
sein	ist	war	ist gewesen	to be
singen		sang	gesungen	to sing
sitzen		saß	gesessen	to sit
sollen		sollte	gesollt	to be supposed to
spazierengehen		ging spazieren	ist spazierengegangen	to go for a walk
sprechen	spricht	sprach	gesprochen	to talk
stehen		stand	ist *or* hat gestanden	to stand
stehlen	stiehlt	stahl	gestohlen	to steal
steigen		stieg	ist gestiegen	to climb
sterben	stirbt	starb	ist gestorben	to die
tragen	trägt	trug	getragen	to carry, wear
treffen	trifft	traf	getroffen	to meet
trinken		trank	getrunken	to drink
tun		tat	getan	to do
umziehen		zog um	ist umgezogen	to move
(sich) unterhalten	unterhält	unterhielt	unterhalten	to converse
unterscheiden		unterschied	unterschieden	to distinguish
verbieten		verbot	verboten	to forbid
verbringen		verbrachte	verbracht	to spend time
verstehen		verstand	verstanden	to understand
vorlesen	liest vor	las vor	vorgelesen	to read aloud
vorschlagen	schlägt vor	schlug vor	vorgeschlagen	to suggest
(sich) waschen	wäscht	wusch	gewaschen	to wash
wehtun		tat weh	wehgetan	to hurt
werden	wird	wurde	ist geworden	to become
werfen	wirft	warf	geworfen	to throw
wissen	weiß	wusste	gewusst	to know
wollen	will	wollte	gewollt	to want to
ziehen		zog	gezogen	to pull

*Only verbs with a vowel change in the third-person singular are listed.

Wortschatz: Deutsch/Englisch

This vocabulary lists all words used in the text. Nouns are listed in the nominative singular and nominative plural. Only those cognates that require an article are listed. Strong verbs are entered according to the following model:

geben (i), a, e
[geben (gibt), gab, gegeben]

An asterisk (*) indicates that a verb is conjugated with **sein** as the auxiliary verb in the perfect tenses. The forms of irregular verbs are written out. Verbs with a separable prefix are listed with a dot between the prefix and the stem: **ab·fahren.**

The following abbreviations are used:

acc. = accusative	*adv.* = adverb	*f.* = feminine
dat. = dative	*fam.* = familiar	*sing.* = singular
adj. = adjective	*m.* = masculine	*pl.* = plural

A

der Abend, -e   evening
  am Abend, abends   in the evening
  heute abend   tonight
das Abendessen, –   dinner
aber   but
ab·fahren* (ä), u, a   to depart, to leave
  die Abfahrt, -en   departure
die Abfahrtshalle, -n   departure hall

ab·fliegen*, o, o   to fly off, to depart
der Abflug, ¨e   flight departure
ab·heben, o, o   to withdraw (money)
ab·holen   to pick up
ab·laufen* (ä), ie, au   to expire, to run out
das Abonnement, -s   subscription
die Abrechnung, -en   settlement (of accounts)

Note: **Wortschatz** = vocabulary (lit., "treasure of words")

254

ab·reisen* to leave, to depart
ab·schicken to send off, to mail
der Abschied, -e farewell, say good-bye
acht eight
das Achtel, – eighth (part)
achtunddreißigst- thirty-eighth
der Adler, – eagle
ähnlich similar
albern silly
der Alkohol alcohol
alle all, everyone
allein alone
alles everything
    Alles in Ordnung? Everything okay?
als as, when
alt, älter old, older
also therefore, well, so
der Amerikaner, – American, *m.*
die Amerikanerin, -nen American, *f.*
amerikanisch American
die Ampel, -n traffic light
an at, on, to, by
die Ananas pineapple
ander- other
andere others
an·fangen (ä), i, a to begin
angenehm pleasant
(sich) an·hören to listen to
an·kommen*, kam an, angekommen to
    arrive
der Anruf, -e telephone call
an·rufen, ie, u to call
an·schauen to look at
an·sehen (ie), a, e to look at, to view
    (sich) etwas ansehen to take a look at
(sich) anstecken to catch an illness
die Antwort, -en answer
antworten, *dat.* to answer
die Anzeige, -n advertisement, ad
sich an·ziehen, zog an, angezogen to get
    dressed
der Anzug, ⸚e suit
der Apfel, ⸚ apple
der Apfelsaft, ⸚e apple juice, cider
der Apfelstrudel, – apple strudel
der April April
arbeiten to work
der Architekt, -en architect, *m.*
sich ärgern to be annoyed

arm poor
der Artikel, – article
der Arzt, ⸚e physician, *m.*
die Ärztin, -nen physician, *f.*
das Aspirin aspirin
auch also, too
auf on, upon
    auf Kriegsfuß stehen to be in conflict
    with
    Auf Wiedersehen! Good-bye!
auf·hören to stop, to discontinue
auf·kommen*, (für), kam auf,
    aufgekommen to pay for, to com-
    pensate
auf·machen to open
aufregend exciting
auf·stehen*, stand auf, aufgestanden
    to get up, arise
der Auftrag, ⸚e order
auf·wachen to wake up
auf·wachsen* (ä), u, a to grow up
das Auge, -n eye
die Augenfarbe, -n eye color
der Augenblick, -e moment
der August August
aus from, out of, by
der Ausflug, ⸚e outing, trip
aus·fragen to quiz, to question
aus·führen to carry out, to implement
aus·füllen to fill out (a form)
der Ausgang, ⸚e exit
ausgezeichnet excellent
die Auskunft, ⸚e information
das Ausland foreign country
    im Ausland abroad
der Ausländer, – foreigner, *m.*
die Ausländerin, -nen foreigner, *f.*
ausländisch foreign
aus·sehen (ie), a, e to look like, to
    appear
aus·steigen*, ie, ie to get off, to disem-
    bark
die Ausstellung, -en exhibition
aus·suchen to choose, to select
die Auster, -n oyster
ausverkauft sold out
ausziehen*, zog aus, ausgezogen to
    move out
(sich) aus·ziehen to undress

das **Auto**, -s car
die **Autobahn**, -nen superhighway,
  interstate
der **Autoschlüssel**, – car key

B

das **Bad**, ̈er bath
  das **Badehandtuch**, ̈er bath towel
die **Bahn**, -nen streetcar, train
der **Bahnhof**, ̈e train station
der **Bahnsteig**, -e platform (train station)
bald soon
der **Balkon**, -e balcony
der **Ball**, ̈e ball
die **Banane**, -n banana
die **Bank**, -en bank
basteln to tinker, to do crafts
der **Baum**, ̈e tree
Bayreuth city in Bavaria, site of Wagner
  festivals
der **Beamte**, -n civil servant, *m.*
die **Beamtin**, -nen civil servant, *f.*
beantworten to answer
sich **bedanken (für)** to thank, to say
  thanks
bedauern to regret
sich **beeilen** to hurry
sich **befinden**, a, u to be located, to be
  situated
die **Beförderung**, -en promotion
die **Begrüßung**, -en greeting
behandeln to treat
bei with, at near
die **Beilage**, -n side dish, garnishing
das **Beispiel**, -e example
  zum Beispiel (z.B.) for example
beißen, i, i to bite
bei·tragen, u, a to contribute
bekannt known
benutzen to use
das **Benzin** gasoline
bequem comfortable
der **Berg**, -e mountain
die **Berichterstattung**, -en reporting
der **Beruf**, -e occupation, profession
berühmt famous
beschäftigt busy, occupied
der **Beschwerdebrief**, -e letter of complaint

sich **beschweren** to complain
besetzt occupied, full
besonders special
best- best
besteigen, ie, ie to climb
bestellen to order
bestimmt certain(ly)
besuchen to visit
die **Betriebsferien** *pl.* company vacation
das **Bett**, -en bed
bevor before
sich **bewerben um** to apply for
die **Bibliothek**, -en library
die **Bibliothekarin**, -nen librarian, *f.*
das **Bier**, -e beer
die **Bierwurst** beer sausage
billig cheap
die **Billion**, -en trillion
die **Biologie** biology
die **Biologin**, -nen biologist, *f.*
die **Birne**, -n pear
bis as far as, up to
  bis bald till then
  bis später until later
  von . . . bis from . . . to
bisschen a little bit
bitte please
  Bitte schön. You're welcome.
blass pale
blau blue
bleiben*, ie, ie to stay, to remain
der **Blindarm**, -e appendix
der **Blumenkohl** cauliflower
der **Blutdruck** blood pressure
die **Blutwurst** blood sausage
die **Bohne**, -n beans
die **Bombe**, -n bomb
das **Boot**, -e boat
die **Bouillon** bouillon, broth
der **Braten**, – roast
der **Schweinebraten**, – pork roast
brauchen to need
braun brown
brechen (i) a, o to break
brennen, brannte, gebrannt to burn
der **Brief**, -e letter
die **Briefmarke**, -n postage stamp
bringen, brachte, gebracht to bring
das **Brot**, -e bread
die **Brücke**, -n bridge

der Bruder, - brother
das Buch, -er book
die Bundesrepublik Deutschland (BRD)
   The Federal Republic of Germany
das Büro, -s office
der Bus, -se bus
   die Bushaltestelle, -n bus stop
die Butter butter

C

charmant charming
der Chef, -s boss, supervisor, *m.*
die Chefin, -nen boss, supervisor, *f.*
das Cola, -s coke
der Chemiker, – chemist, *m.*
das Cola, -s cola
der Computer, – computer
die Cremeschnitte, -n cream-filled cake

D

da there
die Dame, -n lady
damit so that
dämpfen to steam (cooking)
der Dank thanks
   Danke, gut. Fine, thank you.
   Danke (schön)! Thanks! Thank you!
   Nichts zu danken. Don't mention it.
   Vielen Dank! Thanks a lot!
danken, *dat.* to thank
das Dankschreiben, – thank-you note
dann then
das the, that, this
dass that
dasselbe the same
die Debatte, -n debate
die Demokratie, -n democracy
deshalb therefore, that's why
deutsch German
(das) Deutsch German
der/die Deutsche, -n German, *m., f.*
(das) Deutschland Germany
deutschsprachig German-speaking
der Dezember December
der Dialekt, -e dialect
dich you, *fam. acc.*
der Dienstag, -e Tuesday
diesmal this time

direkt direct
diskutieren to discuss
dir to you, *fam., sing. dat.*
der Dokumentarfilm, -e documentary
der Donnerstag, -e Thursday
doppelt double
das Doppelzimmer, – double room
dort there
   dort drüben over there
   dorthin to that place
drei three
dreimal three times
dreißig thirty
dreiundfünfzigst- fifty-third
dreiundsechzig sixty-three
dreizehnt- thirteenth
dritt- third
das Drittel one-third
der Drogist, -en druggist, *m.*
drücken to push, press
du you, *fam., sing.*
duften to smell pleasantly
dumm dumb
durch through
(gut) durchgebraten well done (cooked)
dürfen (darf) to be allowed (to), may
der Durst thirst
Haben Sie Durst? Are you thirsty?
die Dusche, -n shower
sich duschen to take a shower

E

die Ecke, -n corner
echt genuine
das Ei, die Eier egg
   Russische Eier deviled eggs
eigentlich actually
ein(e) a, one
das Einbettzimmer, – single room
die Energie, -n energy
einfach simple
eingebildet arrogant
ein halb one-half
einig in agreement
sich einig sein to be in agreement
der Einkauf, -e purchase
ein·kaufen to shop
ein·laden (ä), u, a to invite
die Einladung, -en invitation

einmal   once
ein·setzen   to implement
eins   one
einseitig   one-sided
ein·steigen*, ie, ie   to board, to get on
einunddreißig   thirty-one
einundzwanzig   twenty-one
einverstanden   agreed
das Einzelzimmer, –   single room
ein·ziehen*, zog ein, eingezogen   to
   move in
das Eis   ice cream
das Eisbein   pig's knuckle
der Eistee, -s   ice tea
elf   eleven
die Eltern   parents
empfehlen (ie), a, o   to recommend
die Energie, -n   energy
der Engländer, –   Englishman
die Engländerin, -nen   Englishwoman
der Enkel, –   grandson
die Enkelin, -nen   granddaughter
entdecken   to discover
entschuldigen   to excuse
   Entschuldigen Sie bitte!   Excuse me,
      please!
der Entschuldigungsbrief, -e   letter of
   apology
entspannt   relaxed
die Entzündung, -en   inflammation
er   he
die Erbse, -n   pea
die Erdbeere, -n   strawberry
der Erfolg, -e   success
erfolgreich   successful
sich erinnern   to remember
sich erkälten   to catch a cold
die Erkältung, -en   cold
erklären   to explain
erlauben   to permit, to allow
erleben   to experience
erledigen   to finish, to settle
erreichen   to reach, contact
erscheinen*, ie, ie   to appear, to be published
erst-   first
   erst (um)   not until
der Erwachsene, -n   adult
erwarten   to expect
erzählen   to tell, to narrate
es   it

das Essen   meal
essen (isst), aß, gegessen   to eat
etwa   approximately
der Euro, -s   euro (currency)
das Europa   Europe

F

fahren* (ä), u, a   to drive, to go
die Fahrkarte, -n   ticket (for travel)
der Fahrplan, ¨e   schedule, timetable
das Fahrrad, ¨er   bicycle
der Fahrschein, -e   ticket
die Fahrt, -en   trip, journey
fallen* (ä), fiel, gefallen   to fall
falsch   false, wrong
die Familie, -n   family
der Familienname, -n   last name
der Familienstand   marital status
die Farbe, -n   color
der Farbfernseher, –   color television set
das Faschierte   minced meat, hamburger
fast   almost
faul   lazy
der Februar   February
fehlen   to miss, to lack
   Was fehlt Ihnen?   What's wrong with
      you?
feiern   to celebrate
das Fenster, –   window
die Ferien   vacation
fern·sehen (ie), a, e   to watch television
das Fernsehen   television
der Fernseher, –   TV set
fett   fat, fatty
das Fieber   fever
der Fiebermesser, –   thermometer
der Filmschauspieler, –   movie actor
die Filmschauspielerin, -nen   movie
   actress
das Finanzamt, ¨er   internal revenue
   office
finden, a, u   to find
die Firma, die Firmen   firm, company
der Fisch, -e   fish
die Flasche, -n   bottle
das Fleisch   meat
   die Fleischpastete, -n   meat-filled pastry
fleißig   diligent, hardworking
fliegen,* o, o   to fly
die Flöte, -n   flute

der **Flug**, ⁝e   flight (airline)
der **Fluggast**, ⁝e   airline passenger
der **Flughafen**, ⁝   airport
die **Flugkarte**, -n   airplane ticket
das **Flugpersonal**   flight personnel
das **Flugzeug**, -e   airplane
folgen, *dat.*   to follow
das **Foto**, -s   photo, picture
die **Frage**, -n   question
    eine **Frage stellen**   to ask a question
fragen   to ask
der **Franken**,–   Swiss Franc
frankieren   to put on postage
die **Frau**, -en   woman
das **Fräulein**   Miss
frei   free
die **Freiheit**   freedom
„**Der Freischütz**"   opera by K. M. von
    Weber
der **Freitag**, -e   Friday
die **Freizeit**   leisure time, free time
die **Freude**, -n   joy
    Freude machen, *dat.*   to bring (give) joy
sich **freuen**   to enjoy, to be glad
sich **freuen auf**   to look forward
    es **freut mich**   My pleasure.
der **Freund**, -e   friend
die **Freundin**, -nen   friend, *f.*
freundlich   friendly
die **Frikadelle**, -n   croquettes
frisch   fresh
frischgemäht   freshly mowed
der **Friseur**, -e   hairdresser, *m.*
die **Friseuse**, Friseusinnen   hairdresser, *f.*
die **Frittatensuppe**, -n   broth with pan
    cake strips
froh   glad, happy
die **Frucht**, ⁝e   fruit
das **Fruchteis**   sherbet, fruit ice cream
früh   early
der **Frühling**   spring
die **Frühlingssuppe**, -n   spring vegetable
    soup
das **Frühstück**   breakfast
frühstücken   to have breakfast
der **Frühstückssaal**, ⁝e   breakfast room
(sich) **fühlen**   feel
der **Führerschein**, -e   driver's license
fünf   five
fünft-   fifth
fünfzehn   fifteen

fünfzig   fifty
für   for
(sich) **fürchten**   to be afraid, to fear
furchtbar   terrible
der **Fußball**, ⁝e   football, soccer
das **Fußballspiel**, -e   soccer (game)

G

die **Gabel**, -n   fork
gähnen   to yawn
ganz   quite, completely
gar nicht   not at all
der **Garten**, ⁝   garden
die **Gartenarbeit**, -en   gardening
der **Gast**, ⁝e   guest
der **Gastgarten**, ⁝   outdoor sitting area of
    a restaurant
die **Gastgeberin**, -nen   hostess
das **Gasthaus**, ⁝er   inn
der **Gasthof**, ⁝e   inn, hotel
die **Gaststätte**, -n   restaurant
gebacken   baked
geben (i), a, e   to give
    es **gibt**   there is, there are
geboren   born
gebraten   roasted
der **Geburtstag**, -e   birthday
gedämpft   steamed
gefallen (ä), gefiel, gefallen, *dat.*   to like,
    to please
gefüllt   filled
gegen   against
die **Gegend**, -en   area
gegrillt   grilled
gehen*, ging, gegangen   to go
    Das **geht nicht.**   That won't do.
    Es **geht los**   It starts, it begins
    Es **wird gehen.**   It will work out. I can
    manage.
gehören, *dat.*   to belong
die **Geige**, -n   violin
gekocht   cooked
das **Geld**, -er   money
gelten (i), a, o   to be valid
das **Gemüse**, –   vegetable
gemütlich   cozy, comfortable
genug   enough, sufficient
geöffnet   open
das **Gepäck**   luggage
gerade   just, at that moment

geradeaus   straight ahead
geräuchert   smoked
gern + *verb*   to like
  Gern geschehen.   You are welcome.
  Don't mention it.
das Geschäft, -e   store
  der Geschäftsbrief, -e   business letter
  die Geschäftsfrau, -en   businesswoman
  der Geschäftsmann   businessman
  die Geschäftsleute, *pl.*   businesspeople
geschehen* (ie), a, e   to happen
das Geschenk, -e   present
die Geschichte, -n   story
geschieden   divorced
geschlossen   closed
geschmort   braised
die Geschwister   brothers and sisters,
  siblings
das Gespräch, -e   conversation
der Gespritzte, -n   wine with mineral
  water
gestern   yesterday
gestrig   yesterday's
gesund   healthy
die Gesundheit   health
das Getränk, -e   beverage
das Gewicht, -er   weight
gewinnen, a, o   win
der Gipfel, –   peak, summit
die Gitarre, -n   guitar
das Glas, -̈er   glass
glauben, *dat.*   to believe
gleich   same, equal, right away
glücklich   happy
das Golf   golf
der Grad, -e   degree
das Gras, -̈er   grass
die Grießnockerlsuppe, -n   cream of
  wheat dumpling soup
Grindlwald   town in Switzerland
die Grippe, -n   flu
groß   big, large, tall, high
die Größe, -n   size, height
grün   green
die Gruppe, -n   group
der Gruß, -̈e   greetings
  Grüß Gott!   Good day! (southern
  German and Austrian greeting)
das Gulasch   goulash
gültig   valid
die Gurke, -n   cucumber

gut   good
  Guten Abend!   Good evening!
  Guten Morgen!   Good morning!
  Guten Tag!   Hello! Good day!
  Gute Nacht!   Good night!

H

das Haar, -e   hair
  die Haarfarbe, -n   hair color
haben, hatte, gehabt   to have
der Hackbraten, –   meatloaf
halb   half
  halb durchgebraten   medium well
die Hälfte   half
die Halle, -n   hall
der Hals, -̈e   throat
halten (ä), ie, a   to stop
halten von, (hält) ie, a   to think of
häufig   frequently
das Hauptgericht, -e   main meal
der Hauptplatz, -̈e   main square
das Haus, -̈er   house
  nach Hause   (to, toward) home
  zu Hause   at home
der Hausarzt, -̈e   family doctor
die Hausfrau, -en   housewife, home-
  maker
die Hausnummer, -n   house number
heiraten   to marry
heiß   hot
heißen, ie, ei   to be called
  Wie heißen Sie?   What's your name?
helfen, (i), a, o, *dat.*   to help
heraus·kommen*, kam heraus,
  herausgekommen   to come out
der Herbst, -e   autumn, fall
der Hering, -e   herring
  Räucherhering, -e   smoked herring
der Herr, -en   gentleman
herrlich   wonderful
her·stellen   to manufacture
herzlich   cordial
heute   today
  heute abend   tonight
  heute morgen   this morning
  heute nachmittag   this afternoon
hier   here
hier·bleiben*, ie, ie   to remain, to stay
hin   (to) there
hinauf   up, upward

die **Hin- und Rückfahrt, -en** round trip
der **Hinflug, ⸚e** flight (to)
hin·kommen*, kam hin, hingekommen
  to get there
hin und zurück back and forth
hinter behind
hoch, höher high
hochachtungsvoll respectfully
hoffen to hope
hoffentlich it is hoped
höflich polite
hören to hear
das **Hotel, -s** hotel
der **Hotelportier, -s** hotel clerk, con-
  cierge, *m.*
hübsch pretty
das **Huhn, ⸚er (Hühnchen)** chicken
der **Hummer** lobster
der **Humor** humor
der **Hund, -e** dog
hundert hundred
hundertmal a hundred times
der **Hundertmarkschein, -e** hundred-
  mark bill
das **Hundertstel** hundredth
der **Hunger** hunger
hungrig hungry
der **Hustensaft, ⸚e** cough syrup

I

ich I
ihm (to) him, *dat.*
ihn him, it, *acc.*
ihnen them, *dat.*
Ihnen you, *formal, sing./pl.*
ihr her, *dat.*
im, in dem in the
immer always
impfen to immunize, to vaccinate
in in, into, to
die **Information, -en** information
(sich) **informieren** to inform
der **Ingenieur,-e** engineer, *m.*
der **Inhalt, -e** content
innen inside
der **Installateur, -e** plumber, *m.*
(sich) **interessieren für** to be interested
  in
(das) **Italien** Italy
interessant interesting

J

ja yes
die **Jacke, -n** jacket
das **Jahr, -e** year
das **Jahrhundert, -e** century
der **Januar** January
die **Jausenstation, -en** snack bar
  (in Austria)
jeder (jede, jedes) each
jetzt now
der **Job, -s** job
der **Journalist, -en** journalist, *m.*
die **Journalistin, -nen** journalist, *f.*
die **Jugendherberge, -n** youth hostel
der **Juli** July
jung young
der **Junge, -n** boy
der **Juni** June

K

der **Kaffee** coffee
das **Kaffeehaus, ⸚er** coffeehouse
der **Kaiserschmarren, –** shredded pan-
  cake filled with marmalade and cov-
  ered with sugar
der **Kalender, –** calendar
die **Kalorie, -n** calorie
kalt cold
(sich) **kämmen** to comb
der **Kanadier, –** Canadian, *m.*
die **Kanadierin, -nen** Canadian, *f.*
der **Kanton, -e** canton, (of Switzerland)
die **Karotte, -n** carrots
die **Karte, -n** card
die **Kartoffel, -n** potatoes
  die **Bratkartoffeln** hash browns
  geröstete Kartoffeln fried potatoes
  Kartoffelbrei mashed potatoes
  Salzkartoffeln peeled, boiled potatoes
der **Käse, –** cheese
  der **Käsekuchen, –** cheese cake
die **Kasseler Rippen,** *pl.* smoked pork
der **Katholik, -en** Catholic, *m.*
die **Katholikin, -nen** Catholic, *f.*
katholisch Catholic, *adj.*
die **Katze, -n** cat
kaufen to buy
der **Kaufhof** German department store
  chain

die **Kaufleute**, *pl.* businesspeople
der **Kaufmann** businessman
der **Kellner**, – waiter
die **Kellnerin**, -nen waitress
kein no, not a
kennen, kannte, gekannt to become
acquainted with, to know
kennen·lernen to meet, to get
acquainted
das **Kennzeichen**, – mark, emblem
das **Kilo**, -s kilogram
das **Kilogramm**, -e kilogram
der **Kilometer**, – kilometer
das **Kind**, -er child
das **Kino**, -s movie
die **Kirche**, -n church
die **Kirsche**, -n cherry
das **Klavier**, -e piano
das **Kleid**, -er dress
klein small, little
das **Kleingeld** change (money)
klingeln to ring (a bell)
klopfen to knock
der **Klub**, -s club
klug smart
der **Knödel**, – dumpling
kochen to cook
der **Koffer**, – suitcase
der **Kohl** cabbage
der **Rotkohl** red cabbage
der **Kollege**, -n colleague, *m.*
die **Kollegin**, -nen colleague, *f.*
kommen*, kam, gekommen to come
der **Komponist**, -en composer
das **Kompott** stewed fruit
die **Konferenz**, -en conference
können, konnte, gekonnt can, be able
to
die **Königinsuppe**, -n beef, sour cream,
and almond soup
das **Konzert**, -e concert
die **Kopfschmerzen**, *pl.* headache
korrespondieren to write letters, correspond
kosten to cost
die **Krabbe**, -n shrimp
die **Kraftbrühe**, -n beef consommé
kräftig strong
krank sick, ill
das **Krankenhaus**, ¨er hospital
der **Krankenpfleger**, — nurse, *m.*

die **Krankenschwester**, -n nurse, *f.*
der **Krebs** cancer
der **Krimi**, -s detective story
die **Küche**, -n kitchen
der **Kuchen**, – cake
kühl cool
der **Kunde**, -n customer
die **Kunst**, ¨e art
der **Künstler**, – artist, *m.*
die **Künstlerin**, -nen artist, *f.*
der **Kürbis**, -se pumpkin
küssen to kiss
kurz short

L

lachen to laugh
die **Lampe**, -n lamp
landen to land
die **Landezeit**, -en arrival time, landing
time
lang long
langsam slow
langweilig boring
(sich) **lassen (lässt), ie, a** to let, to permit
laufen* (ä), ie, au to run
laut loud
leben to live
die **Leber** liver
die **Leberknödelsuppe**, -n
liver-dumpling soup
ledig single
lehren to teach, to instruct
der **Lehrer**, – teacher, *m.*
die **Lehrerin**, -nen teacher, *f.*
leicht light, easy
leider unfortunately
leid·tun, tat leid, leidgetan, *dat.* to be
sorry
leise quiet, soft(ly)
lernen to learn
lesen (ie), a, e to read
letzt- last
die **Leute** people
lieber dear
liegen, a, e to lie, to be located
Es liegt uns viel daran. We are very
much concerned.
der **Liegewagen**, – train compartment
with makeshift beds
die **Limonade**, -n lemonade

links left
die Linsensuppe, -n lentil soup
die Liste, -n list
der Liter, – liter
lokal local
der Löffel, – spoon
die Luft, ⸚e air
der Lufthansaflug, ⸚e Lufthansa flight
die Lungenentzündung, -en pneumonia

M

machen to make, to do
  Das macht nichts. That doesn't
matter.
das Mädchen, – girl
mähen to mow
der Mai May
der Mais corn, maize
man one, you, people
der Manager, -s manager
die Managerin, -nen manager, *f.*
manchmal sometimes
die Mandeln tonsils
die Manieren, *pl.* manners
der Mann, ⸚er man
der Mantel, ⸚ coat
die Marke, -n (Briefmarke) stamp
der Marktplatz, ⸚e marketplace
die Marmelade, -n marmalade
der März March
der Maßstab, ⸚e scale
das Medikament, -e medicine
die Medizin medicine
der Meerrettich horseradish
mehr more
mein my
die Meinung, -en opinion
meistens mostly
die Melone, -n melon
der Mensch, -en human being, person
das Menü, -s special of the day
das Messer, – knife
mich me
mieten to rent
der Mietvertrag, ⸚e rental agreement,
lease
die Milch milk
die Milchbar, -s dairy bar
die Milliarde, -n billion
die Million, -en million

das Mineralwasser, – mineral water
die Minute, -n minute
mir to me
mit·bringen, brachte mit, mitgebracht
  to bring along
mit·fahren* (ä), u, a to drive along, to
come along
mit·kommen*, kam mit, mitgekommen
  to come along
mit·nehmen (nimmt mit), nahm mit,
  mitgenommen to take long
mit·spielen to play (with), to participate
der Mittag, -e noon
  am Mittag, mittags at noon, midday
das Mittagessen, – lunch
der Mittelpunkt, -e center (of attention)
die Mitternacht, – midnight
der Mittwoch, -e Wednesday
möchten would like to
mögen (mag), mochte, gemocht to like to
möglich possible
der Monat, -e month
der Montag, -e Monday
morgen tomorrow
  Guten Morgen! Good morning!
  morgens in the morning
der Motor, -e motor
das Motorrad, ⸚er motorcycle
müde tired
der Mund, ⸚er mouth
die Münze, -n coin
das Museum, die Museen museum
die Musik music
der Musiker, – musician
müssen, musste, gemusst must, to
have to
die Mutter, ⸚ mother

N

nach to, after
der Nachbar, -n neighbor, *m.*
die Nachbarin, -nen neighbor, *f.*
der Nachmittag, -e afternoon
  am Nachmittag in the afternoon
die Nachnahme, -n cash on delivery
(C.O.D.)
der Nachname, -n last name
die Nachricht, -en news
das Nachrichtenmagazin, -e newsmagazine

nach•schauen to look up, to inquire,
  to check
**nach•schlagen (ä), schlug nach,
  nachgeschlagen** to look up
nach•sehen (ie), a, e to look (up),
  to inquire, to check out
die Nachspeise, -n dessert
nächst- next
die Nacht, ̈e night
  Gute Nacht! Good night.
nah(e) near
nähen to sew
der Name, -n name
die Narbe, -n scar
nass wet
der Nationalfeiertag, -e national holiday
die Natur nature
natürlich naturally
das Naturschnitzel, – unbreaded cutlet
die Nazizeit Nazi period in Germany
  (1933–1945)
nebelig foggy
neben next
nehmen (nimmt), nahm, genommen to
  take
nett nice
neu new
neugierig curious, nosy
(das) Neujahr New Year's Day
nicht not
  nicht mehr no more, no longer
  Nicht wahr? Isn't it true?
der Nichtraucher, – nonsmoker
nichts nothing
nie never
noch still
nochmals once more
  Noch einmal, bitte! Again, please!
  noch mehr even more
nötig necessary
der November November
die Nudel, -n noodles
null zero
das Nummernschild, -er license plate
nur only

O

ob whether
oben top, above

der Ober, – waiter (head)
das Obst fruit
die Obsttorte, -n fruit tart
obwohl although
oder or
der Ofen, ̈ oven, range
offen open
öffnen to open
oft often
ohne without
das Ohr, -en ear
der Oktober October
das Öl, -e oil
der Onkel, – uncle
die Oper, -n opera
operieren to operate
die Opernübertragung, -en opera
  broadcast
die Orange, -n orange
der Orangensaft, ̈e orange juice
der Ort, -e place
der Osten East
(das) Österreich Austria
der Österreicher, – Austrian, *m.*
die Österreicherin, -nen Austrian, *f.*

P

(ein) paar a few
packen to pack
das Paket, -e parcel, package
die Panne, -n breakdown (car)
die Papiere, *pl.* documents
der Park, -s park
der Parkplatz, ̈e parking place
der Partner, – partner
die Party, -s party
der Pass, ̈sse passport
passen + *dat.* to fit, to suit well
passend suitable, matching
die Passnummer, -n passport number
der Pastor, -en pastor, minister
der Patient, -en patient
peinlich embarrassing
die Pension, -en boarding house
der Pfarrer pastor
der Pfeffer pepper
der Pfennig, -e penny
der Pfirsich, -e peach
die Pflaume, -n plum

pflegen to take care of, to nurse
das Pfund, -e pound
der Physiker, – physicist
die Pille, -n pill
der Pilot, -en pilot
der Pilz, -e mushroom
der Platz, ⁻e place, seat, spot, public square
der Politiker, – politician
politisch political
die Polizei police force
der Polizist, -en police officer, *m.*
die Polizistin, -nen police officer, *f.*
der Portier, -s portier, desk clerk (hotel)
das Porto postage
die Post post office, mail
  das Postamt, ⁻er post office
der Postbeamte, -n postal worker
die Postkarte, -n postcard
das Postsparbuch, ⁻er postal savings book
predigen to preach
der Preis, -e price
preiswert low-priced
die Presse press, newspaper(s)
die Pressefreiheit freedom of the press
die Privatwirtschaft private industry
der Professor, -en professor, *m.*
die Professorin, -nen professor, *f.*
das Programm, -e program
protestantisch Protestant, *adj.*
die Prüfung, -en test, exam
der Psychologe, -n psychologist
der Pullover, – pullover
pünktlich punctual
putzen to clean
(sich) die Zähne putzen to clean, to brush one's teeth

Q

die Qualität, -en quality
das Quartier, -e quarters, room

R

das Radfahren bicycling
das Radio, -s radio
das Radischen, – radish
der Rasen, – lawn
(sich) rasieren to shave
die Rast rest, break

die Raststätte, -n restaurant (on the Autobahn)
rauchen to smoke
raus·müssen to get out, to have to leave
rechnen to calculate, to figure
die Rechnung, -en bill, invoice
das Recht, -e right
recht, *adv.* really, quite
  recht gut quite well
rechts right (direction)
der Rechtsanwalt, ⁻e lawyer
der Regen rain
  der saure Regen acid rain
der Regenschirm, -e umbrella
regnen to rain
reich rich
rein pure
der Reis rice
die Reise, -n trip
das Reisebüro, -s travel agency
das Reisegepäck baggage, luggage
reisen to travel
der Reisende, -n traveler
die Reklame, -n advertisement
die Renovierung, -en renovation
reparieren to repair
repräsentieren to represent
reservieren to reserve
das Restaurant, -s restaurant
das Rezept, -e prescription
der Richter, – judge
das Rippensteak, -s rib steak
roh rare (meat)
die Rolltreppe, -n escalator
der Roman, -e novel
der Rosenbusch, ⁻e rosebush
der Rosenkohl brussels sprouts
rot red
die Roulade, -n rolled, filled, and braised thin slice of beef
der Rucksack, ⁻e knapsack
rufen, ie, u to call
der Ruhetag, -e day off

S

die Sache, -n matter, thing
die Sachertorte, -n Viennese chocolate cake
sachlich factual

sagen to say
die Sahne whipped cream
der Salat, -e salad
das Salz salt
sammeln to collect
der Samstag, -e Saturday
der Sänger, – singer
der Satz, ¨e sentence
sauber clean
schade too bad
schaffen, schuf, geschaffen to make, accomplish, create
der Schaffner, – conductor, *m.*
die Schaffnerin, -nen conductor, *f.*
der Schalter, – ticket window
scharf sharp
schattig shady
die Scheckkarte, -n credit card
scheinen, ie, ie to seem, to shine
scheu shy
schicken to send, to mail
schi•fahren* (ä), u, a to ski
schi•laufen* (äu), ie, au to ski
das Schild, -er sign
schimpfen to scold, complain
der Schinken ham
der Schirm, -e umbrella
schlafen (ä), ie, a to sleep
der Schlag whipped cream (Austrian)
schlank slender
schlecht bad
schließen, schloss, geschlossen to close, to lock
schlimm bad
der Schlüssel, – key
schmecken, *dat.* to taste
der Schmerz, -en pain, ache
schmutzig dirty
der Schnee snow
schneien to snow
schnell fast, quick
der Schnellimbiss snack bar
der Schnellzug, ¨e express train
das Schnitzel, – cutlet
schon already
schön beautiful
    Wie schön! How nice!
schreiben, ie, ie to write
der Schuh, -e shoe
    die Schuhgröße, -n shoe size

die Schule, -n school
schussen to ski straight downhill
die Schwarzwälderkirschtorte Black Forest cherry cake (chocolate cake with black cherries and whipped cream)
schwarzweiß black and white
Schweden Sweden
der Schweinebraten, – pork roast
die Schweiz Switzerland
der Schweizer, -n Swiss, *m.*
die Schweizerin, -nen Swiss, *f.*
schwellen*, o, o to swell
schwer heavy, difficult
die Schwester, Schwester, -n sister
schwierig difficult
schwimmen, a, o to swim
schwindelig dizzy
sechs six
sechsundzwanzig twenty-six
der See, -n lake
sehen (ie), a, e to see
die Sehenswürdigkeit, -en site, point of interest
sehr very (much)
sein* (ist), war, gewesen to be
sein, *pron.* his
seit since
die Seite, -n page (in a book)
der Sekretär, -e secretary, *m.*
die Sekretärin, -nen secretary, *f.*
selbst (selber) self
das Selbstbiographische autobiographical matter
selten seldom
das Seminar, -e seminar
senden to send
die Sendung, -en broadcast
der September, – September
sicher safe, sure, for sure,
sie she, they
Sie you, *normal, sing./pl.*
sieben seven
siebzehn seventeen
Silvester New Year's Eve
sitzen, saß, gesessen to sit
sobald as soon as
das Sofa, -s sofa
sofort immediately
der Sohn, ¨e son

solange as long as
der Soldat, -en soldier
sollen ought (to), to be supposed (to)
der Sommer, – summer
die Sondermarke, -n commemorative stamp
sondern but on the contrary
die Sonderstellung, -en special place, position
der Sonnabend, -e Saturday
der Sonntag, -e Sunday
sparen to save
der Spargel asparagus
    die Spargelspitzen, *pl.* asparagus tips
der Spaß, ¨sse fun
spät late
spazieren·gehen*, ging spazieren, spazierengegangen to take a walk
die Speise, -n food
die Sperrstunde, -n closing hour, curfew
das Spiel, -e game
spielen to play
    Das spielt keine Rolle. That doesn't make any difference.
der Speck bacon
der Spinat spinach
der Sport sport
der Sportler, – sportsman
die Sportlerin, -nen sportswoman
sportlich athletic
die Sportübertragung, -en sports broadcast
der Sportwagen, - sports car
die Sprache, -n language
sprechen (i), a, o to speak
der Sprecher, – speaker, announcer
die Sprechstunde, -n office hour
die Sprechstundenhilfe, -n receptionist (for a physician)
springen*, a, u to jump
die Staatsangehörigkeit citizenship
die Stadt, ¨e city
    der Stadtplan, ¨e city map
stehen*, stand, gestanden to stand
stehen·bleiben*, ie, ie to stop, to halt
stehlen (ie), a, o to steal
die Stellung, -en position
sterben* (i), a, o to die
die Steuer, -n tax

die Steuerabrechnung, -en tax return
das Stichwort, ¨er key word, cue
der Stil, -e style
die Stimme, -n voice
stimmen to be correct
der Stock, die Stockwerke floor, story
    im 1. (ersten) Stock on the second floor
stören to disturb
die Straße, -n street
    die Straßenbahn, -en streetcar
    die Straßenbahnhaltestelle, -n streetcar stop
stricken to knit
das Stück, -e piece, slice
der Student, -en student, *m.*
das Studentenheim,-e dormitory
die Studentin, -nen student, *f.*
studieren to study
der Stuhl, ¨e chair
die Stunde, -n hour
stündlich hourly
suchen to search, to look for
die Suppe, -n soup
das System, -e system
    das metrische System, -e metric system

T

die Tablette, -n tablet, pill
der Tag, -e day
    Guten Tag! Good day!
das Tagesmenü,-s special of the day
täglich daily
die Tante, -n aunt
tanzen to dance
die Tasche, -n bag, purse, pocket
die Tasse, -n cup
das Taxi, -s taxi
die Technik technology
der Tee, -s tea
das Telefon, -e telephone
telefonieren to telephone, to make a call
die Telefonnummer, -n telephone number
die Telefonzelle, -n telephone booth
der Telegrammstil telegram style (very brief)
(das) Tennis tennis

die Tennisstunde, -n   tennis lesson
teuer   expensive
das Theater, –   theater, playhouse
die Theaterkarte, -n   theater ticket
das Thema, die Themen   theme, topic
der Thunfisch   tuna fish
das Tier, -e   animal
der Tierarzt, ⸚e   veterinarian
der Tisch, -e   table
das Tischtuch, ⸚er   tablecloth
der Toaster, –   toaster
die Tochter, ⸚   daughter
toll!   fantastic! great!
die Tomate, -n   tomato
der Tourist, -en   tourist
tragen (ä), u, a   to carry, to wear
die Traube, -n   grape
traurig   sad
treffen (i), traf, getroffen   to meet
trinken, a, u   to drink
das Trinkgeld, -er   tip
trocken   dry
die Trompete, -n   trumpet
Tschüss!   Bye now!
tun, tat, getan   to do, to make
die Tür, -en   door
das Tournier, -e   tournament

U̱

üben   to practice
über   over, about
überall   everywhere
die Übernachtung, -en   overnight stay
übersetzen   to translate
die Übung, -en   exercise
übertreiben, ie, ie   to exaggerate
die Uhr, -en   clock, watch
　　um 11 Uhr   at 11 o'clock
um   at, around, about, in order to
um·schalten   to switch over, to shift
um·ziehen*, zog um, umgezogen   to
　　move
sich um·ziehen   to change clothes
unabhängig   independent
unbekannt   unknown
der Unfall, ⸚e   accident
unfreundlich   unfriendly
ungefähr   approximate(ly)
ungerade   uneven

unglaublich   unbelievable
die Universität, -en   university
das Universitätskrankenhaus, ⸚er
　　university hospital
die Unkosten, *pl.*   expenses
uns   us
unser   our
unten   below, under, among
unter   below, at the bottom
sich unterhalten (ä), ie, a   to enjoy one-
　　self, to converse
die Unterhaltungssendung, -en   enter-
　　tainment show
unterrichten   to teach (at a school)
untersuchen   to examine
der Urlaub, -e   vacation
usw. (und so weiter)   and so forth

V̱

der Vater, ⸚   father
die Verabredung, -en   appointment, date
verbinden, a, u   to connect (telephone
　　call)
der Verbrecher, –   criminal
verbringen, verbrachte, verbracht   to
　　spend (time)
verdienen   to earn
der Verein, -e   club, association
vereist   icy
die Verfassung, -en   constitution
vergessen, (i), vergaß, vergessen   to
　　forget
vergleichen, i, i   to compare
verheiratet   married
verkaufen   to sell
der Verkäufer, –   sales clerk
der Verkehr   traffic
verlieren, o, o   to lose
der Verlierer, –   loser
vermieten   to rent to someone
vermissen   to miss
verpassen   to miss
verrückt   crazy
versalzen   to oversalt
das Versandhaus, ⸚er   mail-order house
verschieden   different
verschreiben, ie, ie   to prescribe
versetzen   to transfer
sich verspäten   to be delayed

die Verspätung, -en delay
verstehen, verstand, verstanden to
  understand
versuchen to try
der Vertrag, ⁻e contract
der/die Verwandte, -n relative
verwenden to use
Verzeihung! Excuse me, please!
viel, viele much, many
vier four
das Viertel fourth
viertel quarter
vierundzwanzig twenty-four
vierzig forty
der Volksschullehrer, – elementary
  school teacher
voll full
von from, of
von . . . bis from . . . to
vor in front of, before
vor allem above all
voraussichtlich presumably, probably
vorbei over, past, along, by
  nicht vorbei not over yet
voreingenommen biased
vorbei·kommen*, kam vorbei,
  vorbeigekommen to stop by
der Vormittag, -e time before noon
  am Vormittag, vormittags in the
    morning before noon
der Vorname, -n first name
vor·schreiben, ie, ie to order, to specify
vorsichtig careful
die Vorspeise, -n appetizer
(sich) vorstellen to introduce

W

der Wachhund, -e watchdog
wählen to choose, to dial
wahr true
  Das ist nicht wahr. That isn't true.
während during, while, whereas
die Währung, -en currency (foreign)
wandern to hike
die Wanderung, -en hike
die Wanderkarte, -n hiking map
wann when
  Ab wann . . . From what time
    on . . .?

warm warm
warten to wait
warum why
was what
was noch what else
die Wäsche laundry
waschen (ä), u, a to wash
der Waschlappen, – washcloth
das Wasser, – water
wechseln to change
die Wechselstube,-n money exchange
  office
die Wäsche laundry
der Wecker, – alarm clock
der Weg, -e way, path
wegen because, on account of
weh·tun, tat weh, wehgetan to hurt,
  ache
Weihnachten Christmas
weil because
der Wein, -e wine
die Weinstube, -n wine tavern
weit far
weiter farther, further
welch which
die Welt, -en world
wem to whom
wen whom
wenig, wenige few
wenigstens at least
wenn if, when, whenever
wer who
die Werbung, -en advertisement,
  commercial
werden* (i), u, o to become, to get
wessen whose
der Westbahnhof West railway station
das Wetter weather
wichtig important
wie how, as, like
  Wie bitte? What was that?
  Wie geht es Ihnen? How are you?
  Wie heißen Sie? What is your name?
wieder again
das Wiedersehen reunion
  Auf Wiedersehen! Good-bye!
wie lang(e), how long
das Wienerschnitzel, – breaded veal
  cutlet
wie oft how often

wieviel, wie viele how many
  Der Wievielte ist heute? What day is
    today?
der Windbeutel, – cream puff
windig windy
der Winter, – winter
wir we
wirklich really
die Wirtschaft economy
der Wirtschaftsprüfer, – certified public
  accountant
wissen (weiß), wusste, gewusst to know
die Witwe, -n widow
der Witwer, – widower
wo where
die Woche, -n week
  das Wochenblatt, ¨er weekly news-
    paper
  das Wochenende, – weekend
wofür why, for what
woher from where
wohin where to
(sich) wohl·fühlen to feel well
wohnen to live
der Wohnort, -e place of residence
die Wohnung, -en apartment
das Wohnzimmer, – living room
wollen (will), wollte, gewollt to want,
  to wish
das Wörterbuch, ¨er dictionary
wunderbar wonderful
wünschen to wish
die Wurst, ¨e sausage, assorted lunch
  meat
  die Wurstplatte, -n assorted cold cuts
  die Bockwurst large frankfurter

Z̄

zäh tough
die Zahl, -en number
zahlen to pay
zählen to count

die Zahlkarte, -n money order (*but:*
  Erlagschein, -e in Austria)
der Zahn, ¨e tooth
der Zahnarzt, ¨e dentist
zehn ten
das Zehntel, – tenth
das Zeichen, – sign
zeigen to show
die Zeit, -en time
  sich Zeit lassen to take one's time
die Zeitschrift, -en magazine
die Zeitung, -en newspaper
das Zeitungssterben demise of newspapers
zerstören to destroy
ziehen, zog, gezogen to move, to pull
ziemlich rather
das Zimmer, – room
  der Zimmernachweis room reserva-
    tion service
  die Zimmernummer, -n room number
die Zitrone, -n lemon
der Zoo,-s zoo
zu to, at, too
der Zufall, ¨e chance, coincidence
zufrieden satisfied
der Zug, ¨e train
zu·machen to close, shut
zur, zu der to the
**zurück·kommen*, kam zurück,
  zurückgekommen** to come back
zurück·senden to return
zuviel too much
zuwenig too little
zwanzig twenty
zwanzigst- twentieth
zwei two
zweimal twice
zweistöckig two-story
zweit- second
die Zweizimmerwohnung, -en two-
  room apartment
die Zwiebel, -n onions
zwölf twelve

English-German Vocabulary

This selective English-German vocabulary is based on this text and should aid you in completing the English-to-German activities and exercises. We offer it for your convenience, but it is no substitute for a complete English-German dictionary, which we recommend for any student of German. The definitions given are limited to the context of a particular exercise. Irregular and semi-irregular verbs are indicated with an asterisk (*). Check their various forms on the list in the Reference Grammar section.

A

a, an   ein
about   über, etwa
to be acquainted with, to become acquainted   kennen•lernen
ad, advertisement   die Anzeige, -n
address   die Adresse, -n
to be afraid (of)   sich fürchten vor, Angst haben vor + *dat.*
after   nach, später
again   wieder
airport   der Flughafen, ¨
all   alle
almost   fast, beinahe
alone   allein
always   immer
American   der Amerikaner, *m*, die Amerikanerin, –nen, *f.*; amerikanisch, *adj.*
and   und

B

answer   die Antwort, -en
to answer   antworten + *Dat.*
apartment   die Wohnung, – en
approximate(ly)   ungefähr
to arrive   an•kommen*
article   der Artikel, –
to ask   fragen; bitten* um + *Akk.*
at   an, bei, zu
Austria   (das) Österreich
Austrian   der Österreicher, –, *m.:* die Österreicherin, -nen, *f.*; österreichisch, *adj.*
available (room)   frei

B

back   zurück
bad   schlecht, schlimm
baggage   das (Reise) Gepäck
bath   das Bad, ¨er
beautiful   schön; hübsch

271

because weil
to become werden*
bed das Bett, -en
beer das Bier
before vor, bevor
to begin an•fangen*; beginnen*
behind hinter
to believe glauben + *Dat.*
to belong gehören + *Dat.*
between zwischen
bicycle das Fahrrad, ¨-er
big groß, stark
bill die Rechnung, -en
book das Buch, ¨-er
boring langweilig
born geboren
boy der Junge, -n
bread das Brot, -e
breakfast das Frühstück
to bring bringen
brother der Bruder, ¨
bridge die Brücke, -n
to brush putzen
bus der Bus, -se
business das Geschäft, -e
businessman der Geschäftsmann, *pl.*
busy besetzt (Telefon)
but aber
to buy kaufen

C

call der Anruf, -e
to call an•rufen*
can die Dose, -n
can, to be able to können*
car das Auto, -s; der Wagen, –
card die Karte, -n
to change ändern; wechseln; sich
um•ziehen* (clothes)
cheap billig
to check (luggage) auf•geben* (Gepäck)
children die Kinder
to choose wählen, aus•suchen
city die Stadt, ¨-e
classic klassisch
classified ad die Anzeige, -n
clean sauber, rein
clock die Uhr, -en
at eight o'clock um acht Uhr
coffee der Kaffee, -s
cold kalt, die Erkältung (flu)

color die Farbe, -n
to comb (sich) kämmen
to come kommen*
to compute aus•rechnen, berechnen
to complain sich beklagen über + *Akk.*;
sich beschweren
cool kühl
to cook kochen
corner die Ecke, -n
to cost kosten
crazy verrückt
cup die Tasse, -n

D

to dance tanzen
daughter die Tochter, ¨
day der Tag, -e
dear lieb
degree der Grad, -e
to demand verlangen, fordern
to depart ab•fahren*
departure die Abfahrt, -en
dessert die Nachspeise, -n
to develop entwickeln
different verschieden, anders
difficult schwierig, schwer
diligent fleißig
dinner das Abendessen
dirty schmutzig, dreckig
to disturb stören
divorced geschieden
to do tun, machen
dog der Hund, -e
door die Tür, -en
double room das Doppelzimmer, –
dress das Kleid, -er
to drink trinken*
to drive fahren*
driver der Fahrer, –, *m.;* die Fahrerin,
nen, *f.*
dry trocken
during während

E

early früh
to earn verdienen
easy leicht
to eat essen*
education die Erziehung, die
Ausbildung

to enjoy genießen*, gern•haben, gefallen* + *Dat.*
enough genug
evening der Abend, -e
  in the evening abends
even though obwohl
every jeder, jede, jedes
everything alles
to examine untersuchen; prüfen
to exchange um•wechseln (Geld)
to excuse (sich) entschuldigen
to exercise üben, trainieren (Sport)
exit der Ausgang, ⸚e
expense die Ausgabe, -n; die Kosten
expensive teuer
to explain erklären
express train der Schnellzug, ⸚e

F

to fall fallen*
false falsch
family die Familie, -n
famous berühmt
far weit
fast schnell
father der Vater, ⸚
to fear sich fürchten
to feel sich fühlen
to fill out aus•füllen
to find finden*
finished fertig
firm die Firma, die Firmen
to fly fliegen*
flight der Flug, ⸚e
to follow folgen + *Dat.*
for für
to forget vergessen*
fork die Gabel, -n
free frei
friend der Freund, -e, *m.*
friend die Freundin, -nen, *f.*
friendly freundlich
from von, aus
full voll, besetzt
fun der Spaß

G

to gain weight zu•nehmen*
game das Spiel, -e

German der/die Deutsche, *n.*; deutsch, *adj.*
Germany (das) Deutschland
to get bekommen*; erhalten*
to get up auf•stehen*
to get dressed (sich) an•ziehen*
girl das Mädchen
to give geben*
glass das Glas, ⸚er
to go gehen*; fahren*
golf das Golf
  golf game das Golfspiel, -e
good gut
gram das Gramm
group die Gruppe, -n
guest der Gast, ⸚

H

half halb
to happen geschehen*, passieren + *Dat.*
happy glücklich
to have haben
healthy gesund
to hear hören
to help helfen + *Dat.*
here hier
high hoch
to hike wandern
home, *adv.* nach Hause
  at home zu Hause
hope hoffen
hot heiß
hour die Stunde, -n
house das Haus, ⸚er
how wie
hunger der Hunger
hungry hungrig
to hurry sich beeilen
to hurt verletzen
  It hurts. Es tut weh.

I

ice cream das Eis
idea die Idee, -n
if wenn
ill krank
immediate(ly) sofort, direkt
important wichtig
Independence Day der Unabhängigkeitstag

independent unabhängig
inexpensive billig
to inform informieren
inn das Gasthaus, ̈er
inside innen, drinnen
interest das Interesse, -n
    to be interested in sich interessieren
        für + *Akk.*
interesting interessant
invitation die Einladung, -en

J

job der Beruf, -e; der Job, -s
journey die Reise, -n
just gerade

K

to keep behalten*
key der Schlüssel
to kiss küssen
kitchen die Küche, -n
to know wissen*, kennen*

L

lake der See, -n
language die Sprache, -n
large groß
to last dauern
late spät
to laugh lachen
lawn der Rasen, –
lazy faul
to lead führen
to learn lernen
lease der Mietvertrag, ̈e
to lease mieten
to leave verlassen*, ab•fahren*
left links
to let lassen*
letter der Brief, -e
to lie liegen*, lügen
light das Licht; leicht, *adj.*
to like gern•haben
to listen zu•hören
little klein
to live leben, wohnen
long lang
lost, *adj.* verloren
to look schauen, an•schauen

to look forward to sich freuen auf +
    Akk.
to lose verlieren*
(a) lot viel
loud laut
to love lieben
lovely hübsch; wunderschön
luggage das Gepäck
lunch das Mittagessen, –

M

mail die Post
to make machen
man der Mann, ̈er; der Mensch, -en
many viele
to marry heiraten
    to get married heiraten
    married verheiratet
meal das Essen
to mean bedeuten
meat das Fleisch
medicine die Medizin; das
    Medikament, -e
to meet treffen*
menu die Speisekarte, -n
milk die Milch
to miss verpassen, versäumen, vermis-
    sen
Monday der Montag, -e
money das Geld, -er
money order die Zahlkarte, -n
month der Monat, -e
more mehr
morning der Morgen, –
    in the morning morgens
mother die Mutter, ̈
to move um•ziehen*
to move in ein•ziehen*
to move out aus•ziehen*
movie das Kino, -s; der Film, -e
to mow mähen
much viel
too much zuviel
mushroom der Pilz, -e
must müssen*

N

naturally natürlich
to need brauchen
neighbor der Nachbar, -n

never nie
new neu
news die Nachricht, -en
newspaper die Zeitung, -en
next nächst
nice nett, fein
night die Nacht, ¨e
no nein
nobody niemand
noon der Mittag, -e
nothing nichts
now jetzt
number die Nummer, -n

O

occupied besetzt
of von
offer das Angebot, -e
to offer an·bieten*
often oft
oil das Öl
old alt
on auf, an
once einmal
   at once sofort
to open öffnen, auf·machen
open offen
opinion die Meinung, -en
to order bestellen
other ander-
out aus, hinaus
over über
   over there dort drüben

P

page die Seite, -n
pain der Schmerz, -en
parents die Eltern
passport der Pass, ¨sse
to pay zahlen, bezahlen
peace der Frieden
peak der Gipfel, –
people die Leute
perhaps vielleicht
to phone telefonieren; an·rufen*
photo das Bild, -er; das Photo, -s
physician der Arzt, ¨e, *m.*; die
   Ärztin, -nen, *f.*
to pick up ab·holen
picture das Bild, -er

piece das Stück, -e
place der Ort, -e; die Stelle, -n; der
   Platz, ¨e
to play spielen
please bitte
to please gefallen* + *Dat.*
poor arm
police die Polizei
   policeman der Polizist, -en
polite höflich
possible möglich
post office die Post; das Postamt, ¨er
postage stamp die Briefmarke, -n
to practice üben
to prefer vor·ziehen*; lieber haben
to press drücken
pretty hübsch, schön
price der Preis, -e
prohibited verboten
to protect schützen, beschützen
to prove beweisen*
punctual pünktlich
pure rein
to push drücken
to put legen, stellen, setzen

Q

quality die Qualität, -en
quarter das Viertel, –
question die Frage, -n
quick schnell
quiet leise; ruhig
quite ganz, ziemlich

R

railroad der Zug, ¨e; die Bahn, -en
rain der Regen
to rain regnen
rare (cooked) nur schwach gebraten
rather ziemlich
to reach erreichen
to read lesen*
ready bereit, fertig
reason der Grund, ¨e
record der Rekord, -e
to regret bedauern
to remain bleiben*
to remember sich erinnern an, + *Akk.*
rent die Miete, -n
to rent mieten, vermieten

to report berichten
to request bitten* um, ersuchen um + *Akk.*
to require verlangen, erfordern
to reserve reservieren
restaurant das Restaurant, -s
to return zurück•kommen*
right das Recht, -e
right, *adj.* richtig; rechts
river der Fluss, ¨e
road die Straße, -n
room das Zimmer, –
round trip die Hin- und Rückfahrt, -en
rule die Regel, -n

S

salty salzig, versalzen
satisfied zufrieden
Saturday der Samstag, -e
to say sagen
school die Schule, -n
to search suchen, ausfindig machen
to see sehen*
to seem scheinen*
seldom selten
to sell verkaufen
to send senden*, schicken
to serve bedienen, servieren
several mehrere
to shave (sich) rasieren
shoe der Schuh, -e
short kurz, klein
should sollen
to show zeigen
shower die Dusche, -n
sick krank
sign das Schild, -er; das Zeichen, –
similar ähnlich
to sing singen*
single ledig; unverheiratet
single room das Einzelzimmer, –
to sit sitzen*
sister die Schwester, -n
to sleep schlafen*
small klein, schmal
to smoke rauchen
sold out ausverkauft
some einige, irgendein
something irgend etwas
sometimes manchmal

soon bald
Sorry! Es tut mir leid.
soup die Suppe, -n
to speak sprechen*
special (in a restaurant) das Menü, -s
spoon der Löffel, –
stamp die Briefmarke, -n
to stand stehen*
to stay bleiben*
steamed (food) gedämpft
still noch
to stop auf•hören, halten
straight ahead geradeaus
street die Straße, -n
streetcar die Straßenbahn, -en
strong stark
to study studieren; lernen
student der Student, -en, *m.*; die Studentin, -nen, *f.*
stupid dumm
summer der Sommer, -
to swim schwimmen*
to succeed gelingen*
successful erfolgreich
to suggest vor•schlagen*
suitcase der Koffer, –
sun die Sonne, -n
sunglasses die Sonnenbrille, -n

T

table der Tisch, -e
to take nehmen*
taken (table in a restaurant) besetzt
to take along mit•nehmen*
to talk sprechen*, reden
to taste schmecken + *Dat.*
tax die Steuer, -n
to teach lehren; unterrichten
teacher der Lehrer, – *m.*; die Lehrerin, -nen, *f.*
telephone das Telefon, -e
telephone booth die Telefonzelle, -n
telephone call der Telefonanruf, -e
television das Fernsehen
television set der Fernseher, –
to tell sagen; erzählen
thanks danke
that dass, *conjunction*; das, *demonstrative pronoun*
theater das Theater, –

theater ticket　die Theaterkarte, -n
then　dann, damals
there　dort
　there is, there are　es gibt + *Akk.*
thing　das Ding, -e
to think　denken*
thirsty　durstig
ticket　die Karte, -n
till　bis
time　die Zeit, -en
　on time　pünktlich
tip　das Trinkgeld, -er
today　heute
tomato　die Tomate, -n
tonight　heute abend
too　zu, auch
tourist　der Tourist, -en
tough　zäh
town　die Stadt, ⸚e
traffic　der Verkehr
train　der Zug, ⸚e
　train station　der Bahnhof, ⸚e
to translate　übersetzen
to travel　reisen
to treat　behandeln
tree　der Baum, ⸚e
to try　versuchen

U

umbrella　der Schirm, -e; der
　Regenschirm, -e
uncle　der Onkel, –
under　unter
to understand　verstehen*
unfortunately　leider, unglücklicherweise
unknown　unbekannt
unpleasant　unangenehm
until　bis
to use　verwenden*, gebrauchen

V

vacant　leer, frei, unbesetzt
vacation　die Ferien; der Urlaub, -e
valid　gültig
vegetable　das Gemüse
very　sehr
visit　der Besuch, -e
to visit　besuchen

vocabulary　der Wortschatz, das
　Vokabular, -e

W

to wait　warten
waiter　der Kellner, –
　waitress　die Kellnerin, -nen
to wake up　auf•wachen
to walk　gehen,* spazieren
to want　wünschen, wollen
to wash　waschen*
water　das Wasser
way　der Weg, -e
to wear　tragen*
weather　das Wetter
Wednesday　der Mittwoch, -e
week　die Woche, -n
well　gut, wohl
well done (cooked)　gut durchgebraten
what　was
when　wenn, als
whenever　wenn
where　wo
whether　ob
which　welch
whipped cream　die Sahne, der Schlag
　(Austrian)
who　wer
whom　wem
why　warum
to win　gewinnen*
window　das Fenster, –
to wish　wünschen
with　mit
without　ohne
woman　die Frau, -en
word　das Wort, ⸚er, -e
to work　arbeiten
would like　möchten
to write　schreiben*
wrong　falsch

Y

year　das Jahr, -e
yes　ja
yesterday　gestern
young　jung

Index

Hear the words from an expert's mouth.

Here's a 65-minute pronunciation tape to help you with your newly learned German vobaculary and grammar. Including exercises, dialogues, and vocabulary lists from the book, it allows you to practice your pronunciation and compare it with that of a native speaker.

Cut out or photocopy the coupon below and mail it today!

German: A Self-Teaching Guide, 2nd Ed.

Please indicate preferred format:

Quantity	Format	Price
_____	Audio cassette	$15.00 USA
_____	Compact disk	$12.00 USA

All prices include shipping and handling.

Your Name: _____

Address: _____

City/State/Zip/Country: _____

Signature: _____

Offer not valid without signature. Prices are subject to change without notice.

Mail check or money order, payable to Arnold Haas, to:

Arnold Haas
4933 Pear Tree Court
Gahanna, OH 43230-1039

Please allow 4 weeks for processing of your order.